Hitchcock's Stars

Alfred Hitchcock's final on-screen cameo, in *Family Plot* (1976). *Universal Pictures/ Photofest © Universal Pictures*

Hitchcock's Stars

Alfred Hitchcock and the Hollywood Studio System

LESLEY L. COFFIN

ROWMAN & LITTLEFIELD
Lanham • Boulder • New York • Toronto • Plymouth, UK

Published by Rowman & Littlefield
4501 Forbes Boulevard, Suite 200, Lanham, Maryland 20706
www.rowman.com

10 Thornbury Road, Plymouth PL6 7PP, United Kingdom

British Library Cataloguing in Publication Information Available

Library of Congress Cataloging-in-Publication Data

Coffin, Lesley L.
  Hitchcock's stars : Alfred Hitchcock and the Hollywood studio system / Lesley L.
Coffin.
    pages cm
  Includes a filmography of Hitchcock's films.
  Includes bibliographical references and index.
  ISBN 978-1-4422-3077-4 (cloth : alk. paper) — ISBN 978-1-4422-3078-1 (ebook) 1.
Hitchcock, Alfred, 1899-1980—Criticism and interpretation. 2. Motion picture actors
and actresses—United States. 3. Motion picture industry—United States—History—20th
century. I. Title.
  PN1998.3.H58C58 2014
  791.4302'33092—dc23   2014007188

Contents

Acknowledgments

Please consider this a warning: this book is not intended to introduce the reader to the films of Alfred Hitchcock. It seems an odd statement to make as there are so many books that can offer that to readers, and more importantly, I can't imagine there would be much interest in this subject if you are a novice. In order to write this book properly and (hopefully) make it an enjoyable read, I make the assumption in my writing that the reader has seen these films. Endings are discussed, specific scenes analyzed, and twists will be mentioned.

But more importantly, a good deal of what is written is meant to introduce you to the stars of these iconic films by Hitchcock—specifically the image audiences had when seeing these films at the time they were made, and what impact these stars had on the interpretation of these films.

When watching a film from the past, it is vital to understand how the film was known and perceived at the time. Films are not made in a vacuum, where one exists for the audience to stand completely alone without outside forces bumping into their interpretation. To know the image of a star, how audiences perceived a film when first released (especially when audiences did not have the benefit of home entertainment), is part of the pleasure of watching classic films—and enriches how we connect cinema to culture.

It is because of this that I am so grateful to members of the freshman class of New York University's Gallatin School of Individualized Studies. To give me a few hours every week to show Hitchcock movies was a pleasure, but to participate in discussions and give their impressions of watching these films with fresh eyes was invaluable. To sit through a screening of *Psycho* and hear girls refer to Norman Bates as cute or say Janet Leigh might be the killer was hilarious. These students gave insightful, truthful thoughts in our hourly discussions. I also must thank Selma Thompson for helping to arrange these movie nights and allowing them to be casual for the maximum "movie watching" experience—complete with popcorn. The mere fact that New York University's Gallatin School allows for a thesis on the casting of Norman Bates (which ignited this project) leaves me grateful to their department. They encourage new areas of study and experimentation in academia, which is truly remarkable.

Hitchcock is not an area of research that is difficult to find materials on; in fact at times I felt I had taken on an area that was oversaturated and unlikely to yield new information. But for this I'm very grateful to the scholars who came before, academics, authors, and biographers (and the biographers of the stars of Hitchcock's films) for having done so much work before and helping me find the areas that have already been covered and where and how I should focus this book. I also am greatly appreciative of the archives that help with considerable research (and archivists who provided answers to so many questions). The UCLA Film Archive, USC Film Library, New York Public Library, and Museum of Modern Art were all of great assistance. Photos for this book were provided by Photofest (NY), who were wonderful, helping me locate interesting, candid photographs of the stars with Hitchcock.

Finally, on a personal note, I would like to send gratitude to my friends and family who offer such encouragement, especially friends Joanna Chebus, Mia Gomez, Vincent Ford, Joyce Artinian, and Jen McCoy, who provided me the time and patience to complete this, and my family, especially Cecile Purcell, Natalie and Steve Kellet, and Tom and Alice Coffin, who put up with a lot of Hitchcock talk.

Introduction:
Hitchcock's Livestock

Any casual fan of cinema has certainly heard the lore that Hitchcock referred to his actors as cattle. It is a statement that he seemed to spend his entire career clarifying and correcting. He insisted often in interviews that "What I probably said was that all actors should be treated like cattle. Actors can't cut. They don't react to the cutting, the timing of the cutting, the montage. How can they? They have to become secondary to the whole."[1]

If a contemporary director made a similar statement regarding the treatment of actors with such contempt, the media would undoubtedly pounce, questioning that director's lack of respect. Yet Hitchcock's comment about the actors who brought his films to life, many considered some of the greatest actors of the twentieth century, has been referenced and quoted as part of what made the master of suspense a true genius and auteur. Every element of his films was touched by his skill as a director: design, storytelling, and even the performances.

Collaboration will always be an idea in question when discussing and studying the work of Hitchcock. We've accepted the fact that Hitchcock collaborated with designers, cameramen, writers, and composers, and have seen many individual studies of their work. However, Hitchcock was not one to hand out praise and acknowledgment of his colleagues generously. Writers, considered for-hire employees by Hitchcock, ultimately began to demand appreciation for their contributions to Hitchcock's masterpieces.[2] And yet, acknowledging these collaborations has never devalued the remarkable work of Hitchcock the man.

Rarely when authors talk about Hitchcock's filmmaking team do they address the contributions of his actors. There is little or no serious attention paid to them or any in-depth study of their contributions to his films. In the five-hundred-page book *Hitchcock's Notebooks* by Dan Auiler, detailing nearly every detail of Hitchcock's directorial craft, Auiler barely mentions the casting. While actors are often the focus of the gossip surrounding Hitchcock's life, the contributions and performances given are rarely approached with any seriousness.

However, actors and stars are part of the film system and, in the best instances, meant to serve the artistic elements of the film. The best films in Hitchcock's filmography, especially those which have become timeless favorites, are those that had an interesting premise built mostly on strong performances and characters, rather than those films created with gimmicks and stunts. Casting, performance, and the important role stars played in Hitchcock films have been noticeably overlooked.

There are several books, most of them biographies of Hitchcock, which have addressed Hitchcock's relationship with his actors, including Donald Spoto's history of Hitchcock's relationship with his women, *Spellbound by Beauty*. But these works primarily focus on Hitchcock's personal relationship with these stars, rather than the performances given or the cultural impact their stardom had on the films. Because of the legend behind the comments and stories that circulate regarding his inappropriate relationships with his female stars, the performances in these great cinematic arts are largely overlooked. This work is intended to put a new focus and perspective on the performances by the stars of Hitchcock films, and the effect these star personas had on audiences. Nearly every other aspect of Hitchcock's films has been analyzed in scholarly works; except for the actors and their performances from these films.

The memorable statement on livestock is an ironic one considering just how many iconic performances by some of Hollywood's greatest stars he directed. Cary Grant, despite more than forty years in Hollywood, will certainly always be remembered in the cornfield, running for his life in a perfectly fitted suit, in his final Hitchcock film, *North by Northwest*. And there are few cinematic images considered more beautiful than Grace Kelly's introduction in *Rear Window* as her shadowy face gradually comes into focus. But the relationship between Hitchcock and his stars was not only mutually beneficial and both commercially and artistic motivated, but extremely complex. Hitchcock created projects and characters shaped around hopes of casting stars in these roles, occasionally abandoning good scripts when unable to secure the actors he had imagined or completely reworking a project to better fit a new actor.

The relationship between stars and Hitchcock is a story of tension between the powers of director as auteur and the stars, those sending the message and those projecting it. And that tension only became more volatile as the star system changed and Hitchcock's notoriety and name recognition grew. When he first arrived in Hollywood, Alfred Hitchcock had the ability to select his cast within a carefully controlled system established by studios; companies that controlled the amount of power given to both stars and directors and could force these two superpowers to collaborate for mutual benefit. But Hitchcock didn't simply intend to use the star system; he intended to revitalize it. His dislike for the studio system existed because he saw a laziness regarding the manner in which studios used their stars. He believed that despite the power the system had, the studios had become complacent, simply casting actors in the same recycled characters they had played before. Hitchcock saw this as proof of the lack of artistic inspiration that existed among the executives at studios, which both frustrated and inspired him to make changes from within the system.

Hitchcock was well aware of the role Hollywood stars had on the success of films and the impact the right or wrong star could have on how an audience perceived a film. The star system had become a microcosm of society and, when used properly, could provide a shortcut for the audiences to have empathy for the characters.

And this was precisely the effect Hitchcock wanted to bring to movies and the reason he moved from England to Hollywood to make pictures. When it was announced that the famous English director had decided to transplant his family to America, he told an interviewer:

> I'm itching to get my hands on some of those American stars. . . . Some of them are so efficient, that it'll be a pleasure to direct them; and there are others I should very much like to debunk. I should like to humanize Luise Rainer

and show Dietrich sucking a toffee-apple. I should like to cast Clark Gable in a much more penetrating characterization than he has yet played, and I should like to put Myrna Loy into the type of part that Edna Best had in *The Man Who Knew Too Much*. What a boon William Powell would be, in a fast-moving comedy thriller! He is the only actor I know who can really put across a far-fetched piece of slapstick with absolute conviction.[3]

While he never had the opportunity to cast Myrna Loy, Clark Gable, or Luise Rainer, he did cast Marlene Dietrich as a hyper, evil version of herself in *Stage Fright*. And he came close to casting William Powell in *Shadow of a Doubt* and later paid homage to the actor in his last feature, the comedy-thriller *Family Plot*. But despite being unable to get all the actors he so wanted, he did cast some of the biggest names at that time, and often in inspired, unconventional roles that forced audiences to question how they saw their favorite performers. It was an approach based on Hitchcock's idea that the overindulged, apathetic audiences had become used to seeing stars in the same roles over and over; so when they did the unexpected, it could thrill the audience more so than when making conventional casting choices.

Hitchcock played with casting, questioning how to best use an actor's persona to add humor, thrills, and social commentary to his films and allowing the audience to find this commentary without it being spelled out for them. Taking this approach, he and his stars created some of the greatest characters in film history. He sunk his teeth into what the system had to offer him, excited because English cinema could not offer the same powerful impact through casting.

Hitchcock was notorious for finding the film acting community in London to be lacking the star qualities and charisma that were available in Hollywood. A major part of this was the widely held belief that in the land of Shakespeare, cinema was considered an industry merely to subsidize a theater career. Actors with theatrical training might take film roles, but many didn't have the commitment to the art of film acting Hitchcock expected. He claimed to have heard actors referring to accepting jobs on films as "slumming" and noticed they put higher priority on their theater commitments than the film work they had been employed to complete.[4] It was a lack of professionalism that Hitchcock found frustrating, and he also had little patience for temperamental British actors. Arriving in Hollywood he demanded professionalism and respect from his actors immediately. To Hitchcock, film was not recorded theater; it was its own art form and required a different approach to acting that could accommodate the technical qualities that did not exist on the stage. Hollywood stars rarely appeared on Broadway, as the sheer geographical difference made it difficult for actors to be bicoastal, and many film actors first received training at Hollywood studios.

Hitchcock was also harsh in his judgment of English actors, especially women, crediting their inability to show emotion as part of their repressed English temperament:

> Plunge an English actress into a bath of cold water and she still comes to the top trying to look aloof and dignified. Her whole concern is not how best to express her emotions but how best to bottle them up. I do not image that American stars suffer from this inhibition to anything like the same extent. No girl could arrive at the pitch of efficiency achieved by Carole Lombard if her one consideration were how best to appear to "society."[5]

It was a harsh comment to make about actresses, especially considering the pleasure Hitchcock took in the reserved blonde and rarity with which he required his actresses to show visual signs of emotional abandonment (tears are rare in Hitchcock's film). But a majority of his leading actors, male and female, had a unique, minimalistic approach that suited Hitchcock's formalistic style of filmmaking, as it added a realism to anchor the film and evoke emotional responses from an audience. To see this difference in acting is what made Hitchcock such a wise director of actors, and why many of the performances of his actors seem particularly modern and void of the exaggerated mannerisms seen in the acting of so much cinema from the Hollywood Golden Age.

It was the reason Hitchcock went so far as to employ Hollywood actor Robert Young in his film *The Secret Agent*. It was while promoting this film that Hitchcock informed the press:

> There is scarcely a star in Hollywood whose appeal I would not try to alter or develop, according to the part they were playing. One of Hollywood's greatest failings is the way it allows its stars to get into a groove. When an actor achieves fame in some particular type of part the tendency is to grind out all his future roles in the same pattern. When Robert Young came to England to work for me

in *Secret Agent* he had never appeared in a film as anything more than himself. In this picture I gave him a chance to give a genuine characterization, with the result that, in the final sequences of the picture, he developed a power and a conviction that would have done credit to Spencer Tracy. That is what I would like to do with all the stars that come under my control in Hollywood.[6]

His last statement, regarding his desire to take control from the studio for himself, hints at what would ultimately bring about Hitchcock's downfall with actors. For while the studio machine frequently wheeled too much control over actors' careers, most performers did not want to simply trade the control of their careers from studio boss to their directors. And toward the end of Hitchcock's career, during Hollywood's great transition into "new Hollywood," actors began to demand more control over their careers, control Hitchcock did not want to surrender.

1

Rebecca

Alfred Hitchcock did not come to Hollywood with the express mission to direct the film *Rebecca*; he came to Hollywood to make Hollywood films, and his first film happened to be *Rebecca*. Hitchcock arrived from England with a contract in hand from David O. Selznick, hired on the basis of the high-quality work he had done as an English director, especially with his popular *The Lady Vanishes* and *The 39 Steps*. His innovative directorial style was precisely what Selznick wanted under contract as he emerged as the most successful independent producer, and the resources that were afforded to directors under the umbrella of a Selznick contract was precisely the kind of freedom Hitchcock wanted in Hollywood.

For a time it was reported that Hitchcock would make a film documenting the story of the *Titanic*, which promised to be an impressive set piece for him to work with on his first Hollywood feature. However, the project was pushed aside and Selznick selected Daphne du Maurier's novel *Rebecca* as Hitchcock's first film. The best seller was noted for being influenced by the literature of the Brontë sisters and could be described as modern Gothic-romance. Hitchcock claimed he approached the work differently, describing the story of a nameless spinster who married a widow as being a scary fairy tale in which the heroine is "Cinderella and Mrs. Danvers is one of the ugly sisters."[1] After being assigned the "very British novel," Selznick made his wishes clear as to the "approach" he wanted Hitchcock to take. He was to make a lush woman's picture as a cinematic thriller with elements of horror and mystery but also to remain as close as possible to the original narrative. Superficially the property suited Hitchcock's sensibilities and the novel's acclaim elevated the film's importance during production, increasingly finding Hitchcock and Selznick's name in the papers, detailing the status of the film.

But as with every Selznick film, especially those which were considered hot properties, he was an active, opinionated producer, especially regarding who from his stable of contracted stars would be cast for optimum box-office return, critical acclaim, and artistic integrity. During the production, Selznick gave an interview to explain how he worked and the importance he placed on casting.

> Most important of all considerations is casting and in *Rebecca* this presented a major difficulty. It is usually wise to choose popular, experienced stars to play the principal parts in such a film, but only if they suit the roles to perfection; otherwise they will find their rich parts proving boomerangs, for the antagonism that an audience feels against the miscasting of a favorite character is usually directed against the unfortunate actor.[2]

While Hitchcock shared many of these opinions on the effect casting can have on an audience's response to a film, the two men didn't agree on who the audience would accept in these roles.

Almost immediately, there were concerns over the stars, specifically the undiscovered stars, who could bring the already famous roles to life. Selznick insisted that an actress be "discovered" for the role of the unnamed Mrs. De Winter. It was this opinion that kept actress Vivian Leigh out of contention for the role, one she desperately wanted. Selznick, however, was introducing the English Leigh to American audiences as Scarlett O'Hara in the upcoming *Gone with the Wind* and wanted to retain Leigh's strong connection to that role for some time.

While Selznick's decision angered Laurence Olivier, who wanted to appear with his fiancée, it seems that Leigh would have been a poor choice for the role. Part of the quality that made Leigh so ideally suited for the role of Scarlet O'Hara was the spitfire tenacity she projected from her first moments on-screen. She dominates all characters, especially the men, from start to finish, and while it makes her an often unlikable character, it also made her resiliency an admirable quality and made her identifiable to female moviegoers during the Great Depression. Leigh played on the fighting spirit she easily projected in many roles to come, including her iconic casting in *A Streetcar Named Desire*, in which she was cast as damaged Blanche largely in reference to the O'Hara myth she had cultivated a decade earlier.

But the wife of Mr. De Winter was to be fragile from the moment we meet her, and someone who is easy for both her husband and Mrs. Davers to control and manipulate. After seeing Leigh chased by all men in *Gone with the Wind* a year earlier, it may have been impossible to believe that she could also be a lonely spinster who would be putty in the hands of the first man who shows any interest in her. While Mrs. De Winter must be charming and attractive, she couldn't be a head-turner like Vivian Leigh.

With Leigh out of the way and not yet certain that Olivier would take the role of Mr. De Winter, other stars were considered for the leading roles by both Hitchcock and Selznick. Hollywood stars Ronald Coleman and Alan Marshall were considered front-runners for the role of the moody Max De Winter (as were William Powell and Leslie Howard mentioned as possibilities in the press and David O. Selznick's infamous memos). Coleman, one of the actors Hitchcock mentioned wanting to work with when he first arrived in Hollywood, was considered one of the ideal romantic leading men, accomplished in both light comedies and serious dramas, although Hitchcock himself thought he had not yet been given the opportunity to show his true abilities and should take on roles that demanded more humor and "less static" rigidness.[3] He was considered a gentleman and one of the great wits of Hollywood, who also happened to be an Englishman who had already made the transition to American films in the 1930s. Similarly, Australian-born Alan Marshall was best known at this time for lighter fare, often in B musical comedies. In fact, all the actors mentioned by Hitchcock as possible choices were known not only as gentlemen and romantic stars, but for their skills in comedy. It seems likely that had Hitchcock been permitted to make his own selection of leading man, he would have chosen an actor who could bring a bit of levity to the moody character of Max De Winter, which would have been far more intriguing casting.

Ultimately, however, the role of Max De Winter went to the actor Selznick insisted was "the only possible choice,"[4] the predictable casting of Laurence Olivier. Olivier had already played Heathcliff in an English film adaptation of the classic novel *Wuthering Heights*, and the character Max De Winter had obvious ties to this classic figure representing dark romance. Olivier was also a sought-after property, the English actor Hollywood was most eager to import. Selznick was well aware of the star's appeal and the immediate marketability *Rebecca* would have with Olivier playing Max. To appease the actor, frustrated that he couldn't convince them to hire Vivian Leigh, Olivier was given a massive fee and Selznick agreed to cast the couple in the feature film *The Flushing Stream* (a film that never came to fruition).

With Olivier secured in the lead, guaranteed to bring the brooding power he had in *Wuthering Heights* (and his loyal fans into movie theaters), a host of unproven ingénues were considered for the coveted role of Mrs. De Winter. When asked about the casting process by François Truffaut, Hitchcock claimed that it was his idea (and his insistence) that it be an unknown, despite Selznick's claims to the contrary:

> In the preliminary stages of *Rebecca*, Selznick insisted on testing every woman in town, known or unknown, for the lead the picture. I think he really was trying to repeat the same publicity stunt he pulled in the search for Scarlett O'Hara. He talked all the big stars in town into doing tests for *Rebecca*. I found it a little embarrassing myself; testing women who I knew in advance were unsuitable for the part. All the more so since earlier tests of Joan Fontaine had convinced me that she was the nearest one to our heroine.[5]

Dismissed were popular stars who also petitioned Selznick to be considered for Scarlett O'Hara, including Bette Davis and Carol Lombard (a favorite actress of both Selznick and Hitchcock). One actress, Nova Pilbeam, a striking, girlish actress from England, was precisely the kind of "find" Selznick wanted, hoping to make her his next star (at one time even announcing her for *The Flushing Stream*). But his insistence on a five-year contract prevented her and her agent from signing. Hitchcock, however, was not sold on the actress, already passing on her years before as a suitable heroine in Hitchcock's *The Lady Vanishes* (the film that convinced Selznick to bring Hitchcock to America).[6]

The actresses thought to be in highest contention were Margaret Sullivan, Loretta Young, Maureen O'Hara, Anne Baxter, and Joan Fontaine. Unsurprisingly, Sullivan and Young were thought to be unlikely choices, not only because their popularity was on the rise (particularly MGM's Sullivan who had just starred in the hit *The Shop around the Corner*), but by that time, they had lost some of the innocent, girlish qualities desired for the role. Sullivan specifically, at one time Hitchcock's top choice for the role, was called "too quirkily autonomous for the part of a shy, anxious ingénue."[7] Both were exceptional actresses, but complete innocence and weakness were aspects of their personalities that rarely worked in their favor, and both projected a maturity slightly beyond their years. For the same reasons Maureen O'Hara (who had starred in the *Hunchback of Notre Dame*) was still girlish, but seemed far more self-sufficient in her youthful personality than would have been suited to the character. It seems that Anne Baxter and Joan Fontaine were Hitchcock and Selznick final choices.

Anne Baxter, sixteen at the time, was the pick of Alma Hitchcock, largely because she found Joan Fontaine "too coy and simpering to a degree that is intolerable." Alma Hitchcock's thoughts were not necessarily cruel and mirrored many of the opinions critics and filmmakers had of Joan Fontaine at the time.[8] Fontaine's distaste for being compared to her older sister, Olivia de Havilland, was understandable, considering de Havilland was emerging as one of the most respected actresses of her generation and would soon be nominated for her role as saintly Melanie in *Gone with the Wind*. Fontaine was continually called an actress lacking in technique, personality, and presence. Fan magazines had described her as the "Blah Girl" and "Lady Goldbrick" who seemed to lack any audience appeal.[9] At the time that *Rebecca* was being cast, her mere inclusion as a candidate was a surprise, let alone being a major contender.

The constant criticism of her acting ability had understandably left Fontaine fragile and insecure with her abilities as an actress—the very quality Selznick wanted to capture in his Mrs. De Winter. He would turn his find into the star he believed she had the potential to be. Selznick brought her screen test to Hitchcock, stating the insecurity she projected was precisely what was missing from the other actresses, but Hitchcock responded that it was her own insecurity, not her acting, that was on display.[10]

Selznick went so far as to do a "poll" of his staff, asking which screen test they preferred. Overwhelmingly, Fontaine lost to Anne Baxter. Yet Selznick still insisted that he wanted Fontaine for the role, a producer's demand Hitchcock ultimately had to give in to. Selznick defended his choice of actress in press reports regarding the status of the production of *Rebecca*: "The heroine of *Rebecca* should be, both Selznick and Hitchcock reasoned, something of a nonentity, and none of Hollywood's celebrated stars could possibly convey this. Miss Fontaine might be a complete ingénue, but the motivating characteristic of the role was ingenuousness. So Joan Fontaine it was."[11]

After Selznick had selected his two stars, Hitchcock was permitted to populate the rest of the cast with a colorful collection of theater and character actors (most from England, with a talent for light humor). Hitchcock stock company members Nigel Bruce, Reginald Denny, and Leo G. Carroll appeared in small but memorable roles as compassionate, friendly faces to the frightened Mrs. De Winter. George Sanders, with a bellowing voice and harsh features, played the slithering blackmailer, and Judith Anderson the terrifying housekeeper Mrs. Danvers.

Joan Fontaine's happiness around jolly Nigel Bruce, established in *Rebecca* (1940), would translate to their on-screen friendship in *Suspicion*. *United Artists/Photofest © United Artists*

Anderson, the Australian-born star of the Broadway stage, was perhaps the most important casting decision made at the insistence of Hitchcock, as she had only appeared in one other film, seven years earlier. As Mrs. Danvers, Anderson's attractive, strong features, which suggested a regal quality, were transformed to appear almost masculine, adding to Hitchcock's insinuation that Mrs. Danvers was a lesbian who tortured Fontaine out of an obsessive loyalty to first wife Rebecca. Hitchcock also instructed the actress to play the character as a lesbian, though it would never be overtly stated, to add tension to her scenes and keep Fontaine on edge.

Having Anderson to play with the inexperienced Fontaine, intimidating the actress, and Olivier, visibly annoyed that the unproved girl was chosen over Leigh, only added to Fontaine's insecurity on set. It was a trait Hitchcock chose to utilize in order to create a performance. On her harsh relationship with Olivier, which Hitchcock suggested his leading man project openly, she recalled, "He made me so dreadfully intimidated, that I was believable in my portrayal."[12]

According to Joan Fontaine's autobiography, Hitchcock found it necessary to be proactive in shaping her performance, building on the psychological insecurities the actress already had and bringing them to the performance.[13] The reason was based on Hitchcock's opinion that the only way for her to project her feelings on-screen was if she personally felt the same level of insecurity as her character. The confidence of having won such a coveted role would be a boost to any actress, confidence that would have risked destroying her performance if projected on-screen. To keep her in check, Hitchcock would need to keep her feeling the insecurity she felt during her screen test. He explained, "In early stages of the actual shooting, I felt that Joan Fontaine was a little self-conscious, but I could see her potential for restrained acting and I felt she could play the character in a quiet, shy manner. At the outset, she tended to overdo the shyness, but I felt she would work out all right, and once we got going, she did."[14]

His theory of how best to work with Fontaine seemed accurate, as it is an emotional performance Fontaine had never been able to tap into before . . . but the process was agonizing. In recounting her experiences with Hitchcock, as he molded and shaped every aspect of her performance, she explained:

> He was a Svengali. He controlled me totally. He took me aside and whispered, "Now, kid, you go in there and you do this and you do that." And then he said,

"Do you know what so and so said about you today? Well, never you mind. You just listen to me." Now some of what he told me might have been true, but of course it also made me feel absolutely miserable all the time. To be honest, he was divisive with us. He wanted total control over me, and he seemed to relish the cast not liking one another, actor for actor, by the end of the film. This helped me perform since I was supposed to be terrified of everyone, and it gave a lot of tension to my scenes. It kept him in command, and it was part of the upheaval he wanted. He kept me off balance, much to his own delight. . . . But he didn't give me what I needed most, which was confidence.[15]

Fontaine's comment on Hitchcock's unwillingness to motivate his cast is an opinion that is restated over and over by actors. Hitchcock seemed to live by the opinion that actors are the same as any of the other professionals working on a film. To praise their work was to treat them like a child. As he said again and again to actors, he would allow them to act and would only step in if he needed to make a correction. While some actors appreciated his hands-off approach, it could cause anxiety to other actors. His refusal to offer encouragement kept actors on edge while working with him, uncertain how their performances were being accessed throughout filming and aware that any time Hitchcock stepped in was due to a mistake.

Yet the mind games Hitchcock played with Fontaine seemed to work to her advantage in her performance, as she was universally praised by critics. Critic Archer Winsten wrote, "In the case of Joan Fontaine it is impossible to be more assured. She does everything that by common agreement has come to mean girlish innocence. She does it so well that it could pass for a classroom example. This studied perfection will be hailed as a great performance by the pat familiarity of it."[16] David Platt, of the *Daily Worker*, wrote, "The film is a triumph for Joan Fontaine who plays the second Mrs. De Winter with sensitivity and intelligence for which Alfred Hitchcock is to be thanked."[17] Another review wrote, "The surprise sensation of the year is Joan Fontaine's portrayal of the title role. She takes Du Maurier's anemic little mouse of a heroine, and makes her charming and alive, all the while retaining the modesty, appeal, and shrinking terror of people that characterized the girl in the novel. . . . Miss Fontaine has magnetism, beauty and a voice that makes the heartstrings vibrate."[18] Critic Archer Winsten acknowledged that the previously dismissed actress was no longer merely living in the shadow of her sister; instead "Miss

Joan Fontaine described Hitchcock as a Svengali in his control of the struggling actress while filming *Rebecca* (1940). *Selznick International Pictures/Photofest* © *Selznick International Pictures*

Fontaine has developed the rare ability to mingle charm with a sensitive expression, first, of simple timidity, then of fear and finally of bold courage and determination. Hers is a problem of complex dramatic reactions, and it is a problem that she solves with complete conviction. Through it she reveals a splendid young actress—clever, expressive and vastly appealing."[19]

Like Fontaine, Judith Anderson was highly praised, as were the many other character actors who brought color to the gothic story. Yet Olivier was perhaps the performance that truly divided the critics, leaving them questioning the charmless, harsh way Olivier played the role. Archer Winsten, after lavishing praise on Fontaine, wrote, "He must be gruff, rude, and given to moodiness without apparent cause. He gives a sincere if not inspired performance. Frankly, I am at a loss to know what an inspired performance would have entailed. Perhaps a different character would have seemed more satisfactory. If that were the case, then Olivier is not to blame. On the other hand, it may be that small mustache which has caused him to lose so much of his stingo."[20] Another critic was slightly more positive regarding his performance, making a point to compare him to the actor previously in consideration by Hitchcock, writing, "Laurence Olivier, in a mustached and slightly mature guise, is attractive, competent and only occasionally surly as Max de Winter. Never has his physical and vocal resemblance to Ronald Coleman been more pronounced."[21] Years later, Robin Wood described the legacy of Oliver's performance as "charmless, problematic in the romance."[22] Even Hitchcock was somewhat disappointed with the performance Olivier gave, telling Truffaut in his series of interviews that the lack of humor Olivier brought to the role was the biggest problem he had bringing the role of Max De Winter to life, a complaint that in retrospect suggests Hitchcock's initial insights of how the character would have been best cast were impeccable.

In *Rebecca*, the undeniable power Max has over his second wife should be evident, and audiences should be completely charmed and seduced by his romance of the heroine. Only when she discovers his dark side gradually and unexpectedly should an audience feel discomforted by their previous affection. Yet Olivier almost immediately shows his true self to the audience as one not to be trusted, only further complicated by the memory audiences had of his all-powerful and dangerous performance of Heathcliff. The disturbances on display from *Wuthering Heights* ultimately remain in the audience's memory and are suggested throughout *Rebecca* in Olivier's performance. Olivier's sinister qualities and his charmless, humorless performance keep audiences from being won over by him. We sympathize with Ms. De Winter for the way she is tortured (especially by Judith Anderson), but it is hard to rationalize the devotion she has toward Max.

His approach to the role makes even less sense because of the one major change Selznick demanded when adapting the novel: in the film, Mr. De Winter is innocent of killing his first wife, whereas in the novel, he is guilty. The new ending seems ridiculous considering the cruel intensity we've just witnessed. Ultimately, Olivier seems to be overplaying the character of Max, especially when compared to the screen performances given by Joan Fontaine and the supporting cast.

Despite any critique one has of Olivier, one of the greatest stars of his era, it was undeniable that it was Joan Fontaine who was the standout of the film for the sheer depths she reaches as an actress playing such a complex character. When first introduced, Fontaine plays the role with a girlish shyness who elicits sympathy. One only needs to watch the breakfast scene between Joan Fontaine and Laurence Olivier to see the warmth, sensitivity, and fear of simply being in the presence of a man Fontaine projects, and one sees precisely what Selznick first saw in her. In just that one scene she goes from buttoned up and nervous, eyes down and fearful of focusing on Olivier, to finally relaxing in his presence. Her body language, the way her shoulders go from rigid to relaxed, is subtle but expressive. And Fontaine continues to bring a layer of complexity to the role without losing grasp of the character. She is charming when hiding a broken statue in the desk drawer and frightened when in the presence of Mrs. Danvers.

It was her role in *Rebecca* that would make Joan Fontaine a star and was one of the great discoveries of 1940. However, all her accolades seemed to come with a grain of salt. Not only was she frequently compared to her sister, still a bigger name in Hollywood, but the role Hitchcock played in establishing her career was forever in question. The debatable method that Hitchcock used to help her craft this performance was brought to light many years later. But within the industry, filmmakers were well aware of the hands-on approach Hitchcock had taken, as they did see the difference between her performance in *Rebecca* and those films where she had been left on her own to craft a performance. Many reviewers suggested that the performance was built by Hitchcock, and therefore, most of the credit belonged to him.[23]

Considering the poor performances she had previously given, was she simply a puppet who could take precise direction but an incompetent actress? Did she have to be handled and manipulated to get any performance of merit from her? Or was she simply an untrained actress who needed instruction?

While promoting the film, Hitchcock made a point to reintroduce Fontaine to the press and sing her praises. Hitchcock insisted she had star qualities that were beyond her technical struggles as an actress. And Fontaine's talents as an actress would be addressed a few years later when she was cast in Hitchcock's film *Suspicion*. However, there would always be that towering question regarding her performance in *Rebecca*.

2

Foreign Correspondent

If *Rebecca* is Hitchcock's first Hollywood film, *Foreign Correspondent* is his first American film and was promoted as such when released in theaters as his "first American-made movie." Ironic as it is for a film about European travel, it functions as the spiritual link between his last English film, *The Lady Vanishes*, and the Hitchcock masterpiece about cross-country travel through the states, *North by Northwest*. *Foreign Correspondent* was not only a hit with audiences and his second best picture nominee in 1940 (*Rebecca* would win that year), but it gave Hitchcock the opportunity to take on new challenges as a studio director.

For the story of an investigative reporter sent to Europe as a war correspondent to uncover a traitor, Hitchcock initially hoped to cast the most trusted actor in Hollywood, Gary Cooper, as war correspondent Johnny Jones and sultry actress Barbara Stanwyck, an actress who always added a considerable bite, intelligence, and tension to films.[1] However, for a film considered a B movie (as much as a Hitchcock film could be called one), A-list stars were not available to him.[2] Hitchcock, used to dealing with the British film industry, was alarmed to discover the Hollywood "class structure" that deemed thrillers as B pictures, regardless of their merits or potential at the box office. Hitchcock made attempts to cast the stars, but his requests had been dismissed, recalling, "I went to Cooper with it [the script], but ended up with the next best thing . . . in this instance Joel McCrea. Years later, Gary Cooper told me, 'That was a mistake. I should have done it.'"[3]

The inability to cast these big stars forced Hitchcock to seek out some of the undervalued actors within the studio system. Joel McCrea, named "the All-American Boy" by W. R. Hearst[4] and a real-life rancher by this time in his career, was a popular leading man too often compared to other leading men as a second-best or lesser version of A-list stars. McCrea was often cast in forgettable romantic comedies that were patterned out of the films of Cary Grant. One year after *Foreign Correspondent*, McCrea's career would get a major boost due to his collaborations with writer/director Preston Sturges, starting with 1941's *Sullivan's Travels*. But one quality McCrea did have that became signature to him was a sincerity and trust with his audiences.

The sincerity of an actor is rarely addressed as it seems such a natural characteristic, but in the films of Hitchcock it is especially important to note, considering the number of times characters switch loyalties or hide identities. Very few actors could be trusted implicitly, and often Hitchcock cast those actors that his audiences assumed would be trustworthy in roles that called that

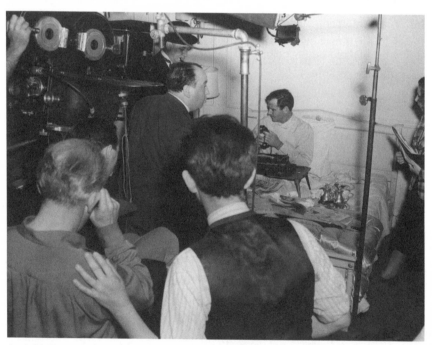

Joel McCrea anchored the film *Foreign Correspondent* (1940) with his inherent sincerity. *United Artists/Photofest © United Artists*

assumption into question. While Hitchcock frequently cast actors whose loyalties were in question to create thrills, *Foreign Correspondent* benefits from having an anchor like McCrea who is completely trustworthy, as the audience is left to question the loyalties of so many surrounding him.

Laraine Day had a similar sincerity in her performance style and was about as different from Barbara Stanwyck as an actress could have been. For three years, her primary focus had been cultivating her image as the leading lady in the Dr. Kildare series with Lew Ayres. Her first film since being "killed off" in the Dr. Kildare series, Day brought to the role a brainy, independent quality. Compared to the characters of wealthy heiresses and women who marry for wealth that were popular in the day, her character's status as an unmarried woman never identifies her as a spinster (as it had Joan Fontaine in *Rebecca*) nor does it suggest she is unwanted by the male sex. Rather it is she who rejects them, focusing instead on her own interests and intellectual pursuits.

One only needs to watch the scene of Day and McCrea at the Conference for Peace to see what each actor brought to the film. As she speaks to hundreds of delegates and businessmen with authority and intelligence, he struggles to "seduce" her, unable to play the cool Cary Grant type. Overcome by her beauty and intelligence, he finds himself simply distracting her, unable to keep from smiling.

Day represented a certain type of heroine rarely mentioned in Hitchcock lore but very common. While a classic blonde and quite beautiful, Day's type is more closely associated with the nonsexualized good girl, often described as All-American, who could be a pal to the everyman. There is a sense of equality between Day's and McCrea's characters, and as Day often projects, she is more a "Girl Friday" than damsel in distress. Hitchcock would go back to this character type often in films, often casting feisty brunettes (*Shadow of a Doubt*, *Stage Fright*, and *The Trouble with Harry*) to differentiate them from the mysterious blonde image he elevated to its own character type. And this is part of the reason the film dates remarkably well. Despite being made in 1940, the sexism that frequently creeps into Hitchcock films is largely absent from *Foreign Correspondent*, which allows for the fun of the thriller to emerge for contemporary audiences, despite the overarching narrative connected to World War II and the war effort.

It also helps that these two actors, who seem to represent decency and trustworthiness, are also surrounded by a collection of actors whose alliances are impossible to predict. *Rebecca* costar George Sanders is one of the first stars for which Hitchcock not only altered his established image (one he previously reinforced by casting him as the blackmailer in *Rebecca*), but played him against his public image. In the press, he was a favorite personality to write about because he was noted for his particularly odd, droll sense of humor, which allowed him to get away with an unusual amount of open distaste for Hollywood reporters, gossip columnists, and critics. He was known as a cad (a term he enjoyed so much he titled his autobiography *Memoirs of a Professional Cad*), and as he said when promoting that very book, "I'm always rude to people. I am not a sweet person. I am a disagreeable person. I am a hateful person. I like to be hateful."[5] But despite all of this misbehavior, which had been going on for years, he was somehow still a likable cad or at least one whose unapologetic wickedness audiences loved to delight in.

Oddly, upon introduction to Sanders, it was assumed that he would be an ideal "hero" for his tall build, soft features, and personal polish (high living was a vice he was well known for, especially good suits and going into unapologetic bankruptcy). His exterior didn't hint at the villainy he was capable of. But once this darkness had been exposed, his appearance and public personality only enhanced his image as one not to be trusted on film. But in *Foreign Correspondent*, Sanders is downright honorable, certainly the noblest character in the film. And by casting Sanders in the role, Hitchcock not only forces an audience taught to distrust him to question how they perceive "the villain type" but also adds a tension to this thriller. His smile is untrustworthy to audiences who have been conditioned to distrust him, allowing Hitchcock to create suspense, not through narrative structure but purely through creative casting.

When Sanders first enters the film, we expect the double agent will certainly be him, and the audience remains hyperfocused on what he does in the film, looking for signs of what is to come. Our attention is elsewhere until Herbert Marshall's character, Stephen Fischer, proves to be the villain in question we've been looking for, right under our nose. And like *North by Northwest*'s Vandamm (played by James Mason), Marshall's character is especially devious because we would never expect him to be guilty. Furthermore, the fact that his personality doesn't change after the reveal only adds a greater chill to the discovery.

Unlike Sanders, however, Marshall had avoided being typecast, largely because of the variety of work he had performed on the stage. He was a strong comic thespian (appearing in many Philip Barry plays when first beginning his career), but had also played plenty of villains and spoke to theater critics with pride over never having been typecast. However, while his on-screen image had not been fully established, his public image was that of a war hero. For example, in 1937 one fan magazine declared:

> He has been here for a long time and has proven a "goodwill ambassador." Because of him we like Englishmen better. We know that during the war he fought and suffered. We have seen him as soldier, as a scamp and in many other parts, but whatever the role is we enjoy the culture in his voice, the character in his face and his ever present kindly humor. You have to like a chap like that.[6]

Who better to play a man guilty of spying and treason than a man who had become an ambassador of England in Hollywood? The audience, and therefore the film's heroes, would never be suspicious of such a man.

George Sanders and Herbert Marshall switched typical character types in *Foreign Correspondent* (1940). *United Artists/Photofest © United Artists*

Like Marshall, Edmund Gwenn, as hit man Rowley, is delightfully under-
playing the character's villainous side, playing Rowley as lighthearted and
mischievous (even the name suggests a harmless chap). Gwenn was a favorite
character actor of many directors on both stage and film, but was often asked
to simply flesh out or enhance characters with his natural charms. While the
true nature and deeds of his characters in *Foreign Correspondent* and *The
Trouble with Harry* are considerably different, the mannerisms of both characters are similar: sweet, lovable, talkative, slightly unkempt, and lower class.
He had been a sailor in real life (like many of his characters) and was a thirty-
year veteran of the stage before finally breaking into films. Even his Cockney
accent was authentic and only added to the lovable, teddy-bear quality audiences saw in the grandfatherly actor. In Hitchcock's stock company, of which
Gwenn was a beloved member, he often seems to be the lower-class version
of Nigel Bruce's characters in *Rebecca* and *Suspicion*. After being brought to
Hollywood by Hitchcock to appear in *Foreign Correspondent*, Gwenn would
appear as another seaman in the acclaimed Broadway production of *The
Wookey*, which would elevate his name recognition considerably in America
. . . and would be a role to influence Hitchcock a decade later.

But of all the stars to make an appearance in the film, the best-known personality for American audiences was arguably the comic wit Robert Benchley. Best known as a humorist in print and later in short films (including
his clever "how to" parodies), Benchley was brought in to punch up *Foreign
Correspondence*'s dialogue. Hitchcock and wife Alma (herself a strong writer)
found several of their best character actors to be writers (Hume Cronyn,
Patricia Collinge) and simply created the role of Stebbins for Benchley to
play—one which was very similar to the oblivious professor character he had
played in the short films he had written and directed.

The role of Stebbins isn't one that moves the story along, but it is nonethe-
less entertaining and sets the humorous tone that will run throughout the
thriller. However, in regard to Benchley's career, his role in *Foreign Correspondent* is arguably the saddest he ever played. Benchley's persona was based
on a man who suffered from depression and alcoholism until his premature
death at fifty-six in 1945. Benchley's melancholy funnyman always had sadness, having come to regret leaving his literary career as a critic, humorist,
and editor at *The New Yorker* to become "Hollywood's only actor-author."
He considered himself a hack for making the move to Hollywood, despite his

popularity with audiences. Anyone familiar with Benchley certainly finds his few scenes in *Foreign Correspondent* difficult to watch, as he discusses being a hack reporter while drinking a glass of milk at a bar because "I've been doing it for twenty-five years, twenty-five years and end up drinking milk." It is a memorable character, and a happy cameo from a well-liked personality at the time of the film's first release, which to contemporary audiences plays as a sad reminder.

Despite the surprisingly strong cast assembled, only one star received attention from the Academy Awards: Albert Bassermann, who was, like Robert Benchley, a fellow writer and who had returned to acting after pursuing a second career in chemistry. Once a star of theater (including the original plays of Ibsen), Bassermann played the character of Van Meer, a character not remarkably different from the intelligent, ethical characters he played in several other films the same year: a priest in *Knute Rockne, All American* and a doctor in *Escape*. But his performance in *Foreign Correspondent* caught the attention of the Academy because in the otherwise breezy thriller, Bassermann sells the film's honorable message for the war effort without making the film seem disjointed or tonally inconsistent. His scenes are also the most dramatic in the light thriller, adding weight and substance to the film.

Foreign Correspondent was, despite the comparisons made to *Rebecca* at the time, widely considered an exceptional war film full of thrills and generally entertaining, despite not having the A-list stars Hitchcock initially developed the film around. All the actors were widely praised, including Joel McCrea, who was described as amiable and casual and "somewhere between Gary Cooper and Cary Grant,"[7] which was precisely the comparisons Hitchcock wanted to evoke with audiences, even if he would have preferred to have the originals rather than an imitation.

3

Mr. and Mrs. Smith

I liked Lombard very much. She had a bawdy sense of humor and used the language men used with each other. I'd never heard a woman speak that way. She was a forceful personality—stronger, I felt, than Gable.[1]

When you consider the career Hitchcock had when he first arrived in Hollywood and the grasp he had for such a variety of films, it was remarkable: a quickie thriller, romantic epic, and classic screwball comedy were all done in less than a year, and each showed the vast knowledge Hitchcock had of film genres. But of his first films, *Mr. and Mrs. Smith* is the greatest enigma, perhaps the greatest in his career, not because it is comic, but for the general lack of thrills or mystery in it. There is no murder, no horror, and no people of questionable morals. The worst thing these characters do is trick and lie to each other when the long-married couple discovers they are not legally married.

Decades later, Hitchcock came to dismiss the largely forgotten screwball comedy, telling Truffaut, "That picture was done as a friendly gesture to Carole Lombard. At the time, she was married to Clark Gable, and she asked whether I'd do a picture with her. In a weak moment I accepted, and I more or less followed Norman Krasna's screenplay, since I really didn't understand the type of people who were portrayed in the film, all I did was photograph the scenes as written."[2] Hitchcock's inspiration to take on the film was his genuine affection for Carole Lombard, an actress he felt had been misused and unappreciated for almost a decade, and whom he had wanted to work with for some time. Hitchcock made this fact known to the press, even citing her as one of the actresses who inspired him to work with American actresses, explaining:

> Plunge an English actress into a bath of cold water and she still comes to the top trying to look aloof and dignified. Her whole concern is not how best to express her emotions but how best to bottle them up. I do not imagine that American stars suffer from this inhibition to anything like the same extent. No girl could arrive at the pitch of efficiency achieved by Carole Lombard if her one consideration were how best to appear to "society."[3]

According to Hitchcock, Lombard's career had not elevated beyond the screwball films she was so beloved for due primarily to the lazy, uninspired casting decisions made at studios, the same people who had kept her from taking the many roles she campaigned for. Hitchcock saw a potential Hollywood had overlooked, explaining:

> I should like to cast Lombard not in the type of superficial comedy which she so often plays but in a much meatier comedy-drama, giving her plenty of scope for characterizations. I believe that, imaginatively treated, Lombard is capable of giving a performance equal to that of any of the best male actors, like [Paul] Muni and Leslie Howard.[4]

It was a statement of considerable honor to Lombard, and one of note, considering Hitchcock's notorious treatment of his actresses. As disparaging as he could be toward women ("certainly don't think they are as good actors as men"[5]), fine actresses such as Lombard (along with Myrna Loy, who he mentioned in the same interview) were given due respect, even if always paying homage to them by comparing them to men. But Hitchcock did note that female actors were treated considerably worse in the studio system, with those with any power over casting often unable to see new possibilities that would keep themselves fresh and continue to evolve their star image. It wasn't until 1934 that Lombard was given a leading role of any merit (*Twentieth Century*), and another two years passed before she received her one and only Oscar nomination (*My Man Godfrey*). And still Lombard, one of the most popular actresses in Hollywood, struggled to find roles.

Having become a close friend of Carole Lombard, Hitchcock was eager to work with the "Hoosier Tornado" and lent his services to one of her signature screwball comedies, but one that required her to be considerably more "refined" and reactive, rather than the hyperactive crazy girls she had been playing. Despite her popularity with audiences who delighted in her antics, which always seemed surprising for an actress who often looked like an American Marlene Dietrich, critics sensed Lombard was maturing out of these childish roles, as mentioned in a 1939 article profiling the actress:

> American Girl is precisely what Carole Lombard is. A little pert, a little too prone to wisecrack and pretend to be hard boiled, but very genuine and likable underneath it all. . . . I don't think she's ever going to be a great dramatic actress. I hope she'll never get too inextricably mixed up in crazy comedy again.[6]

Hitchcock had no intention of making another crazy comedy for his friend; instead, he created a more sophisticated variation on the classic "comedy of remarriage" variety, and one that today would be considered quite modern. According to RKO record, Hitchcock proposed himself as the director of Lombard's next film, promising, "The typical comedy has its character slip, figuratively speaking, on a banana peel, and thereby gets its laugh. But the slip is not funny to the victim. I prefer to have my comedy examine his reaction."[7] *Mr. and Mrs. Smith* was the ideal project to allow him to challenge Lombard (and Robert Montgomery), to direct them in performances that required the same refinement they would approach in one of his dramas. The press was informed that in his new approach to comedy: "He does not want his stars to screw their faces around in funny ways. He doesn't want them to read funny lines as though they had just popped them out of a joke book. He says that, when two people live and work together, they are not conscious of being funny; people are funniest when they're serious."[8]

While Lombard was adept in comedy, Hitchcock needed a certain type of actor who, much the way Joel McCrea could play the ridiculous fool in a thriller like *Foreign Correspondent*, had the ability to play the dope who loses his wife when he doesn't tell her they aren't married and spends the rest of the film trying to win her back. As Peter Bogdanovich explained, a sophisticated actor like Cary Grant would never have worked in the roles because failures never register as failures on Grant, and it is impossible to embarrass him.

Robert Montgomery is pictured filming a scene from the comedy *Mr. and Mrs. Smith* (1941), with Hitchcock serving as his scene partner off-camera. *RKO Radio Pictures/ Photofest © RKO Radio Pictures*

Instead, Hitchcock selected the likable, rubber-faced Robert Montgomery, who like Carole Lombard was active in proving his versatility and had an uncharacteristic amount of control over his career for an actor in 1940, including being president of the Screen Actors Guild. Although he had already proven himself comic, he was primarily known as a dramatic actor at the time, including a best actor Oscar nomination in 1937. More importantly, he was easy to embarrass and, because of this, quick to elicit sympathetic laughs from audiences.

But the third leading character, the wedge between Montgomery's Mr. Smith and Lombard's Mrs. Smith was an unexpected appearance by Gene Raymond. When he first arrived in Hollywood, he was considered a dashing leading man who actively "wanted to fill the void of Douglas Fairbanks Sr." and was described as a nervy, arrogant, smart-aleck type, "too conscious of his appeal to women."[9] But five years after arriving in Hollywood, his image had drastically changed, now more reminiscent of Van Johnson and still known for his debut film *Golden Boy*.

Married to one of the most popular musical stars in Hollywood, Raymond was also better known as Mr. Jeanette MacDonald. All this made his appearance in *Mr. and Mrs. Smith* as the opportunistic cad Jeff Custer a joke on the unsuspecting audiences, particularly the change in his appearance with his signature blond hair dyed black and his light skin darkly tanned. Like George Sanders' surprising casting in *Foreign Correspondent* (whose real personality was closer to the character of Custer), Hitchcock understood that by casting against type, he could enhance the audience's reaction, this time getting a laugh from audiences who didn't expect Raymond's appearance.

Ultimately, *Mr. and Mrs. Smith* did, as Hitchcock intended, show the stars in a different light. Lombard was capable of retaining her elegance while being comedic. Montgomery was given an opportunity to show his skills in physical comedy. And Gene Raymond played against type. And yet their

Stars Robert Montgomery, Carole Lombard, and Gene Raymond (with his blond hair dyed black) in a scene from *Mr. and Mrs. Smith* (1941). *RKO Radio Pictures/Photofest* © *RKO Radio Pictures*

work has been overlooked in the history of the film's production because of the infamous livestock comment. Asked during production if he had in fact referred to actors as cattle, Hitchcock spent his life revising and correcting his comments, insisting he said actors should be "treated like cattle." Spitfire Lombard took a humorous approach to these comments, with a prank even Hitchcock could appreciate. As Hitchcock recounted:

> When I arrived on the set, the first day of shooting, Carole Lombard had had a corral built, with three sections, and in each one there was a live young cow. Round the neck of each of them there was a white disk tied on with ribbon, with three names; Carole Lombard, Robert Montgomery, and the name of a third member of the cast, Gene Raymond.[10]

This publicity stunt cemented the notoriety of this comment, which would go to the grave with the master of suspense. Hitchcock claimed he suspected Lombard agreed with his assessment that actors should be treated purely as employees and she showed a good deal more professionalism than a number of the spoiled studio stars did.[11]

However, when considering the origins of *Mr. and Mrs. Smith* and how he cast the film, such a comment doesn't translate to how he really wanted to use actors. A constant professional, yes, but Lombard was also one of the most unique stars of her time; so special Hitchcock would take a job outside his comfort zone simply to work with her. Lombard, Montgomery, and particularly Raymond were each cast because of a quality unique to their personalities. If actors were (or should be) treated like cattle, Hitchcock would not have taken such efforts to cast with the creativity and intelligence he had.

4

Suspicion

In light of some of the comments regarding Joan Fontaine's standout performance in *Rebecca*, critics claiming it was nothing more than an anomaly or owed purely to Hitchcock's directorial talents rather than her abilities as an actress made her follow-up film, *Suspicion*, vitally important in the trajectory of her career. In her performance in *Suspicion*, the creation of the character of Lina would fall on her shoulders, as she would have to establish a noticeable difference between her roles in *Rebecca* and *Suspicion*—a challenge she took with intensity and seriousness, and more than succeeded in accomplishing.

In *Rebecca*, Fontaine was girlish, insecure, and naive, called a spinster but also far from unapproachable, simply the overlooked wallflower. In *Suspicion*, her Lina is quite cold, composed, and even a bit intimidating. In the presence of men, she is frigid (rather than frightened) and detached (aware she holds back her affections but fearful of rejection). Her downfall is not her naiveté; but the loss of control she gives in to when she finally gives up her rational mind for her emotional desires for the first time by falling in love with Cary Grant's Johnnie. In *Rebecca*, Hitchcock wanted her to be an empty vessel for the audience, but in *Suspicion*, Lina had to be a full character, for the film is told entirely from her perspective, and the audience's acceptance of the film depends almost exclusively on the degree to which they sympathize and connect to this fuller and more dimensional character.

Ironically, her character in *Suspicion* was one with which Joan Fontaine had a personal identification, described by many (even when she wrote her memoir decades later) as a woman who "lacked human warmth and compassion" and had a stoic quality, which when presented in just the right angle could appeal to audiences because of her mysterious coolness but quickly became outright cold and made her unlikable to audiences. It was this quality that made her initially struggle as an actress; her reserve was interpreted as pretension or boredom, rather than cool mystery for sheer female self-preservation. While in *Rebecca* she largely had rid herself of that hardness, in *Suspicion* she remains just on the line between reserved and cold, which makes her character unique but still likable. Fontaine earned high praise for her performance in *Suspicion*, and her Oscar was not simply a correction for not honoring her for *Rebecca*.

While Fontaine is at times a bit cold and shrewish in *Suspicion*, she had the benefit of working with a familiar face (and her *Rebecca* costar) Nigel Bruce. Played with the playful lovability of an overgrown teddy bear, the undeniable affection Lina feels for his character makes it easy to warm to her, especially as his relationship with Johnnie begins to disintegrate and the two become allies. When the horrific events surrounding the death of Bruce's character in the third act come to light, the audience feels much like Lina, distrustful of Johnnie and mourning the loss of Nigel Bruce's warm presence.

With a far more substantial role in *Suspicion* than he had in *Rebecca*, Bruce created a persona and character type that was easy to like. Having played Watson in the Sherlock Holmes films with Basil Rathbone, audiences viewed the actor much as they viewed the character Bruce described as a "rather amusing fellow, Watson. A little pompous. Maybe not too bright. Good sound stuff there, though. I always enjoy playing a character I think I'd like if I knew him in real life."[1] Bruce's view of how he selected characters, playing a character he would like to know, was the reason people had such affection for the lovable Englishman. He projected characters who seemed not only likable, but as individuals the audience would want to spend time with in their lives.

While Fontaine's performance is a lovely, complex performance, which made her a true star with sustainability, *Suspicion* will always be known as the first film to unite Hitchcock and star Cary Grant. As Johnnie, the financially irresponsible playboy, Grant is asked to give one of the most challenging performances of his career: remaining vague as a character in order to increase suspense, playing the character with an element of both fear and humor, and challenging the public image he had spent decades creating for himself.

Joan Fontaine and Alfred Hitchcock created a far more complex character in *Suspicion* (1941) than as the nameless vessel she played in *Rebecca*. *RKO Radio Pictures/ Photofest © RKO Radio Pictures*

Hitchcock had a theory that the standard (and publicly accepted) career transition of a star was from villain to straight man to comedian.[2] It had certainly been the transition of some of his favorite stars (especially in America). Yet during the golden age of Hollywood, Hitchcock's desire to experiment with and challenge the conventions of the star system casting drove him to continually cast not only villains as heroes but also heroes as villains. While he did this somewhat with the often likable Herbert Marshall in *Foreign Correspondent* and Gene Raymond in *Mr. and Mrs. Smith*, the casting of a star as iconic as Cary Grant in *Suspicion* was his first noble but ultimately troubled attempt to truly revolutionize the Hollywood casting structure.

In a more conventional film, an actor who represented something threatening or had no defining persona would have been the more likely casting choice. And for some time, reports circled that Hitchcock's *Mr. and Mrs. Smith* star Robert Montgomery or *Rebecca*'s Laurence Olivier would star. Either actor would have been a far more accepted and conventional choice for the role of Johnnie at that time.[3] But the actor who would have the strongest visceral impact on an audience was the ultimate image of lighthearted romantic hero Cary Grant. And Grant was himself eager to "stretch" as an actor, the same way Hitchcock wanted to test his stars.

Casting Cary Grant as Johnnie would not only be casting against type but asking audiences to completely reexamine the Cary Grant playboy image as something not to fantasize about but perceive as a possible threat or menace. The character is a man who presents himself as so charming that his most personal inadequacies are forgiven by those who fall for him. Yet it is gradually revealed that Johnnie has the potential to be more than simply a rogue but genuinely dangerous. Calling attention to the fact that Johnnie is essentially a dangerous version of the Grant persona suggests that the master of playing the carefree playboy hides a sinister motive behind his light comedy—an individual whose charms kept him hiding in plain sight. The role would be a balancing act for Grant, for if that threat did not exist, the film would be without any suspense whatsoever and become a directionless melodrama. But if Johnnie is too dangerous and suspicious, Lina's attraction to him is called into question and destroys the audience's alliance to her. It was a daring request for Hitchcock to make of the giant star, especially considering the approach Grant takes with the role; rather than playing Johnnie as a significantly different character, his performance is not that different from how he plays so many of his comic characters. As one review stated:

> The work of Cary Grant as an irresponsible charmer of women who is not above living off one or borrowing without a thought of paying back is surely as fine as he has ever done. Though he has been seen in charmer roles, there are frequent suggestions here of something beneath the surface, of a truly complex character. The gradual unfolding of his various aspects is accomplished with complete assurance.[4]

Suspicion is the very definition of a star vehicle, which was defined by film theorist Richard Maltby as being when the character is adapted to fit the star. A frequently used mechanism centers the plot on a character who eventually

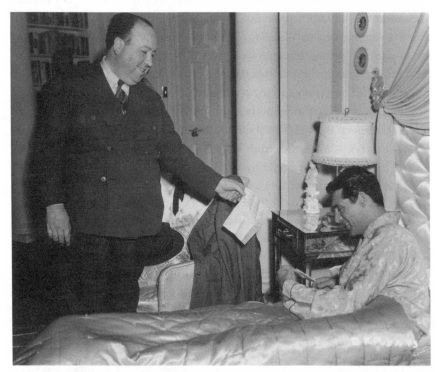

Cary Grant's performance as irresponsible playboy Johnnie in *Suspicion* (1941) was far closer to his screwball heroes than fans of the star were willing to accept. *RKO Radio Pictures/Photofest © RKO Radio Pictures*

displays the skills that the audiences already know the performer possesses. A convincing performance is thus one in which the character becomes the star persona as the movie progresses.[5] *Suspicion* achieves this with both Grant and Fontaine. While Grant's character and even the superficial structure of *Suspicion* is similar to screwball romance, the presence of Grant made the film thrilling as Hitchcock slowly turns our expectations; yet at the same time the Fontaine persona is established throughout the film, emerging to be a popular star of unique qualities by the end.

We are won over by Grant as Johnnie at the same time that Fontaine's character is being seduced; we can't judge her as weak or foolish because we are just like her. Grant plays Johnnie for a majority of the film with the same carefree, comic charms he did in films such as *The Awful Truth*, *Holiday*, or *Penny Serenade*. The latter (made two years earlier and earning Grant an Oscar nomination) is an especially good comparison, as a film that casts working-class Grant as a man incapable of holding down a job, the very same shortcoming Johnnie has in *Suspicion*. We pass no judgment on his behavior, as his boyishness is precisely what we expect, and want, to see from Cary Grant. And at first, Fontaine's shrewish nagging of him keeps him in our favor a bit longer than he deserves. As she berates him for doing wrong, our alliance falls in Johnnie's favor. But when his behavior becomes possibly sinister, our entire interpretation of the belief in the myth of Grant is called into question, not only in *Suspicion* but in the entire image of Hollywood's Cary Grant.

Theorist John Ellis wrote in his essay "Stars as a Cinematic Phenomenon" on the effect of Grant in *Suspicion*, stating:

> At its limits, the fictional figure can go against the grain of the circulated image, creating a specific tension in the film. Such is the case with Hitchcock's *Suspicion* where Cary Grant is cast as the likely murderer and swindler. The whole film is constructed on this dislocation in order to render Joan Fontaine's suspicions incongruous at first, and then increasingly irrefutable even to the most incredulous audience as the "evidence" mounts. Despite the reconciliatory ending, this film represents something more than "casting against type." *Suspicion* needs the star image of Cary Grant in order to function at all. Its effect would have been totally different with Reginald Denny.[6]

Suspicion is a movie that is structured, from start to finish, around the cultural impact Grant's image represented; its suspense does not come from whether

"Johnnie" (the character) could possibly be a murderer, but if Cary Grant could possibly be a murderer. If played by another actor, the audience would have quickly accepted what Fontaine's Lina doubts.

But while the film does as it must, convincing an audience slowly that he could in fact be a murderer, however much we resist such an idea, the ending makes the entire film seem a bit off, especially Grant's performance. If he is in fact innocent of the crimes of the film, his behavior still seems off-kilter and raises new questions as to the reason for his moody, sinister gaze. While we can accept a charmer hiding a dark side, a person showing his or her dark side can rarely be accepted as the reverse of true innocence. It is why, perhaps, modern-day audiences are more willing to accept that the film simply has an ambiguous ending rather than a happy one; while Fontaine may accept and be complicit with his behavior, Johnnie will always be a manipulative and possibly dangerous man.

According to Cary Grant biographer Charles Higham, Grant approached *Suspicion* as his great dramatic role but was ultimately disappointed with the outcome of the final film, explaining "He [Hitchcock] did kill me in the original cut, but at the preview, the audience objected, so they had to reshoot it. We were told later that the audience simply refused to accept him as the murderer. In the new version, the film just stops—without the proper ending."[7] Hitchcock claimed in the ending he really wanted, Fontaine is killed by the poison milk Grant gives her, but gives Johnnie the letter confessing her husband's crimes to mail before allowing herself to be poisoned.[8]

While many audiences resisted the film, unwilling or unable to believe Grant could be possible of such mischief no matter how Hitchcock insists or its ending, the film did well at the box office and critics praised the performances of both Grant and Fontaine. Critics noticed that the comedic approach Grant had taken added a layer of exciting complexity and thrills to the film. And Fontaine was universally praised for the delicate performance she gave, which only proved that her breakthrough in *Rebecca* had been far from a flash in the pan. One critic raved that Fontaine had,

> in the character of Lina Aysgarth, a part which enables her to carry on successfully her reputation as an emotional actress of ability. Smoothly she develops from a shy provincial creature, apparently fated for spinsterhood in the lush English countryside into a young woman whose attractive possibilities blossom

under the influence of a sudden, sincere love. . . . She maintains a fine balance in portraying the anguish of a woman weighing the love for her husband and what she knows is right, against what she has been taught is wrong.[9]

The film deservedly won Fontaine the best actress statue many believed she had been robbed of for *Rebecca* and secured her place as an A-level film star. But perhaps more importantly, the film was the first of four Hitchcock films Grant would star in and the first time Hitchcock would attempt to manipulate his "irresponsible audiences" through casting for added thrills.

5

Saboteur

The supporting parts are excellently cast, but Hitchcock could have done better with the leads. Miss Lane is acceptable, if little more, but Cummings's acting is a handicap which a picture has to overcome. This one does.[1]

From one of the most charming men in Hollywood with Cary Grant in *Suspicion*, Hitchcock turned to perhaps the blandest of any of his leading men: Robert Cummings's performance in *Saboteur* as a man wrongly accused of arson in a military airplane factory. As an actor, Robert Cummings was likable enough, and by all accounts he was a lovely, gracious man who made a name for himself on television with the comedy series *The Bob Cummings Show* and *My Living Doll*. But Hitchcock preferred actors who made a strong impression on audiences, and Cummings seemed to be lacking any noticeable identity in Hollywood (if one believes the story Cummings told of coming to Hollywood: he didn't believe in his own star quality and made up a false identity that he was a Texan from a wealthy family). Cummings used two different names in film: Bob Cummings when appearing in comedies and Robert when in a drama. Considering Hitchcock's preference for blending comedy with his thrillers, it should have been expected that "Robert Cummings's" performance in *Saboteur* would lack any charisma.

Hitchcock acknowledged that the casting of Cummings is one of the primary reasons the film is today dismissed:

A major problem with this sort of film is getting an actor of stature to play the central figure. I've learned from experience that whenever the hero isn't portrayed by a star, the whole picture suffers, you see, because audiences are far less concerned about the predicament of a character who's played by someone they don't know. Robert Cummings played the hero of *Saboteur*; he's a competent performer, but he belongs to the light-comedy class of actors. Aside from that, he has an amusing face, so that even when he's in desperate straits, his features don't convey any anguish.[2]

It comes as little surprise that despite the active role Hitchcock played in getting *Saboteur* finally made after Selznick had abandoned it, Hitchcock did not have absolute authority regarding the casting of the leading roles. Although he suggested, once again, matching up Gary Cooper and Barbara Stanwyck (a screen relationship he found very exciting), Universal insisted Hitchcock use actors from their studio in the leads. Cummings was a contract player and Priscilla Lane had a contract to make a picture for Universal at the time, so they were assigned to the film. Like with Cummings, Hitchcock initially resisted the casting of Lane, believing she was too much of a good girl to play the role, and described having her forced on him as a case of being double-crossed by producers.[3] It is undeniable that the film would have been considerably better if there had been a big star to anchor the film. However, considering the difficult circumstances she had been put in, and the awareness that she was not wanted by Hitchcock, actress Priscilla Lane gave a surprisingly spirited and intelligent performance in a forgettable movie.

At the time of *Saboteur*, Lane's career was on a bit of an upswing after years of her talents being squandered at Warner Bros., her home studio until 1941. Although her sisters were slightly better known, the press (especially the British papers) had made it well aware that they considered Priscilla Lane to be the only one of the actresses to possess any comic abilities. At the time Hitchcock was casting *Saboteur*, she had just utilized those comic abilities alongside *Suspicion* star Cary Grant in Frank Capra's *Arsenic and Old Lace*, but the film would not be released for nearly three years due to its extended run on Broadway.

Unlike Hitchcock's other leading men, including Joel McCrea and Robert Montgomery, Robert Cummings was best known for playing second bananas to stronger females. Opposite Barbara Stanwyck, Jean Arthur, and Deanna

Pictured with actors Mary and Billy Curtis, actor Robert Cummings was one of Hitchcock's few uncharismatic leading men, despite appearing in both *Saboteur* (1942) and *Dial M for Murder. Universal Pictures/Photofest © Universal Pictures*

Durban, he had been the supporting male in some of their star-making films; and while *Saboteur* was not a film that would make her an A-list star, Lane did steal the attention from Cummings's leading man. Ironically, her biggest scene, and one of the best in the film, is not opposite Cummings but the film's villain, Norman Lloyd, when she follows him to the Statue of Liberty by boat and uses her feminine wiles to trap him. In the scene, Lane shows some of her comic ability, and she finally shows some of the star potential she had hinted at throughout her career—stardom that seemed to always be just out of grasp.

It helped in that scene that Lloyd was such a strong actor for Lane to work opposite. This was Lloyd's first film, making a memorable appearance in a brief scene at the beginning before disappearing until the last act. According to Lloyd, who would work with Hitchcock again in *Spellbound*, Hitchcock wanted an unknown for the role of the saboteur, and Lloyd was recom-

Priscilla Lane's best scene in *Saboteur* (1942) was opposite Norman Lloyd, who played the villain, rather than leading man Robert Cummings. *Universal Pictures/Photofest ©
Universal Pictures*

mended by John Houseman. Theater-trained Lloyd was an ideal choice; unlike the athletic, rugged, and always healthy-looking Cummings, Lloyd was fair and slender and had slightly effeminate features, establishing an immediate contrast between the two men, which would make Lloyd memorable, as he is absent from the entire second act of the film. As Hitchcock so often did with actors inexperienced working on camera, he gave Lloyd precise directions regarding his every physical movement. However, unlike so many who found this approach from Hitchcock overbearing or disruptive to their performance, Lloyd was unbothered and found it easier to create an internal performance while taking precise "direction."

With similarities to the likes of Peter Lorre in Hitchcock's *The Man Who Knew Too Much* (1934), Lloyd is arguably the first villain who truly overshadows a hero in one of Hitchcock's Hollywood films. And the same is true of costar Otto Kruger, who like Herbert Marshall in *Foreign Correspondent*, possessed a lovable, paternal quality that made his character far scarier than if played as a mustache twirler or evil genius. Hitchcock, despite how memorable the performance was, didn't like the casting of Kruger; he had intended to make a subversive comment with the casting of that role:

> We were in 1941 and there were pro-German elements who called themselves American Firsters and who were, in fact, American Fascists. This was the group I had in mind while writing the scenario, and for the role of the heavy I had thought of a very popular actor, Harry Carey, who generally played the good guy in westerns. When I approached him, his wife was very indignant. She said, "I am shocked that you should dare to offer my husband a part like this. After all, since Will Rogers's death, the youth of America have looked up to my husband!" So the loss of that counterpoint element was another disappointment. In the end we wound up with a conventional heavy.[4]

Like Norman Lloyd, who is undeniably villainous but a delight to watch on-screen, Kruger is similarly enjoyable as the villain. Smooth as he always was on film, and known also as a symbol of urban sophistication, the mere way Kruger reads his dialogue about his acts of terrorism with the delight of a Hollywood dandy makes his character chilling, funny, and fascinating to watch. And despite knowing all the while that Cummings is in the right, the audience is far more interested in watching Kruger and Lloyd. Kruger's line to Cummings "You have the makings of an outstanding bore" sadly reflects the audience's own frustration with Cummings's hero.

The problem with casting a flat actor like Cummings in the lead is evident in the fight on the Statue of Liberty between he and Lloyd, when Lloyd missteps and hangs from the statue until he falls to his death. Although Lloyd claimed Hitchcock later thought it was ultimately an anticlimactic scene because it showed the villain in danger, rather than the hero,[5] had Cummings been in the same danger, the audience wouldn't have been on the edge of their seats the way they were watching Lloyd's terrified face.

Yet, despite all this, Cummings received some of the best reviews of his career, with Archer Winsten of the *New York Post* writing, "Robert Cummings turns in one of his best acting jobs under the master's direction."[6] And even Hitchcock saved face by insisting that the casting of Cummings and Lane was to his benefit, telling the press:

> I was lucky doubly for I not only had young players, but unmistakably young Americans. It was easy to bring out the familiar qualities to make Bob seem the lovable boy at the next lathe or around the next corner. In Priscilla, too I had the resolute and daring attributes typical of American girlhood. I wanted the boy and girl in *Saboteur* to suggest the thrilling importance of the unimportant people, to forget they were movie stars, to remember only that they were free and in terrible danger.[7]

Saboteur serves as one of the key examples of how casting can fundamentally alter how audiences see and perceive characters, despite script and directorial intention. In writing, Robert Cummings's character is our everyman, the individual audiences should identify with and root for. But the mere casting of Cummings not only allows the character to be overshadowed by the supporting characters, but also prevents the audience from connecting emotionally, so we are hardly even concerned with the character's fate. It is unsurprising that Hitchcock initially wanted to cast Gary Cooper in the role of an American patriot wrongfully accused, which would have made *Saboteur* a completely different film. Years later, Hitchcock would tell a very similar story about a good man wrongfully accused; however, that time he would be able to cast his first choice to star in the film, Henry Fonda in *The Wrong Man*.

6

Shadow of a Doubt

The casting of *Shadow of a Doubt* is in some ways as much about who was considered for the leading roles as who was ultimately cast. In addition to considering Joan Fontaine for the role of young Charlie, Hitchcock originally intended that the role of her Uncle Charlie be created for William Powell. The beloved, mustached actor was one of the Hitchcock's favorite actors, insisting,

> Usually when I prepare a script, I tend to hold myself back a bit because I have the constant fear that my actors will not be able to go as far as my own imagination. If I were going to direct Powell I should let myself go completely; both in the melodramatic and the comedy sequences, convinced that no matter how fanciful it became he would be able to bring it to life.[1]

He had even used Powell as the quintessential example of the way leading men evolve (like Cary Grant):

> Very few heavies succeed in staying the course if they don't change their styles. This is why you'll find that most screen villains reform, unless they are content to remain in small parts. Among the straight and comedy stars of today, there are a good many that began their film careers as bad men. The best example, of course, is William Powell, who was once a very suave villain indeed. He is typical of the development of a heavy. The process is: villain; straight actor;

comedian. It is easiest to be a villain; less easy to be a straight actor; considerably more difficult to be a comedian. As a rule, the development from villain to straight actor is gradual, and it is largely due to an attractive personality breaking through the label of "heavy." Thus William Powell's likable qualities slowly but surely dominated his screen characterizations. From straight actor to comedian is equally gradual, though not so frequent. It is done more or less by the player himself taking over the comedy relief instead of leaving this to small-part actors, and then developing into a full-blown comedian.[2]

Just as he had done with Grant's personality in *Suspicion*, challenging the audience to believe it possible that he was a murderer, he wanted to do the same with Powell's image. And apparently Powell was seriously considering the role and would in fact go on to star as Uncle Charlie in the radio version of the film with the film's star Teresa Wright. But ultimately, Powell (and particularly his management) considered the role too great a risk to his image. Unable to secure Powell, Hitchcock went in a very different direction in the casting of Uncle Charlie.

The radio play version of *Shadow of a Doubt* presents an Uncle Charlie very similar to Johnnie in *Suspicion*: a man who is so charming and warm, he is able to hide his darkness from his family. The audience's suspicion of Charlie emerges at the same time that young Charlie begins to question her uncle. The film, however, informs the audience immediately that Uncle Charlie is not to be trusted. Part of this change in the direction of the character may be the fact that for a considerable time, the writers Thornton Wilder, Sally Benson, and Alma Reville (Mrs. Hitchcock) were unsure who would be playing the risky role. Without a star to write the screenplay for, Charlie's true nature had to be evident from the first scenes, rather than hope that audiences would have the patience to wait for young Charlie to reveal the truth. Hitchcock did not know who would be cast as Uncle Charlie for such a long time, three sets of clothing were selected before finally going with the tall actor Joseph Cotton.[3]

Joseph Cotton was a highly respected actor whose theatrical performance as C. K. Dexter in the Broadway hit *The Philadelphia Story* served as the basis for Cary Grant's performance in the film of the same name in 1940 (a film role Cotton had wanted to take on himself, but he was not considered a big enough star). Also a member of the Mercury Players, Cotton was best known for appearing in Orson Welles films, most notably as the loyal friend Jedidiah Leland in *Citizen Kane* and the Amberson mother's love interest in the troubled film *The Magnificent Ambersons*. He was in the process of building a film career when cast in *Shadow of a Doubt* but was still far from a major name or leading man; he entered *Shadow of a Doubt* without an established public image that could dramatically influence the way audiences would view Uncle Charlie.

Shadow of a Doubt was a major opportunity for Cotton, and many critics thought Cotton exceptional as the threatening Uncle Charlie, one writing that "Joseph Cotton plays the role of the menace in uncle's clothing as only Joseph Cotton, aided and abetted by Alfred Hitchcock, can do";[4] and Alton Cook, who adored the film, wrote Cotton's performance "throws an air of power and sheeted wickedness about his stalwart young Uncle Charlie."[5] But other critics thought his performance was less impressive, with one writer questioning why "Hollywood" had chosen him as the actor to watch, feeling he lacked considerable star quality.[6]

With a lesser known actor playing Uncle Charlie, the majority of the responsibility to lead the film fell on the small shoulders of Goldwyn contract actress Teresa Wright, at the suggestion of screenwriter Thornton Wilder, who knew the actress well.[7] Wright had starred as Emily in a production of his *Our Town* in 1938, which is precisely the type of character young Charlotte represents: a small-town, innocent, spirited girl on the verge of womanhood. More importantly, Wright was considered one of the outstanding leading ladies of the time, described in the same review that disparaged Joseph Cotton as lacking in star quality as "the first lady of the American screen. I think her performance in *Shadow of a Doubt* with its change of pace from her other outstanding roles, is final proof."[8] In another review she was called "just about the most wonderfully endowed ingénue Hollywood ever found. Her gentle grace that can slip into intensity of feeling so effortlessly is a miracle of acting. It would be shameful if ever she is cast in a bad picture, a fate she has escaped."[9] Stephen Talty wrote in his critique, praising her almost fifty years after *Shadow of a Doubt*'s first release, that "she had a genius for decency and a gentleness of spirit that has gone out of style. Hitchcock often ravished his actresses with horrified open mouthed reaction shots, but here, he was satisfied to let Wright play almost the entire progression of niece Charlie's tragedy in her eyes and face."[10]

Rising star and recent Oscar winner Teresa Wright was highly praised for her interpretation of young Charlie in *Shadow of a Doubt* (1943). *Universal Pictures/ Photofest © Universal Pictures*

Coming into *Shadow of a Doubt,* Wright had been on a winning streak, with her first three film performances earning her three consecutive Oscar nominations and finally winning her a statue for best supporting actress for *Mrs. Miniver* (she lost the best actress honor for *Pride of the Yankees* to her *Mrs. Miniver* costar Greer Garson). She had already stolen the show from Bette Davis in *Little Foxes* and arrived with a strong stage résumé, having first found success in the comedy *Life with Father* and *Our Town.* But *Shadow of a Doubt* was the first film that presented her as the clear lead in the film, a status she would not have had if a bigger star had been cast to play Uncle Charlie.

Wright was an interesting personality in Hollywood, well known for a film contract (after carefully choosing her studio) that demanded she would not be obligated to appear as a homemaker or in "cheesecake photos" (sexy images of ingénues in tight sweaters and bathing suits). Her contract clause read as follows:

> I will not pose for publicity photographs in a bathing suit—unless I'm doing a water scene in a picture. I will not be photographed on the beach with my hair flying in the wind, holding aloft a beach ball. I will not pose in shorts, playing with a cute cocker spaniel. I will not be shown happily whipping up a meal for a huge family. I will not be dressed in firecrackers for the Fourth of July. I will not look insinuatingly at a turkey on Thanksgiving. I will not wear a bunny cap with long ears for Easter. I will not twinkle for the camera on prop snow, in a skiing outfit, while a fan blows my scarf. And I will not assume an athletic stance while pretending to hit something or other with a bow and arrow.[11]

Her reason behind insisting on such a clause was in her mind very simple, saying, "I was no sweater girl, and knew it. I had heard much about new actresses spending most of their time posing for bathing suit and leg pictures. I didn't want a career in picture magazines. I wanted to be an actress."[12]

When first arriving in Hollywood, audiences were struck by her unique and refreshing sensibility at a time when so many girls came to Hollywood to become cookie-cutter glamour girls created in movie studios. She was described by Ward Morehouse as "representing a startling departure from the accepted movie star pattern. She wears almost no make-up. Her voice is soft and she is very gentle. She dresses well but inconspicuously. . . . For her entire, but all too brief film career, she was a delicate youthful woman, with soft wavy dark hair, and tremble in her voice whether happy or sad . . . and a walk which Hitchcock noted as being particularly unique."[13] She was a favorite of Samuel Goldwyn, who praised her for never complaining or fussing about anything,[14] praise Hitchcock also offered to the press regarding their working relationship on *Shadow of a Doubt*: she was an easy actress to get along with.

Sadly, however, her relationship with Goldwyn ultimately ended disastrously when the two debated in the press her unwillingness to participate in any promotional activity. Wright informed the press that the inciting incident was due to an illness, but she went so far as to offer an editorial on why she felt the studio contracts were unfair, explaining, "When we sign such contracts we say in effect 'we have no privacy that can't be invaded. Treat us like children. Send us wherever you like and work us as long as you want, only as long as you give us a big pay check.' The time has come for actors to stop being tax collectors. It has come time for them to say, 'Pay me less, only treat me with respect.'"[15]

Like her cheesecake clause, such statements showed an intelligent and opinionated woman behind the soft-spoken girl with good manners. She could and did speak up when necessary, often with eloquent statements that caught the press off guard, but without shouting or becoming a childish star who made demands as a way of showing her power. Wright was a protégé of the more demonstrative Katharine Hepburn, who took notice of Wright and considered Wright to be demure and well mannered, but told her that upon first impression she thought Wright's lack of forcefulness "would make it unlikely for her to succeed." However, Wright's quiet tenacity began to show the feisty, opinionated side that she kept just underneath the surface, and like a weapon she would take out only when needed, adding depth to the ingénue image she had cultivated before arriving in Hollywood that impressed even Hepburn.[16] When Wright did speak up, Hollywood took young Wright seriously because she was both unexpected and so articulate.

It is that quality that comes out in Young Charlie in *Shadow of a Doubt*: a resourceful survivor existing just under the overprotected, good-girl exterior. It is what makes her battle of wits with Uncle Charlie such a surprising development halfway through the film, as the audiences, and Uncle Charlie, do not expect that from her. When she first discovers the horrific truth of who her uncle truly is, it seems to nearly destroy her until she finds the inner strength to confront Uncle Charlie in order to protect her mother.

Likewise, the supporting cast is uniformly excellent, each bringing a homey, but never hayseed, quality to the film and excellent juxtaposition to the dark and urban Uncle Charlie. Her love interest, for example, popular radio actor MacDonald Carey, is far from a dashing leading man, but a rather gangly, soft-spoken man with large, almost comic features. Truffaut especially disliked the performance and actor, stating (during his series of interviews with Hitchcock), "Whereas the script requires him to compete in terms of stature with Uncle Charlie, he strikes one as being such an ordinary sort of fellow that it somehow spoils the end for me." Hitchcock claims he would have preferred a bigger name for the film, agreeing with Truffaut that he isn't much of a rival to Cotton.[17] However, while Cotton is far more elegant and urbane, the ordinary charms of Carey make his character instantly likable

Teresa Wright and MacDonald Carey played their young lovers in *Shadow of a Doubt* (1943) as innocents in the mold of Emily and George from screenwriter Thornton Wilder's play *Our Town*. *Universal Pictures/Photofest © Universal Pictures*

without seeming simple or unworthy of young Charlie; and their courtship scenes are some of the most realistic romantic scenes in any of Hitchcock's films.

Wright's *Mrs. Miniver* costar Henry Travers (also Oscar nominated) adds a welcome familiarity, as does Wright's *Little Foxes* costar Patricia Collinge (Oscar nominated along with Wright), who played her mother. Both older actors were described as very much as they appeared on screen: Irish Travers was a good-natured man of easy humor and Collinge a nurturing mother figure to the younger actors—even rewriting the love scene for Wright and Carey.[18] The chemistry of all four of these actors gives the film its warmth, so Cotton can bring the cold with his icy Uncle Charlie.

Ultimately, Cotton would become a much bigger star. Wright is the star of *Shadow of a Doubt*. It is important to note that this is Hitchcock's first Hollywood film that undeniably had a female main character and protagonist; it was an actress very different from the stereotypical "Hitchcock blonde." As much as is made of "the Hitchcock blonde," there were in fact two very different types of iconic Hitchcock women: the mysterious blonde and the fresh-faced girl. Wright is the quintessential fresh-faced girl (the American counter to his leading actress Margaret Lockwood in *The Lady Vanishes*) and perfectly reflects the qualities Hitchcock described as essential to selecting his heroines:

> The chief point I keep in mind when selecting my heroine is that she must be fashioned to please women rather than men, for the reason that women form three-quarters of the average cinema audience. Therefore, no actress can be a good commercial proposition as a film heroine unless she pleases her own sex. Screen aspirants please note! My contention will probably be challenged by the supporters of the "physical" school of screen art who assert that sex appeal is the most important quality which can be possessed by a screen actress, but ignore the fact that the woman stars whose popularity has been long lasting, such as Mary Pickford, Lillian Gish, Betty Balfour, Pauline Frederick, and Norma Talmadge, have no sex appeal, as the phrase is used in the jargon of today. They owe their success not only to their natural talent and charm, but to the fact that they invariably appear in roles which in respect of suggestion and ultimate achievement, appeal to the best in human nature.[19]

7

Lifeboat

Considering Hitchcock's preference for casting stars for his Hollywood films, the casting of *Lifeboat* is a bit of a rarity. With a cast so large, he wanted only one legitimate star in the cast, Tallulah Bankhead, and surrounded her with a host of lesser-known character actors whose names audiences would barely recognize. One needs only to look at the credits on the feature, with Tallulah Bankhead's name dwarfing the others, to understand the effect Bankhead's mere presence would have on the film. And while the only star in the film, Bankhead couldn't even be described as a movie star as much as she was a notorious personality who happened to star in movies and theater (at the time best known for the plays *The Little Foxes*, *Dark Victory*, and *The Skin of Our Teeth*). Audiences certainly knew the name Tallulah Bankhead, but her presence in films did not evoke a character type, but the public image of her celebrity, a woman constantly at the center of scandal and gossip. For Hitchcock to select her to star in *Lifeboat* was not simply a case of perfect casting; her presence was of vital importance as no other actress would be able to evoke the reaction among audiences that Bankhead could. As Hitchcock explained when planning the movie, he wanted the one personality an audience would never expect to see stranded on a lifeboat, and that name could only be Tallulah Bankhead.

Tales of Bankhead's behavior on the set have become just a small part of the legend of the larger-than-life personality that was Tallulah Bankhead.

Already she was known for her flamboyant personality, sexual liberation, and battle with the bottle, so the story that dominated the making of *Lifeboat* was almost tame: her simple refusal to wear undergarments. Although she did get into an argument with one costar, Hume Cronyn, over the situation, Alfred Hitchcock was apparently disinterested in participating in the battle over her decency and joked that he wouldn't tell her to put something on because it was neither hair nor makeup. However, his joke does lead to the grander topic of Hitchcock's acceptance of and friendship with Bankhead while making the film. Although Hitchcock's own attraction to women tended toward those who were "well-behaved" (which often translated to passive), Hitchcock had a professional respect for Bankhead that had nothing to do with gender. Both were individuals who wanted to live the good life, especially in regard to their food. They both tended to take pleasure in being showmen and provocateurs

Hitchcock cast Tallulah Bankhead in *Lifeboat* (1944) to shock audiences who would never expect a star of her status deserted on a lifeboat in the middle of the ocean. *20th Century Fox / Photofest © 20th Century Fox*

in the press. And while neither was easy to work with, they both had a belief in professionalism while filming.

But the greatest difference between the two, besides being director and actor, was the fact that Hitchcock was a man, living a conservative, domestic life, while Bankhead was a sexually liberated, divorced female. The sexual freedom she expressed openly was fascinating to the press and public, despite outraging many who felt she did not behave as a proper woman. And it is this aspect of her persona that is on-screen in *Lifeboat*.

While there are ten characters in *Lifeboat*, the lack of character development of the majority of them is surprising. While the performers all show themselves to be capable actors, the smaller roles are more than a bit forgettable, ironic considering part of the pleasure in films about the isolation of a small group is to see which "types" emerge and how they come to coexist in their claustrophobic spaces. But in *Lifeboat*, the characters frequently seem rather content with one another from the very beginning, though not especially productive, with the exception of Bankhead and "the German" Willi (Walter Slezak).

On the boat with Bankhead's Connie and Willi are Hume Cronyn's Sparks (the English seaman), Mary Anderson's Alice (a nurse), William Bendix's Gus (an injured shipmate), John Hodiak's John Kovak (a healthy shipmate), Henry Hull's Ritt (a wealthy industrialist), Canada Lee's George (a porter), and Heather Angel's Mrs. Higgins (the mother of the dead baby). With the exception of Angel (who kills herself in grief over the death of her infant son) and the pedestrian love story between Anderson and Cronyn (which seems shoehorned into the plot), the rest of the film focuses on the other survivors' mistrust of the Connie and Willi characters—he because he is a Nazi and the captain of the U-Boat that sunk their ship, and Connie because they perceive her to be a self-centered and ungenerous woman of the upper class.

It at times is suggested that the lower-class crew members (especially Kovak) dislike Connie due to their mistrust of the wealthy. And yet, Henry Hull's Ritt, who is part of the idle rich (Connie works as a photographer at the very least) and is far less resourceful than Connie, is tolerated far better by "everyman" Kovak. The outright dislike that Kovak has for Connie is spread throughout the boat. She is a woman who has overstepped her place in society, unlike Mary Anderson's passive and obedient Alice, who is favored by the crew but rather unimportant to the audience.

It's been discussed in many readings of the film that Connie's arc is of a woman who needs to be "brought down" to be seen as a true woman by Kovac. However, Connie never fully gives herself over to changing for a man; she adapts in order to survive. After conversations regarding her willingness to give up her expensive bracelet, she finally takes it off not to appease or win over Kovac, but to catch fish and save herself and the others from starvation. Likewise, there is Connie's flirtation with Kovac, smiling at him as he looks through the binoculars or telling him, "You can call me Connie. I like it when you call me Connie." It's like a "sock in the jaw," both a way of teasing Kovac for insisting he isn't attracted to her and then seducing him, and merely to pass the time, suggesting sex is simply meant for pleasure. This is precisely how Bankhead herself saw the world, speaking openly about her love for sex (and disinterest in marriage) and love for the finer things in life without feeling guilt for such extravagances. We are not watching "Connie" on a boat; rather we are watching Tallulah Bankhead on a boat.

More importantly, we are watching how the "common people" in the audience might react if forced onto a lifeboat with Bankhead. Distracted and annoyed by Connie the celebrity (ignoring her advice), they overlook the danger possessed by Willi. When Connie asserts to the other survivors, "What's the matter with us? We not only let the Nazis do the rowing for us but do our thinking," there is an awareness that their focus on the unimportant has prevented them from focusing on survival on the boat and at war.

Besides Bankhead's Connie, William Bendix and Walter Slezak are certainly the performers who leave the strongest impression on audiences. Paul Jones of the *Atlanta Constitution* wrote that "[Slezak] was one of its most memorable characterizations, while William Bendix is nothing short of terrific in his part of the Brooklyn jitterbug addict whose leg is amputated after gangrene sets in."[1] But more important are the similarities Hitchcock draws between them, one an American born of German descent, the other a German Nazi, now face-to-face. Bendix and Slezak were cast partially because of their physical similarities in face and body, to create an instant connection between the two men, showing them as the flip side of the same coin. They were likely raised in families with similar values, similar heritage, and similar education, yet one is a Nazi trying to kill the other.

Willi's torture of Gus's character seems all the crueler because of these similarities. Willi's singing, unlike the music Gus loves to dance to, is his

Walter Slezak and William Bendix's similar physical appearance juxtaposed their German bloodlines as German Nazi Willi and German-American Gus in *Lifeboat* (1944). *20th Century Fox/Photofest © 20th Century Fox*

victory song mocking his captives. And after talking to the delirious Gus, Willi pushes the helpless man overboard and watches him drown, an act of cruelty by the German that was preventable if the others on the boat had simply listened to Gus when he said Willi had water. Instead Kovak and Ritt gamble for money they may never see while Sparks and Alice begin a love affair they may never continue.

Critic Abe Hill, who was one of the writers who called the film unpatriotic and pro-Nazi, found this aspect of the characters most unsettling because "the characters did an excellent job of acting, though they were revealed as quarrelsome, weak, nincompoops, outwitted by the Nazi Captain. The spectacular was made to dislike the whole lot. Stripped to the bone, they left a negative taste."[2] The claims of the film being unpatriotic enraged Bankhead, who was known for her outspoken patriotism and came forward to defend the film against the press's claims that it was pro-Nazi, even as producer Darryl Zanuck and the film's studio, Fox, began to pull promotion of the film. She went so far as to say it was the only film of merit she made at that time in her career. For this, and her performance in the film, she won the prestigious New York Film Critics Circle Best Actress Award.

Ironically, while Bankhead was far from a pleasure to work with on the film, apparently yelling at beloved actor Henry Hull for not knowing his lines, Hull wrote a column for Hedda Hopper on the experience of making the claustrophobic film, saying of his experience working with Bankhead:

> Now we come to Tallulah, a lady whose brusqueness of manner is exceeded only by the warmth of her heart. Tallulah, victorious veteran of numberless encounters with Thespis, Venus, Vulcan, Neptune, and lesser gods. Tallulah alone of all of us survived *Lifeboat*, still the master of her fate and the captain of her soul. She also survived bronchitis, laryngitis, pneumonia, and housemaid's knee. Her only regret was that she was unable to direct the picture, write it, light it, photograph it, edit, and handle the prop department, in addition to acting all the parts. I feel sure that when Charon takes her for her last long voyage home, she'll be heard to remark, "What a hell of a way to row a boat! . . . As for myself, I can only repeat, I'm too damned old for this kind of nonsense."[3]

Spellbound

Spellbound, though a Hitchcock/Selznick collaboration, is unlike *Rebecca* as it is less a "Selznick Production" and more a problematic collaboration between the two men. Each had their demands, which ultimately made the film noticeably unbalanced. The film has an unpleasant tendency to have exquisite individual scenes that never come together as an entirely satisfying feature. The dream sequence designed by Salvador Dali and Hitchcock's first collaboration with Ingrid Bergman are the highlights of the film.

One of the greatest challenges Selznick and Hitchcock faced was the casting of the leads. Ingrid Bergman had, like Hitchcock, been brought to America by Selznick as a major name from European films and was considered to have tremendous potential to cross over as an international star. Her soft smile and internal warmth was what captured Hitchcock's and the public's attention. And while Hitchcock insisted that movement on-screen (rather than acting) was what made films dramatic, no actress could hold attention with her stillness better than Bergman. Robin Wood wrote that Bergman's appeal in Hitchcock films was due to her being a "natural and healthy" image of womanhood, which was in stark contrast with the artificial glamour of so many stars of the 1920s and 1930s (such as Garbo and Dietrich), and the accessibility Bergman projected, which rejected the "feminine mystique" of these manufactured Hollywood representations of the ideal woman.[1]

Considering the method in which the film is framed, starting and ending with Bergman's psychiatrist, Constance, it is undeniable that she (rather than Gregory Peck) is the dominant character. Like *Suspicion*, it is a story of a woman losing herself over love, but unlike the earlier film and Joan Fontaine's Lina, Constance takes enough control back in her life to clear the name of her great love. We are immediately told who Bergman is playing in her first scene, reserved but kind, elegant but not overtly "sexual," which is accentuated by the arrival of her first patient, a nymphomaniac played by Rhonda Fleming, who slithers in the room. Bergman is immediately introduced as the proper woman who wants to cure Fleming, but has no love of her own because she is consumed by her career.

It is the contemporary quality of Bergman, far from the fragile victim Joan Fontaine played, that allows her to play her character as cool and reserved. Bergman's natural warmth always exists just underneath the cold, defensive shield she has around her male colleagues. The only area of her performance in *Spellbound* in which she falters is the lack of romantic chemistry between her and Peck. Her scenes with Hitchcock favorite Reginald Owens are playful and familiar, making her realization of his crimes seem far sadder to know she has lost him than happy that she has cleared John's name. Even her brief scene with the house detective, Bill Goodwin, has a comic charm that enlivens the film considerably. However, her scenes with Peck never appear "romantic" and read simply as a maternal figure interested in helping a damaged child. One only needs to watch their courtship scene, when they are supposedly falling in love during a picnic, to note how it reads as no more than a friendly outing.

Truffaut considered Peck the primary problem with *Spellbound*, informing Hitchcock, "Whereas Ingrid Bergman is an extraordinary actress, ideally well suited to your style, Gregory Peck isn't a Hitchcock actor. He's shallow for one, but the main thing is the lack of expression in his eyes."[2]

Like Joan Fontaine, Peck had been discovered by David O. Selznick, and it was the producer's mission to turn him into a star. He had found considerable success as a maverick priest in *Keys to the Kingdom* and had a true warmth and kindness that translated from his person to the screen. However, he did not yet have the polished technique or professionalism that Hitchcock considered key to film acting. While Hitchcock had trained Fontaine to be the type of actress he wanted, he never accomplished this with Peck. Peck was an actor with definitive ideas of his own who resisted the instructions Hitchcock gave because, as Peck admitted, "I was not quite flexible enough,

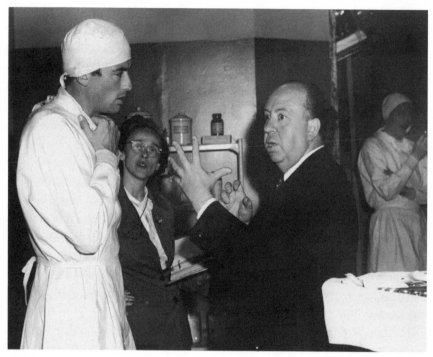

Gregory Peck believed he was simply too inexperienced to adapt to Hitchcock's directorial style on *Spellbound* (1945). *Selznick International Pictures/Photofest* © *Selznick International Pictures*

nor indeed professional enough yet—it was quite early in my film career. To do everything he wanted and needed and at the same time provide my own inner truth. Because it is quite possible to act the other way. From the externals in. Many, many great actors do this. But I wasn't experienced enough to do that."[3]

Peck was a student of the Stanislavsky method of acting, which stressed that an actor must feel the internal motivation in order to play the character and create accurate physicality in a performance. Peck insisted that in order to play the character of the mentally ill amnesiac, he needed internal motivation and couldn't be limited by Hitchcock's strict direction of where to stand, look, and react. Peck insisted that Hitchcock was never cruel to actors, at least him, saying, "The fact is that he treats actors with great affection, great delicacy. I've never seen him browbeat or put down or humiliate an actor on the set. He's far too wise and too human to do a thing like that. But, of course, he does put great stock in preparation, and has every foot of film in his head before he begins." It was that aspect of filmmaking with Hitchcock, the rigidity of having to follow his preplanned storyboards, that frustrated Peck, believing he was "creating a moment that is truth and therefore the externals are right."[4]

It was a tension Hitchcock experienced with other method actors such as Montgomery Clift and Paul Newman, both actors who insisted on playing their characters as they particularly felt, rather than partaking in the rigid plans Hitchcock created by storyboarding the film. It was a struggle because while actors are motivated by what works for their characters, Hitchcock was concerned with the entire film and took a far more formalistic, rather than naturalistic, approach to filmmaking. One only needs to see the extreme formalism when Hitchcock filmed Bergman's extreme close-ups to witness this quality in his films. Yet Bergman's naturalism and authenticity anchors the film and prevents it from becoming a piece of pure formalism without emotions behind it.

Hitchcock preferred directing Bergman, who could enliven characters and bring something unique to the scene that was not written on the page without improvising or refusing to take technical direction. Bergman's performance in *Spellbound* has become one of the quintessential examples of how an actor can infuse a character with the inner qualities of a star that may not be on the page and elevate the picture. As a reviewer wrote, Bergman's performance in *Spellbound* was "the essence of romance in the film. Her soft and luminescent revelation of sincerity of a woman's love is the basis of credibility for an often implausible plot."[5] Similarly, the *Los Angeles Times* critic Edwin Schallert wrote in his review of *Spellbound*:

> Ingrid Bergman's acting is destined especially to exert a compelling charm over all beholders. She has both art and artfulness in her work in her depiction of a psychoanalyst, who is cold toward all romantic persuasion, until Gregory Peck arrives on the scene. She falls madly in love, and nothing that might appear to diminish his worth alters her devout vindication that he is right. The talents of a Bergman are definitely required to make these scenes fully convincing, as well as certain other portions of the cinema, wherein it might be in danger of falling apart.[6]

Ingrid Bergman captivated audiences and Hitchcock with the naturalism she brought to roles, even in formulistic films such as *Spellbound* (1945). *Selznick International Pictures/Photofest © Selznick International Pictures*

Donald Spoto has made much of the amount of patience Hitchcock had for Ingrid Bergman. A perfectionist, she often asked Hitchcock for additional takes and voiced her concerns over having played a scene incorrectly, with Hitchcock reassuring her by saying, "Ingrid, it's only a movie." Beyond Hitchcock's personal affection for Ingrid, the very quality she brought to life and showed on-screen is what could keep a director like Hitchcock, who claimed to often be bored on sets, interested in the action. Bergman could entertain him in a way his storyboards could not and bring that something extra that would have been missing from both *Spellbound* and their next collaboration: *Notorious*.

9

Notorious

There are films by Hitchcock that exist narratively because of the inspiration of a star. *Suspicion, Lifeboat, Marnie,* and *Vertigo* are all films that were developed with a star in mind, their persona not only fleshing out a character but inspiring it. *Notorious* was such a picture in the collaboration between Ingrid Bergman and Hitchcock. After having worked with Bergman on *Spellbound,* captivated by her, Hitchcock approached her with a film that would cast her as a modern-day Mata Hari who infiltrates the Nazi party to clear her name (destroyed by her father's Nazi connections) and for the love of the government agent who approaches her with the mission. The scandalous role enticed Bergman, a character willing to use her body to destroy her maligned reputation and win the affection of Devlin.

It was also a role perfectly suited to the actress Bergman. Just as Alicia had become a notorious woman for her bad reputation, Bergman lived her life under the microscope tied to a virginal image of sound womanhood. The Swedish actress's private life was far from the "perfect" domestic life the public was exposed to. In real life, all of Hollywood seemed well aware that despite having children with her husband, Bergman was promiscuous and carrying on an open affair with Larry Adler. Her behavior was strategically kept secret within Hollywood, as they wanted to keep the far more powerful (and profitable) false image. But these hidden truths of Bergman's true self were inspiring to several in Hollywood who wanted to suggest the darker side behind the persona, an idea that especially excited Hitchcock.

In her performance as Alicia, Bergman received a majority of the attention and critical praise, as she had for her work in *Spellbound*. It captivated critics that Bergman could play a character so dark, while retaining the character's humanity. Despite Alicia's dangerous reputation as a playgirl and lush, "Mr. Hitchcock has not overlooked the actress's wholesomeness or her suggestion of tremendous sensitivity and awareness. He uses these qualities to build a contradictory character. Miss Bergman shows in her characterization what can happen to an artistic nature when it has become disillusioned."[1] Another review for the film declared, "Bergman is eternally handsome whether she is drunk, violently in love, or dying from poison."[2] Once again, Bergman and Hitchcock's partnership proved to be a mutually beneficial success, as was his experience with Cary Grant, once again casting him in an antiheroic role.

Ironically, although Grant had protested having a secondary role to Joan Fontaine in *Suspicion*[3] Grant accepted the role of Devlin in *Notorious* without

Hitchcock's two iconic stars, Cary Grant and Ingrid Bergman, brought their most attractive and mysterious qualities to their roles in *Notorious* (1946). *RKO Radio Pictures/Photofest © RKO Radio Pictures*

question, which may be even smaller. In fact, with the exception of one film, *North by Northwest*, all of Grant's collaborations with Hitchcock featured him in "support" of his more dominant leading ladies—as the object of their desire. It was an intelligent and rather inspired approach for Hitchcock to take with the image of Grant, whose mere presence, more than any other actor's, evoked an immediate reaction from audiences that mirrored the females in his films. Joan Fontaine softened in his presence, Eva Marie Saint protects him, Grace Kelly is obsessed with him, and in *Notorious* Bergman is powerless against his charms, risking her life just to be with him.

One only needs to watch the first scenes, when Bergman is at the party, talking to him, to see the hold Grant has on her. Watch Bergman's face, well aware just by his noted profile that she is speaking with Cary Grant, anticipating his reactions. At times he is almost emotionless in his behavior, and Bergman's eagerness for his approval is very much the audience's own. But unlike *Suspicion*, which shows the "work" Grant had to put into his deceptive role of Johnnie, his role in *Notorious* is far more subtle, manipulatively simpler, and as Andrew Britton wrote in his profile of Cary Grant, his Devlin was "the most detestable leading man in American popular cinema."[4]

After being unable to include the ending of *Suspicion* because audiences would not accept Grant as a murderer, Hitchcock had to almost hide the darker elements of Grant's character, and once again, Grant used the romantic charm that had made him a star to convince Bergman's Alicia to put herself in danger, causing the audience to fear for her safety.[5] Grant could do nearly anything on-screen without provoking his loyal audiences to dismiss or turn against him, and when viewed for the first time, the coldness of Grant's Devlin is not immediately noticed because of the charm he pours on. Only when the audience steps back do we realize what Grant is guilty of. Critics and audiences took notice, mentioning the fact that "Cary Grant acts with the sophisticated emotional restraint which used to characterize his best work, but which he rarely uses now unless he is sufficiently challenged."[6]

It helped that Bergman and Grant had remarkable chemistry, more than Grant had had with Joan Fontaine during *Suspicion* or Bergman had with Gregory Peck in *Spellbound*. And just as Robin Wood described Bergman as being appealing for her naturalism and approachability, the pairing of fantasy Grant and real Bergman captivated an audience as women vicariously lived through Bergman's experience. It would become a trend in Hitchcock's great romances to cast one "common star" against the fantasy, to reflect the audience's desire to fantasize about their favorite stars. He would do it again, reversing the sex, with James Stewart and Grace Kelly, signally the fact that it is the male fantasy, while *Notorious* is a woman's and Grant the ideal on display. As Hitchcock told Truffaut when describing their iconic kissing scene, "I felt it was indispensable that they should not separate, and I also felt that the public, represented by the camera, was the third party to this embrace. The public was being given the great privilege of embracing Cary Grant and Ingrid Bergman together. It was a kind of temporary ménage a trois."[7]

But what also sells the film's romance, besides the chemistry between Grant and Bergman, is the strong chemistry between Claude Raines and Bergman, creating a dynamic and plausible love triangle. Unlike so many cinematic love triangles, in which one side is unlikable, Hitchcock strived to create relationships in which the audience is convinced that both are real and plausible. Although Raines is playing a Nazi, there are moments in which the audience perceives the genuine affection he has for his wife, Bergman, and acknowledges the pain he feels when he not only realizes his wife is a spy, but their relationship is a fraud.

At the time, Claude Raines was known as a star of the theater world that could not have been more unlike Grant. Unlike the nonregional accent Cary Grant created for himself in Hollywood, Raines had a distinct, crisp voice and perfect diction, along with a knack for disguising his voice with accents. That voice came in handy with his first starring role in *The Invisible Man*, in which there was only his voice to identify himself and he remained unseen or wrapped in bandages. Being self-deprecating regarding his physical appeal as a film actor, Raines said of his role in *The Invisible Man*, "I daresay it was the best thing they could do with this face. Now if they could keep it invisible, I might get by in the cinema."[8] But even with hit films, he never would be the kind of star Grant became, who as Hitchcock knew was unable to divorce himself from his public image. Raines could easily take on any role, but publicly, he was always self-critical of his talents, discussing how he always played weak characters and the fact that he only had a strong, posh voice because of a childhood lisp and therapy that forced him to learn proper English.

The making of the film proved to be remarkably easy for Hitchcock, and so easy that he accepted input from Bergman regarding how she wanted to play her role and even took suggestions.[9] But this did not prevent Bergman from

Despite her anxious perfectionism, Ingrid Bergman enchanted both Cary Grant and Hitchcock during the production of *Notorious* (1946). *RKO Radio Pictures/Photofest ©️ RKO Radio Pictures*

still suffering from anxiety, which at times could cause her to freeze and begin to stammer. However, on *Notorious*, Hitchcock showed patience, as Grant recalled of one particularly difficult day for Bergman:

> She was a splendid, splendid performer, but she wasn't very relaxed in front of the camera. Ingrid spoke English beautifully, of course, but she would occasionally have problems with some of its nuances. One morning, when we were working on *Notorious*, she had difficulty with a line. She had to say her lines a certain way so I could imitate her readings. We worked on the scene for a couple of hours. Hitch never said anything. He just sat next to the camera, puffing on his cigar. I took a break, and later, when I was making my way back to the set, I heard her say her lines perfectly. At which point Hitch said, "Cut!" followed by "Good morning, Ingrid."[10]

Although Hitchcock enjoyed working with both, he noted the very different approaches they had to acting. While Bergman became ultra-focused, struggling to find her characters, Grant embraced being "easy." It would affect how Hitchcock used both stars in the future. He would demand far more character development from Bergman, who embraced the acting challenge despite the anxiety it caused. On his next two films with Cary Grant, Hitchcock would embrace the light effortlessness of simply being Cary Grant.

10

The Paradine Case

I would have brought in Laurence Olivier. I also considered Ronald Coleman for the part. For a while we hoped we might get Greta Garbo to make her comeback in the role of the wife. But the worst flaw in the casting was assigning Louis Jourdan to play the groom. After all, the story of *The Paradine Case* is about the degradation of a gentleman who becomes enamored of his client, a woman who is not only a murderess, but also a nymphomaniac. And that degradation reaches its climactic point when he's forced to confront the heroine with one of her lovers, who is a groom. But that groom should have been a manure-smelling stable hand, a man who really reeked of manure. Unfortunately, Selznick had already signed up Alida Valli—he thought she was going to be another Bergman—and he also had Louis Jourdan under contract, so I had to use them, and this miscasting was very detrimental to the story.[1]

The Paradine Case was a film Hitchcock considered ideal as his next collaboration with Ingrid Bergman, who desperately wanted to stretch and take on more challenging roles. However, she had no interest in working with David O. Selznick again, who had partially written the screenplay to the court drama and would be an instrumental producer on set. Hitchcock had little interest in working with Selznick himself and was eager to finish his contract, the primary reason he agreed to direct *The Paradine Case* without Bergman.

However, that obligation came with the requirement that Hitchcock agree to the casting of the producer's choosing, which included Gregory Peck, Louis

Jourdan, and Alida Valli.[2] Although Hitchcock thought nothing was wrong with the casting of Alida Valli, he considered the pairing of her with Gregory Peck and Louis Jourdan as the great mistake of the film because their rivalry "screwed up all the values" of the film.[3] Once again he felt Peck was all wrong for the role.

Even as a young man, Peck had the ability to evoke the inner decency that showed through his characters. It was that very quality that made his work in films such as *The Gentleman's Agreement* and *To Kill a Mockingbird* stand out in his career, and why years later, he could be cast against type for dramatic effect. But at the time that he made *The Paradine Case*, just a few years after *Spellbound* and his breakthrough in *Keys to the Kingdom*, he did not have the experience, technique, or persona to make his amoral attorney, seduced by a beautiful client accused of murder, shocking or convincing. The moral complexity other actors would have sunk their teeth into was simply absent from his performance. With his black hair colored gray, when he says to his wife, Ann Todd, "I hardly recognize my lost ideals," he still seemed to be an innocent young man and is completely unconvincing.

His presence at the center of the film threw off the entire tone of the film, a problem Hitchcock made well known during his conversations with Peter Bogdanovich and François Truffaut. He claimed that a more mature, naturally elegant man would have worked much better in the film, such as Laurence Olivier or Ronald Coleman, adding the detached sensibility necessary for the character. But he also felt there were problems with the casting of the young servant who worked in the Paradine house. In the film, he is played by Louis Jourdan, a rather elegant young man—too elegant for a role Hitchcock referred to as "the kind of man who should smell of manure." His first choice had been Robert Newton, who he said had horny hands like the devil.[4] Having starred in Hitchcock's *Jamaica Inn*, he would soon play two of the great rouge's in literature, Sykes in *Oliver Twist* and Long John Silver in *Treasure Island*. The rough quality of Newton would have accentuated the gravities of the privileged, well-to-do life of the attorney. Only then would the ultimate theme of the film, the capacity a beautiful woman has to bring out the animalistic, amoral qualities of men, have been evident to the audience.[5]

But Hitchcock admitted to being somewhat withdrawn from the film due to restrictions of casting but also his own confusion regarding the plot.[6] In development since Selznick had been at MGM, it was originally conceived as

Star of *The Paradine Case* (1947) Alida Valli, pictured in conference with Alfred Hitchcock, received very little guidance from the director in her first English-language film. *Selznick International Pictures/Photofest © Selznick International Pictures*

a vehicle for Lionel and John Barrymore and Ginger Rogers.[7] Even the idea of making a courtroom drama was not sufficiently inspiring for Hitchcock, telling Peter Bogdanovich, "The courtroom is less promising a setting for such nuances of Hitchcock than the straightforward story of original crime—as so often, the whodunit, or did she do it, keeps us on the periphery of action, expressing, perhaps that particularly middle-class combination of pervasive suspicion of others, and veil distance."[8] Hitchcock would have preferred to simply direct the crimes in question rather than the legal drama recounting them. His reservations about simply making the film and Selznick's choices in casting prevented Hitchcock from acknowledging the exceptionally good acting he gets in the film, particularly from a trio of actresses: Valli, Ann Todd, and Joan Tetzel.

Valli was a highly respected actress in her native country of Italy making her English-film debut. She had been brought over from Europe by Selznick, specifically to become "the next Bergman."[9] Hitchcock thought an actress with the style and notoriety of Greta Garbo or Marlene Dietrich, both of whose continental style had made them international stars, and their power to seduce and conquer men was precisely what was needed of his Mrs. Paradine. Valli's name was not as widely known as Garbo, Dietrich, or Bergman, especially in America, as she was yet to appear in the superior *The Third Man*. However, she had a similar presence as Garbo and Dietrich, whose hands and eyes could seduce without saying a word, and she had the additional quality of eliciting sympathy from men, making her dialogue with Peck some of the most compelling in the film. Although underused by Hitchcock, who failed to create any genuine excitement on-screen (Hitchcock supposedly all but ignored Peck and Valli on set), at times her ability to overpower Peck throws off the balance of the film and makes him appear impotent rather than seduced.

Hitchcock was generally disinterested in directing Gregory Peck in *The Paradine Case* (1947) but was extremely controlling of Ann Todd's performance. *Selznick International Pictures/Photofest © Selznick International Pictures*

But the seductive qualities Valli showed juxtaposes the difference between herself and Ann Todd, part of a love triangle with Gregory Peck. Unlike the rivalry between Peck and Jourdan, which does not fully express their differences or obsession for Valli, the juxtaposition between Valli and earnest Todd is instantly recognizable and dynamic, from the moment they appear on-screen. Unlike the exotic Valli, angelic Ann Todd represented Englishness because of her prim, proper, and reserved disposition. As with look-alike Hitchcock female Joan Fontaine, Hitchcock focused most of his time and attention with actors on crafting Todd's performance. Only with her was he willing to discuss the character, physically moving her in scenes (once hurting her hand when he grabbed it too hard).[10] *Variety Magazine* took notice, writing, "Ann Todd delights as his wife, giving the assignment a grace and understanding that tug at the emotions,"[11] and *Time Magazine* similarly leveled praise on Todd's all too brief appearance, writing, "The only characters who come sharply to life are the barrister's wife (Ann Todd) and her confidante (Joan Tetzel)."[12]

Joan Tetzel, who stands out to audiences today, was a screen newcomer with a spirit and appearance that reminds one of Teresa Wright from *Shadow of a Doubt,* just a few years before she would become one of the first ladies of English theater. In her relatively brief role as Todd's confidante, and the gossipy daughter of Charles Coburn, she is both refreshingly lively and completely natural on-screen. It is because of her presence that Peck has one scene that shows the appeal he had as a film actor that is missing throughout the rest of the film: when Teztel questions his fidelity to his wife and her best friend, played by Ann Todd.

But Hitchcock overlooked Teztel's bright performance, as well as those of character actors Charles Colburn, Ethel Barrymore, and Charles Laughton, who were completely underused characters. These all-stars' appearances are close to extended cameos and distracting performances for the lack of character and importance they have in the film. Although Hitchcock was working with a troubled script and had little control over certain elements of production, as the film's director, he approached the work as if it had already failed. He allowed his frustrations with his cast to control his work, and he ignored the exceptional performances some of his actors were capable of giving.

11

Rope

Under the banner of Hitchcock's films, *Rope* is more a noble experiment than cinematic masterpiece, or as Hitchcock himself described it, "an ill-conceived experiment."[1] Hitchcock was initially attracted to do the film as an experiment after watching an adaptation of the play on English television in 1939. Finally away from Selznick, Alfred Hitchcock's first film would also be his first color film. He selected as his first property to produce an adaptation of Patrick Hamilton's play *Rope*, inspired by the infamous Leopold and Loeb murders. The story focuses on the crime committed by characters Brandon and Philip, claiming it is all an experiment to see if they can commit the perfect murder of an intellectually inferior person, David Kentley. Using the trunk they've kept the dead body in as a buffet table, they host a dinner party for friends, which include Kentley's father and fiancée. Also in attendance is their former teacher, Rupert Cadell, who first suggested in classes the Machiavellian idea of superior individuals.

The original play had been explicit regarding the homosexuality of the two main characters and presented the teacher as having had an inappropriate relationship with Brandon while he was a student. Due to censorship in Hollywood, these elements could only be hinted at in the film and would therefore require the performances to evoke what couldn't be spoken. To suggest the homosexual relationship of his characters, Hitchcock planned to cast the dapper, romantic Cary Grant and the effeminate, delicate Montgomery Clift as the professor and student who had had an affair. Unfortunately, both Grant and Clift said they didn't want to be associated with "it": the word censored Hollywood used to describe homosexuality.

The role of Brandon, originally intended for Montgomery Clift, was eventually given to actor John Dall, a talented screen and stage actor who was a friendly associate of Hitchcock's and rumored to be a gay man in Hollywood, though he would never discuss such matters openly. The character of Brandon truly is an amoral, manipulative character able to seduce people to do as he desires. Montgomery Clift was known in Hollywood to have had this capacity sexually with both men and women, an innocent beauty that hid his manipulative nature. John Dall, despite being a skilled character actor, projected an average Joe persona and lacked the sheer magnetism that seemed necessary for a leading character capable of manipulating another boy into committing a murder.

John Dall was a respected theater actor whose first screen role, in *The Corn Is Green*, garnered him an Oscar nomination. Dall was the devoted protégé of a teacher, played by Bette Davis, in the populist drama. Memories of this role would add dimension and plant seeds in the audience's minds of his character's ability to be influenced by a teacher, for good (as in *The Corn Is Green*) or bad (as in *Rope*). Unfortunately, the noticeable lack of chemistry he had with both the teacher, played by James Stewart, and his partner in crime, played by Farley Granger, did not express what had been intended.

Farley Granger, in later interviews following Dall's death, felt their lack of chemistry came from a definite dislike Dall had for Granger for being open (though not public) as a homosexual.[2] On the set, though the studios disliked his association with him, Granger was known to be in a relationship with *Rope*'s screenwriter, Arthur Laurents. Laurents informed Granger that the English play had been explicit in its homosexual content, but he had been forced to remove these aspects (along with any of the English slang that made it dirtier and funnier) from the screenplay. He instructed him of the romantic bond between Brandon and Philip, Philip's obsessive desire to please Brandon, and Brandon's history with the professor.

Unlike Dall, who was entering the film with an Oscar nomination, Farley Granger's career had never been as respectable and had slowed considerably since being introduced to audiences as a teen actor during World War II. His first films, *The Purple Heart* and *North Star*, allowed the studios to introduce

Filming a scene from *Rope* (1948), stars John Dall, Farley Granger, and James Stewart struggled with the physical limitations of filming long takes, lack of chemistry, and the little direction they received from Hitchcock. *Warner Bros/Photofest © Warner Bros*

him to the public as an earnest young man, promoting him as a boy who loved animals and wanted to take care of his family with his hundred-dollars-a-week salary and describing him as a boy scout. Picking up a five-year contract from Goldwyn at seventeen, the studio's press release describing their latest acquisition stated:

> A typical American boy, whose proudest possession is the electric shaver which he began using on his 17th birthday, he swims, rides, hunts, fishes, and ice skates at every opportunity. His fondness for dogs and horses is such that until 18 months ago his prime ambition was to be a veterinarian. He says he has yet to meet a girl who has such beautiful eyes and teeth as his wire haired terrier Boots. He has made himself an authority on breeds of dogs and has collected 200 china canine miniatures as well as a small library on dogs.[3]

After a brief period in the army, which only emphasized this All-American boy image, he became frustrated with the limitations placed on him by the studio system. He was being given few adult films and his popularity was wavering, with one fan magazine suggesting he should marry "girlfriend" Shelley Winters to save his career.[4] He claimed he was offered but not allowed to accept roles in *A Place in the Sun* and *Sunset Boulevard* because the studio wanted to keep his "sensitive boy-next-door" image, hoping to turn him into a young Rock Hudson.[5]

It was only after he had been permitted to film *They Lived by Night* that he seemed to make the transition to adult films. It was also this film that convinced Hitchcock that the sensitive boy could play a killer in *Rope*.[6] Granger embraced the role, believing it an opportunity to revive his stalled acting career, as was his recent decision to buy out his Goldwyn contract in order to work in New York theater, select his own film roles, and avoid the studio's interference regarding his personal life.[7] Granger took Laurents's advice to "emphasize" his character's homosexual tendencies and suggest that the boys' relationship was a romantic obsession, rather than mere friendship. However, Dall refused to engage with him, which, along with Stewart's choice to underplay his character's sinister qualities and homosexuality, certainly put the movie off balance.

The pivotal role of the teacher who planted the ideas of "the perfect murder" and Machiavellian views of a higher class into the boys' heads required an actor whose sexual appeal suggests an ability to manipulate and control the admirers he's corrupted. While Cary Grant enjoyed playing up his dark side, real-life family man Stewart embraced the good-guy persona the studio had cultivated, and he was leery at the time of tapping into the dark sides of his personality. With his average appearance, quacking voice, and slight build, Stewart lacked the qualities that dripped effortlessly off of Grant with ease as a person who could manipulate with charm. Arthur Laurents described his miscasting as "Jimmy Stewart never had an affair with anyone. He was just a boy scout."[8] Years later, with Anthony Mann and Hitchcock, the fractured good guy would emerge in memorable films, played with conviction by Stewart. However, at the time that he was making *Rope*, Granger felt Stewart's genuine nice, sweet nature hurt his ability to find his dark side as an actor, especially considering the lack of guidance he was given by his director, and told an interviewer:

> I thought it needed to have been somebody like James Mason. Stewart is a fine actor, but he just cannot express any kind of a sinister quality, which this

professor needs to have, so that you can feel the influence he's had on these boys. He is really the heavy. He is the one who's destroyed them and made them think the way they do. That's really the point of the thing. And with Stewart, you simply never believed that.[9]

Arthur Laurents, who protested the casting to Hitchcock when first decided, explained that it was the casting of Jimmy Stewart that "destroyed a motive and a relationship unintentionally,"[10] writing:

I suppose they got what they wanted in muting the homosexual undercurrents by bringing Jimmy in, but I can't help but think that's all they got. Jimmy never really got comfortable with the idea of playing this real heavy, a true villain. After all, no matter what he says at the end, his is the character that has triggered the killing in the story. He was extremely conscious of being his dark figure, and that made him edgy all the way through. He was a pro, of course, and he worked

James Stewart was generally unhappy with his experiences working on *Rope* (1948), his first of four films for Hitchcock, who he found disinterested in working with actors during the production. *Warner Bros/Photofest © Warner Bros*

at it. But off camera he wasn't especially friendly, and on camera, I really never got the feeling that we were building a scene together. Of course, a lot of that also had to do with the fact that we were all a little distracted by Hitchcock's technical considerations.[11]

Arthur Laurents also made claims that Stewart was drinking heavily at the time because of his misery on set and barely sleeping over the tension. Press took notice of his anxiety, which he was unable to hide when the set was opened to the public.[12]

Much the way Gregory Peck's casting in *The Paradine Case* hurt that film, and audiences resisted Cary Grant as the murderer in *Suspicion*, the Stewart performance throws off the intention and balance of the film. *Rope* was meant to be one of Hitchcock's films featuring charming villains (along with *Shadow of a Doubt*, *Strangers on a Train*, *Psycho*, and to a lesser extent *North by Northwest*) who could hold the audience's interest despite the crimes. Hitchcock himself felt the audience should be primarily interested in Brandon and Philip, for "crime is a most fascinating subject. But it is not the detection of crime that holds one's interest—it is the motivation."[13] However, Stewart's star was so high and trusted at the time, audiences were anticipating his arrival (which is close to halfway through the film) and expected him to play the hero, so they never invested interest in the characters of Brandon and Philip and were ultimately disappointed by Stewart's character for his ambiguous role in the murder he ultimately solves.

Vince Canby wrote, "It seems highly unlikely that the man we see on the screen could ever have spouted the nonsense attributed to him. He's also too down-to-earth and pragmatic ever to have been intrigued by the foppish manners and mini-intellect of the murderous Brandon."[14] Because of his detachment from this triangle of homosexual men, Stewart's character seems more like a detective, and his role in the crimes never comes to the surface. Laurents, ultimately disappointed with the film, said, "Jimmy Stewart was Jimmy Stewart. Which meant not a whiff of sex of any kind. He does dominate the picture, though, with ease and authority. His Rupert is intelligent, attractive, laced with humor—teasing, though, rather than sardonic."[15] Indeed even this difference was problematic, as the true dark comedy of such a macabre story, played up with visual gags and the cool humor of John Dall, is lessened by Stewart's everyman earnestness.

Stewart's inability to commit, Dall's reserve, and Granger mania were problematic, but not completely the fault of the actors. Rather, they showed the flaws in the way Hitchcock directed films. Although he often claimed storyboarding and planning out so much of the film caused him to be bored on sets, it can't be ignored that part of his directorial responsibility was to keep an eye on the performances to ensure actors projected what was required of the narrative and characters. However, the technical challenges of a film with extended one-shots and a camera on a moving track kept him from taking notice of the actors, who were struggling even more with the technical challenges of re-creating such precise movement so as to not ruin takes and avoid disturbing the camera's flow. The cast reached the point of exhaustion having to refilm their ten-minute scenes over and over again, and tensions began to rise when one would blow a line or make a mistake.[16] Stewart complained that he was never actually directed by Hitchcock, who was preoccupied with the camera work necessary for the film, only shouting unhelpful comments such as "The scene is tired," which Stewart found disparaging and far from instructive. Granger noticed years later that Hitchcock failed to even offer technical instruction, despite the difficulties they faced,[17] a fact he only realized years later when he made *Strangers on a Train*, a Hitchcock collaboration he found far more fulfilling and enjoyable.

It is somewhat remarkable to think that despite the difficulties they had working with Hitchcock, and cold treatment they felt they received from him, both Granger and Stewart would work with the master once again—and more importantly, that despite feeling *Rope* was a disappointment, they made films that are today considered some of Hitchcock's best.

12

Under Capricorn

Since suggesting Ingrid Bergman for the role of Mrs. Paradine in *The Paradine Case*, Hitchcock had been tickled by the idea of showing Bergman as a woman who, like Alicia at the beginning of *Notorious*, was of a questionable moral position, but who, rather than being rescued and saved by a man, is able to bring down a man. He told Peter Bogdanovich his theory (one he would return to over and over again) that "any beautiful woman is a compromise for evil—meaning, perhaps, that beauty always appeals to the animal, the base, the non-moral in man."[1] He thought it possible to address the theory in his feature *The Paradine Case*, but failed to convey Peck's downfall because of the lack of passion the actor had with costar Alida Valli.

The notion made such a strong imprint on his mind that rather than make another thriller, he made his first and only historic period drama during his time in Hollywood about this very theme with *Under Capricorn*. *Under Capricorn* is the story of an alcoholic who has become a pariah in Australia despite her reformed convict husband's (Cotton) rise to wealth and societal respectability. Michael Wilding played the brother of Bergman's childhood friend, whose professional association with Cotton brings them together and reignites something long dead in Bergman. She ultimately has a brief affair with him, which enrages Cotton to the point of shooting him, only to have it revealed that Bergman is guilty of the murder that led to Cotton's relocation to Australia.

Although Hitchcock claimed to be inspired by the thought of showing a woman usually as pure as Ingrid Bergman as dangerous and capable of corrupting decent men (a femme fatale), years later he would recount the film's inception differently, placing responsibility (and its faults) largely on Bergman:

> I had no special admiration for the novel, and I don't think I would have made the picture if it hadn't been for Ingrid Bergman. At that time she was the biggest star in America and all the American producers were competing for her services, and I must admit that I made the mistake of thinking that to get Bergman would be a tremendous feat; it was a victory over the rest of the industry, you see. That was bad thinking, and my behavior was almost infantile. Because even if the presence of Bergman represented a commercial asset, it makes the whole thing so costly that there was no point to it. Had I examined the whole thing more carefully from the commercial angle, I would not have spent two and half million dollars on the picture. At the time that was a lot of money you see. . . . I looked upon Bergman as a feather in my cap. We were making it with our own production company and all I could think about was, "Here I am, Hitchcock, the onetime English director, returning to London with the biggest star of the day." I was literally intoxicated at the thought of the cameras and flashbulbs that would be directed at Bergman and myself at the London airport. All of these externals seemed to be terribly important. I can only say now that I was being stupid and juvenile.[2]

Hitchcock's casting decisions for the Australian historical novel were a sign of his many missteps on how to tell the story effectively. No longer able to claim casting choices were pushed on him by studios, Hitchcock's usually inspired choices seemed off with all three leading roles.

English critics questioned casting American Cotton instead of any number of respected English actors.[3] By that time a close friend of Hitchcock, Cotton had become a profitable leading man in films such as *Portrait of Jenny* and *Since You Went Away*. However, Cotton's suave refinement, the dominant quality that had made him the ideal choice to play the urbane Uncle Charlie, made him poorly suited for the role of a hard-living man who had risen up by the bootstraps to become respectable. Much the way he felt Robert Newton would have been a better choice to play Andre Latour in *The Paradine Case*, Hitchcock later admitted the same would have been true with the role of Sam

Hitchcock made *Under Capricorn* (1949) specifically for the opportunity to work with Ingrid Bergman once again, but when it failed, he placed considerable blame on the actress. *Photofest*

Flusky in *Under Capricorn*. Cotton was simply too "posh" and nonthreaten-
ing an actor to play the character Hitchcock felt would have been better with
a hearty actor such as Burt Lancaster.[4]

There was also simply not a large enough variation between Michael
Wilding and Joseph Cotton, so only in temperament do the actors show any
significant differences; Cotton played Sam as angry and gruff, compared to
Englishman Michael Wilding's constantly foolish grin. Typically a likable,
comic actor, Wilding is easily forgettable and completely unconvincing as a
potential rival for Bergman's affections.[5]

Ironically, poor as the reviews were for the film when released, critics generally praised the acting Hitchcock considered so problematic. Film magazine
Cue wrote that Hitchcock had gotten lazy and the film was just behind *The
Paradine Case* as his worst film because it was "overlong, overblown and
overdone." However, the review did claim, "The master still can wield remarkably fine performances out of his actors."[6] But not all praise was positive,

Joseph Cotton, Ingrid Bergman, and Michael Wilding were considered miscast in
Hitchcock's first and only costume drama, *Under Capricorn* (1949). *Warner Bros/
Photofest © Warner Bros*

especially toward Ingrid Bergman. Roy Kohler wrote in his review, "It's too bad Miss Bergman can't shut down some of the feminine catcalls with a great performance. But Ingrid, while a good actress, never has been a great one. So it isn't surprising she is unable to rise above her vehicle in *Under Capricorn*."[7]

Russell Rhodes called Cotton the standout, but suggested Bergman was miscast as well and thought the film would have been helped if Hitchcock had selected an actress such as Vivien Leigh instead.[8] Ironically, although the film would arrive in theaters two years later, the idea that Leigh would have been an ideal choice hints at the kind of performance the actress would eventually give in *A Streetcar Named Desire*. It was precisely that level of performance, fragile but shrill and unlikable, which was lacking from Bergman. Although Bergman's efforts are evident throughout, there is a general sense that the actress was concerned with making the character truly unlikable, holding back when she should be revolting.

Bergman, however, not only wanted to be in her pet project *Under Capricorn*, but considered the film an opportunity to take on one of the best female characters she'd ever run across. In an editorial she wrote for a gossip columnist, she described how she played the role in her latest Hitchcock film:

> From this distance and in this perspective, my work with Alfred Hitchcock shapes up as probably the most important thing to remember about *Under Capricorn*. Is it my confidence in him? Is it the fact that he always knows exactly what he wants to get on the screen? Is it his long experience in the craftsmanship of film direction? Is it all of these and more? I know I put myself completely in his hands. In the making of that picture Hitch was the boss—and, within the four walls of the sound stage, his word was law. . . . For me this scene was a physical strain that led to almost complete exhaustion. Merely acting for 10 minutes at a stretch is no problem to anyone with stage training, but doing a 10-minute tense emotional scene without a break for the screen is a different matter. Your positions and your movements must be correct to the fraction of an inch for camera focus. Walls and doors are constantly disappearing to make way for the camera as you move from room to room. Property men are crawling under foot removing obstacles in your path. And a Technicolor camera on a 30-foot crane is constantly pursuing you, coming in swiftly for a close-up and then sweeping away—all these make demands upon an actress that go far beyond the realms of mere acting. But a lot of people do exhausting work and are happy to do it because the results are gratifying. And that's how it is with

me. I have seen *Under Capricorn* and I know the experiment, if you care to call it that, has succeeded. Hitch sees, and commits to paper, every movement of the cast and camera six months before hand. He has the whole production in mind, from beginning to end, on the day the camera starts turning. And it is not only a general idea; it is the detailed development, with every camera angle and every movement, worked out to the last quarter.[9]

Ironically, the ten-minute takes she referred to as "an experience" were aspects that seemed to cause the greatest strain to Bergman and Hitchcock's working relationship. As the producer of *Under Capricorn* (and *Rope*), Hitchcock was frustrated with Bergman's singular focus on her own performance and felt she simply wanted to elevate her status as a great actress rather than make a great movie. He also resented the high price tag she earned as an actress, especially now that being the producer obligated him to make the payments.[10] When Bergman insisted on reshooting the ten-minute confession scene over and over again, Hitchcock lost patience with the actress he once spent all morning working with on a single line and walked off set.[11] What Hitchcock overlooked, however, on both *Under Capricorn* and *Rope* was the fact that one-takes are used primarily in films to focus the audience on the "pure performance" of an actor and allow them to capture the entire, emotional moment on film, which Bergman was trying to do take after take.[12]

After having been accommodating and kind to Bergman on the set of *Spellbound* and *Notorious*, Hitchcock placed blame of *Under Capricorn*'s failure on her shoulders, insisting he made the film only because she liked the property, but that "from that, I learned that it was better to look at Ingrid than to listen to her."[13] It was, and is, the opinion of many Hitchcock biographers that Bergman's affair with Roberto Rossellini not only hurt the box office of the film, but severed the relationship she had with Hitchcock. Part of Hitchcock's discontent was the fact that while he wanted to "suggest" the former Joan of Arc was capable of scandalous behavior, by the time *Under Capricorn* was in release, Bergman was embroiled in the far more titillating true story of her affair with Rossellini.[14] Bergman claimed the intrusions into her personal life were the reason she choose to leave Hollywood behind, and for some time she did, moving to Italy and making films primarily in Europe. This decision to give up Hollywood not only for another man but another director seemed to be what severed her professional relationship with the rejected Hitchcock.

13

Stage Fright

I ran into great difficulties with Jane. In her disguise as a lady's maid, she should have been rather unglamorous; after all, she was supposed to be impersonating an unattractive maid. But every time she saw the rushes and how she looked alongside Marlene Dietrich, she would burst into tears. She couldn't accept the idea of her face being in character, while Dietrich looked so glamorous, so she kept improving her appearance every day and that's how she failed to maintain the character.[1]

One of the most common commentaries when studying Hitchcock in connection to his actors was his tendency to chastise his actors for the faults of a film—particularly in consideration of the minimal amount of praise he was willing to extend to the stars of his most successful films. He was quick to say no actor was ever the key to a successful Hitchcock films yet he was quick to point out the mistakes of casting actors or how they failed him. But an individual who seemed victimized to a ridiculous extent by Hitchcock was Jane Wyman, who starred in 1950's *Stage Fright*. During interviews with Truffaut and others, he made the point to single Wyman out, claiming that she vainly refused to be shown in a physically unattractive manner, hurting the film's character development. This claim by Alfred Hitchcock proved to be ridiculous.

As Donald Spoto pointed out, the decision to gradually improve Wyman's appearance made logical sense for the narrative as a way to improve the audience's connection to Wyman's character of Eve. In the film, her drama student character pretends to be a dresser for Marlene Dietrich's diva star, Charlotte Inwood, and dresses plain and unattractive as a disguise (a very funny scene). However, the film calls for Wyman to also anchor a love story (with Michael Wilding), and she appears in the thrilling, dramatic climax of the picture when Richard Todd confesses. If dressed as she was when she first appeared in disguise during the confession, it would have been a ridiculous scene, like a clown discovering Norman Bates.

Furthermore, in terms of the power a person had on set, Hitchcock was not one to give in to the whims of even the biggest stars. Even tearful pleas or reasoned debates would not move him to make such changes with the likes of Ingrid Bergman or Kim Novak. Wyman was a considerable talent and a star at the time that she appeared in *Stage Fright*, but far from as big a name as Hitchcock. Wyman was known in Hollywood for being a remark-

Hitchcock complained that Jane Wyman, pictured with actress Pat Hitchcock, was overly concerned with her appearance while filming *Stage Fright* (1950). *Warner Bros/ Photofest © Warner Bros*

ably agreeable actress; under contract from the age of nineteen, she was never suspended from a contract and spent more than a decade with Warner Bros. Wyman was more than familiar with the type of actress Hitchcock tended to prefer and was surprised but delighted when Hitchcock wanted neither her earlier blonde image nor the melodramatic woman she had been playing recently. Hitchcock wanted the girlish comic known as Ronald Reagan's "Little Miss Button Nose" from the Midwest. And Wyman was delighted to be encouraged to use her comic skills again after so many dramatic films.

It seems this tension between Hitchcock and Wyman resulted not from any vanity on her part, but the fact that the agreeable and passive actress found the courage to speak her mind—from the grand dame of Hollywood, Marlene Dietrich. Dietrich was the biggest name in *Stage Fright* and one of the biggest names in Hollywood; despite having the smaller role, she was a considerable draw. She was at her most popular in 1920 as a star of Berlin and later in the 1930s and 1940s, despite a minor downturn before a comeback with the Jimmy Stewart western parody *Destry Rides Again*. However, after World War II, she had made the transition to working primarily on the stage and as a cabaret singer—a character very similar to the grand dame of theater she plays in *Stage Fright*. And Dietrich's performance was entirely wrapped up in the expectations audiences had about who Dietrich the woman was. Charlotte is a remarkably underwritten character, far from a lead. But as played by Dietrich, all the aspects audiences found true of her personality seemed to be true on-screen.

As with Tallulah Bankhead in *Lifeboat*, or even Cary Grant in *Suspicion*, Dietrich is playing a character based almost entirely on her persona, and the thrill for the audience comes from seeing that image repurposed. But to hire such a name comes with a high cost (literally and figuratively), and Dietrich seemed to live out the character she was playing on set. A diva in every sense of the word, she was both demanding and unprofessional. She would arrive on set late and demand her own costuming (always Dior) and began an affair with Michael Wilding. But it was especially frustrating to Hitchcock that, along with her own demands of how she was to be filmed, she encouraged Michael Wilding and Jane Wyman to do the same.

Wyman recalled being treated as a protégé by the senior actress and began making similar requests and questioning Hitchcock's choices. It is a common occurrence on film sets for an actor to want to understand the directorial

Hitchcock found himself frustrated with Marlene Dietrich, who played a villainous version of her stage diva persona in *Stage Fright* (1950). *Warner Bros/Photofest © Warner Bros*

choices being made, especially when it related to how they would be filmed and therefore perceived by an audience. However, Hitchcock wanted absolute loyalty, which included no questioning of his directorial choices.

It was not surprising that the seductive Dietrich and playboy Michael Wilding would begin an affair on set, no matter how disruptive it was. While the casting of English Wilding as the gangly fool with ridiculous costumes in *Under Capricorn* did nothing to improve his public image, it certainly did little harm. Even in *Under Capricorn*, the overall character trait projected by Wilding in the overly dramatic film was a certain goofy charm, romantic indeed, but far from elegant or regal. Wilding, a self-deprecating actor with the press, knew his limitations well, insisting, "Considering I was the worst actor I ever came across with no talent at all, except perhaps a penchant for mimicry, I did pretty well."[2] Along with a slightly clipped accent, he had already established his own distinct "look" he dubbed "the Wilding way." With cigarette in hand and hat slightly to the side, he was far better suited to the role of the detective who puts Eve at ease, as he does with the audience, and reminiscent of Macdonald Carey's detective character in *Shadow of a Doubt*. The reviewers took note of the pleasure of watching him in such a role, Philip Scheuer comparing him to a young Noel Coward.[3]

Ironically, although a considerably flasher role, as the villain with a fractured love for Dietrich's character (finally demonstrating a woman's ability to corrupt a man), Richard Todd received little notice from critics. Todd was a considerable star at the time, having been nominated for an Oscar just a year earlier for *The Hasty Heart* and considered the most popular English actor of 1949. Despite his Irish roots, he was the quintessential Englishman with perfect diction (an ear which could rival Claude Raines), and he would go on to play Robin Hood and Heathcliff in *Wuthering Heights* and was the first actor offered the role of James Bond (for the first film of the franchise, *Dr. No*), before it was given to the star of Hitchcock's *Marnie*, Sean Connery. However, a large part of his popularity grew out of his very well-known war record as a parachuter and his involvement in the D-Day landing (events he would re-create as part of the ensemble film *The Longest Day*). For a national hero to appear as a villain in only his second film was a risk. Fortunately, the mediocre *Stage Fright* was rarely mentioned as part of his respectable and quintessentially English filmography.[4]

The reason the film was a failure, despite all (or reported) difficulties Hitchcock had with the cast, had nothing to do with the generally strong performances from the ensemble and is primarily due to the mistake he made of showing a "false flashback" told by Todd's character. Hitchcock noted that it was ultimately a mistake to have the character lie—but in fact the audience did not reject the liar, but the fact that Hitchcock lied to them. To film the figment of a lie was itself a lie. Today, the primary pleasure one gets from watching the most forgotten Hitchcock film is the enjoyment of watching the impressive ensemble, the most noteworthy aspect of the film being Alastair Sim's role as Wyman's father, who was just a year away from his iconic role as Scrooge and already one of the most beloved English character actors of his time. However, the stars are satisfying. Todd is memorable but underused as the villain, but gives an especially impressive last scene. Likewise, to see larger-than-life Dietrich "taken down" is itself a thrill, and the charming romance between Wyman and Wilding adds some humanity to the film.

14

Strangers on a Train

After several box-office and critical flops, Hitchcock was in desperate need of a hit. Ironically, rather than return to the romantic thrillers that had been so popular for him (*Rebecca*, *Spellbound*, or *Notorious*), Hitchcock chose one of his darkest projects, *Strangers on a Train*, about a stalker who murders the wife of a famous tennis player. Guy (Farley Granger) and Bruno (Robert Walker) are coconspirators in the murder of Guy's wife, but unlike *Rope*, in which Granger is the willing but regretful participant, his involvement is purely forced upon him by Bruno.

Granger was on the outs with his home studio, having made two consecutive failures (*Edge of Doom* and *Our Very Own*), both of which he refused to promote and led to his being suspended. Considering the failure of *Rope* and disinterest Hitchcock had taken working with actors, a second collaboration was a surprise to Granger. Years later, Hitchcock made it no secret that the still-living Granger was his second choice, explaining, "I must say that I wasn't too pleased with Farley Granger; he's a good actor, but I would have liked to see William Holden in the part because he's stronger. In this kind of story the stronger the hero, the more effective the situation."[1] However, this time Hitchcock did not pout over his inability to have exactly the actor he wanted. Instead, Granger found Hitchcock to be fully engaged in the project and performances. Not only was he willing to discuss some of the personality and backstory of Guy, but he also explained some of the directorial aspects of his storytelling, which had been a mystery to Granger while on the set of *Rope*. Upon reflection of the film, over and over in interviews, Granger would call *Strangers on a Train* "the nicest experience I had ever had working in films."

His happiness on-screen didn't simply relate to his work with Hitchcock, but also the opportunity to work with Robert Walker, a man whose performance he would be quick to praise for the rest of his life. John Dall had been unfriendly to Granger and refused to play his character of Brandon as being in a homosexual relationship with Granger's Philip. However, almost immediately Granger was delighted meeting Robert Walker, who also looked at *Strangers on a Train* as an opportunity to improve a stalled and frustrated movie career. Walker fully committed to the truth of the situation (including the homoerotic elements of his character) and, like Granger, found Hitchcock willing to work with him on developing the character.

Despite their cold relationship on *Rope,* Farley Granger considered his experience working with Hitchcock on *Strangers on a Train* (1951) his most enjoyable filmmaking experience. *Warner Bros/Photofest © Warner Bros*

Walker was so focused on the character and opportunity he had been given, he spent months working on the character. A friend of Walker, Jim Henaghan, recalled:

> During all the time I knew him, Bob had never shown any excitement about a part or a picture. But he was damned excited about Strangers and about the prospect of working with Alfred Hitchcock, and vastly flattered that Hitchcock had wanted only him. As I've said, Bob was the last person to be impressed by his own career—he considered acting a crock. Suddenly there was a radical change in his attitude. Now, for the first time, he wanted to be accepted as a real actor.[2]

Although Walker's biographer Beverly Linet felt the role cast Walker against type, calling his screen image "outwardly good-natured,"[3] one only needs to recall the fact that Walker's personal image was disconnected from his screen image and had for some time overshadowed his career. Robert Walker had in fact a certain understanding of the character of Bruno.

Unlike the likable boys he typically played, Walker also suffered mental illness, which occasionally made it into the papers. Introduced to play "cute boys" and "shy guys,"[4] his marriage to Jennifer Jones and family life were part of the selling point as the "fresh-faced family entering Hollywood." During his first years, fan magazines published reports of him being a polite, well-mannered young man, one article introducing him as "Robert Walker: Aside from a Few Annoying Habits, He's Simply a Nice Kid from Utah."[5]

But despite a $2,500 seven-year contract (with a $1,000 raise every year), his personal problems began hurting his career. He told Hollywood reporter Emily Cowan, "You've seen me in pictures, but I'm not as nice as those boys I played in *Hargrove* [*See Here, Private Hargrove*] and *Since You Went Away*. Really I'm psychologically difficult. I used to be a difficult child; my parents had a bad time with me. I used to fight with my brothers and I didn't get along at school. That's why they sent me to the San Diego Army and Navy Academy."[6] Similarly, he told Hedda Hopper during one of her profiles of him that "from childhood I was up against mental walls. I was always trying to make an escape from life," citing his parents' divorce as the inciting event that began his struggles with mental illness, believing these problems only improved when an aunt took notice of him and he was accepted to the American Academy of Dramatic Arts in New York.[7]

In 1945, his tortured relationship with wife Jennifer Jones ended when she left him to marry David O. Selznick, and his depression and anxiety only grew. Paranoid, he was convinced Selznick was trying to hurt his career, particularly because none of his films released at that time grossed more than $50,000. He was arrested on charges of drunk and disorderly conduct (with a $50 fine), and a few months later he married actress Barbara Ford, only to legally separate one month later. He briefly left the production of *What Next, Corporal Hargrove?* when it was determined that he was suffering from a lack of sleep and stress after walking off the set in a rage in the middle of production. Finally, he was committed to the Menninger Clinic Psychiatric Ward after starting a physical fight with a policeman, and his studio was forced to put his contract on a one-year hold until he had been released and deemed well enough to work.[8]

Even after these events he remained an unusual celebrity, giving odd interviews that were surprisingly personal and addressed intimate matters. His idiosyncratic character, like a young George Sanders, led him to frequently disparage his film work and discuss highly personal matters rarely mentioned to the press, such as his fetish for girls with glasses (a comment often repeated and almost chilling when thinking of Bruno and his victims). He could aggravate and frustrate Hollywood reporters, but was such a compelling and charismatic individual, they continued to conduct and publish interviews, even after his career slowed.

But despite all his struggles, Walker was an actor who desperately wanted a screen comeback and considered the role of Bruno in *Strangers on a Train* to be exactly the role that could "start my career,"[9] as he told Hedda Hopper just after being cast. And the casting of Walker was an inspired choice by Hitchcock, as the character of Bruno played by Walker would not only play into the image Walker did not regret creating, but show the charismatic side of his oddness. As Bruno, he would dress in the same suits in which he had conducted so many interviews and wear the glasses he wore only in real life (never on film).

Strangers on a Train, despite the intelligent, sensitive, leading-man performance Granger gave, was praised primarily because of Walker and the oddly charismatic yet indiscreet way in which he played the character of Bruno. Bosley Crowther described the character as "a queer, unbalanced fellow with no evident importance in life, other than that of an idol to his mother and a

Robert Walker and Farley Granger established a strong bond on and off camera while making *Strangers on a Train* (1951). *Warner Bros/Photofest © Warner Bros*

nuisance to his frankly detested old man."[10] François Truffaut told Hitchcock that Walker gave "a rather poetic portrayal; he's undoubtedly more attractive [than Guy]. There is a distinct impression that you prefer the villain."[11] While Granger is far more engaging than Robert Cummings, the struggle between Guy and Bruno is reminiscent of the conflict in *Saboteur*, particularly reminiscent in the final set-piece fight and ultimate ending met by the villains.

Granger himself agreed that Walker's performance is what elevates the film, calling his performance the predecessor to Norman Bates and quick to discuss Walker whenever asked about making *Strangers on a Train*.[12] Granger was well aware of the fact that Walker hoped *Strangers* would revitalize his career[13] and help him move past the events that had derailed it. All of which made his untimely death just before the film's release so tragic; what he committed to celluloid was also his greatest performance and would be remembered as one of the iconic characters in film history.

15

I Confess

We shouldn't have made the picture.[1]

Although critically well received and a moderate success, *Strangers on a Train* was far from the successes Hitchcock had experienced with his earliest films in Hollywood. By this time, television was beginning to become the dominant form of entertainment, stealing audiences away from theaters evening after evening. And with this new competition, films had to be both more fantastical and visually expansive, or appeal to the intellectual desires of older audiences. Along with finding properties from the Great White Way, Hollywood was also seeking out the emerging theater actors who brought a new style of acting to film, many trained under the approach commonly described as "method" acting.

Popularized by Lee Strasberg and the Actors Studio, the most popular young stars all seemed to be coming out of this new school of thought and began appearing in gritty, realistic films. Those who thought the approach to be anticinematic referred to these films as "kitchen sink dramas"—drab movies about adult issues with humorless characters. Hitchcock was one of the most vocal critics of the new trend in cinema, telling a journalist:

> They're all right but I've never seen one in white tie and tails. No real elegance. We need ladies on screen. We used to have plenty—Carole Lombard, Irene Dunne, Myrna Loy, Norma Shearer. I call those downbeat films sink to sink

94

pictures. The wife's home washing dishes, her mate says "get a sitter and we'll see a movie." She's elated, gets dressed up, and they go. What does she see? A woman at the sink, washing dishes.[2]

Since working with Gregory Peck, an early student of the Stanislavsky method, Hitchcock had deemed these actors as difficult to direct because of their resistance to technical instructions. Actors were asked to immerse themselves completely, mind and body, into the psychology of their character in order to truly experience their emotions. If they were compelled by this process to move right when instructed to move left, it was part of the truth of the character, and many younger directors were willing to improvise and accommodate them in order to work with them.

Hitchcock was not such a director and insisted his actors do specifically as he asked—it was the responsibility of an actor to find the motivation to do what was asked of him or her. But Hitchcock also admitted that many of these young method actors were extremely talented, and took particular notice of Montgomery Clift. Having considered casting him in *Rope*, he still had the desire to cast him in a role that required him to show the tremendous emotional depth he was able to tap into so completely on film.

Fortunately, the film *I Confess*, one that also deals with the subject of guilt through complicity, was a film Clift found especially compelling, and he accepted the role of a Catholic priest. Clift had an intellectual fascination with theology and this role of a priest tried for murder because of his refusal to give the name of a confessor was a story he found moving and provocative. Not only was Clift considered an excellent actor, perhaps the most respected in his generation, the casting of Clift also promised to improve the film's marketability as the tall, handsome actor was certainly a box-office draw. The definition of the delicate leading man, his little-boy-lost persona made him a heartthrob of his time; George Kingsley wrote in his profile of Clift that "his sadness is one of the qualities that makes him so enormously attractive to female moviegoers. It seems to arouse their maternal instincts."[3]

Yet despite all Clift would bring to *I Confess* and the thoughtful (although quite distant) performance he gave, Hitchcock found him to be an extremely difficult actor. Hitchcock recalled that "there are some actors I've felt uncomfortable with, and working with Montgomery Clift was difficult because he was a method actor and neurotic as well."[4] Clift's costar and friend Karl Malden spoke in detail of the problems he witnessed on set, saying, "Monty was a friend, but he was already a sick man, in the grips of terrible addictions to drugs and drink. As a person, he was wonderful, a great talent, good enough to have been a protégé of the Lunts and Wilder—but he was an accident waiting to happen."[5] Malden was convinced that the biggest problem in Clift's life was the constant presence of Mira Rostova, an acting coach who "Monty was absolutely dependent on. No one could understand why, and this created constant tensions for everyone."[6]

The temperamental Clift could be especially hard on other actors, particularly those Clift felt were beneath him or less talented. Hitchcock had no desire to cast an entire film with New York method actors. Instead, he cast easygoing actor Karl Malden as the detective, who despite being a student (and teacher) of method, was far from neurotic and brought a hard-boiled

Despite considering her for the lead in *Rebecca,* Anne Baxter felt rejected by Hitchcock when she was assigned to *I Confess* (1953) by Warner Bros. *Warner Bros/Photofest © Warner Bros*

realism to the role of the detective. Also assigned to the film was Hollywood actress Anne Baxter, an actress Clift seemed to dislike with venom and who received the cold shoulder from Hitchcock.

Baxter's role of Ruth Grandford was originally created for Jennifer Jones[7] (the former Mrs. Robert Walker), but Hitchcock eventually chose to cast Anita Bjork instead.[8] Ms. Bjork arrived from Sweden with an illegitimate child and in the middle of an affair. The panicked Warner Bros. feared another Ingrid Bergman scandal.[9] As so often happened, the exchange of one actor with another threw Hitchcock into an internal tantrum, years later declaring, "I didn't want Anne Baxter to play the feminine lead; I wanted Anita Bjork, who had played Miss Julie. However, Warner backed her and I was informed by a phone call that Anne Baxter had been assigned to the picture. I met her for the first time a week before the shooting in the dining room of Quebec's Hotel Chateau Frontenac. When you compare Anita Bjork and Anne Baxter, wouldn't you say that was a pretty awkward substitution?"[10]

Hitchcock's dismissive comments, while cruel, had very little to do with the talent or personality of Baxter, who had once been considered for the lead in *Rebecca*. From the moment the twenty-seven-year-old arrived and her dark hair was dyed an unnatural blonde, Baxter was uncomfortable with the manner in which Hitchcock made it constantly known that she was unwanted:

> He gave me the impression that I wasn't attractive enough to be in his film, so he ordered my hair to be dyed bright blond, and he merely had Anita Bjork's costumes quickly altered to fit me. I didn't object to any of that, but there was a lot of Pygmalion in him—he was very proud of his practice of transforming actresses in order to fit them into his rather fixed ideal.[11]

Hitchcock's dislike of Baxter seems especially odd considering she possessed so many of the qualities he admired in actresses: professionalism, confidence, and the ability to take his technical direction. In her role as the former love of Clift's priest, she is the emotional anchor of the film, especially compared to Clift's detached performance. Baxter had a cool, confident persona that made her a favorite of Orson Welles (who cast her in *The Magnificent Ambersons*) and Jean Renoir (who cast her in *Swamp Water*), who called her America's Janie Marese. In truth, however, Baxter was hard to classify, an

actress who even at the tender age of sixteen had seemed far older than her actual age. Baxter was singularly unique, and Hitchcock had no use for her kind.

Hardest for Baxter, however, was the lack of support she received from costar Montgomery Clift, who "was so ill and distraught that his eyes wouldn't
focus. I needed something from him—some response—but there was nothing, just a blank and distant gaze. He was so disturbed and unhappy."[12] Hitchcock had similar difficulties working with Clift and often was frustrated with
behavior he considered childish and temperamental. Unable to address Clift's
poor behavior, Hitchcock frequently expressed his frustrations on set toward

Karl Malden and Anne Baxter (pictured) struggled while making *I Confess* (1953) with
Montgomery Clift, whom they found temperamental and already struggling with
addiction. *Warner Bros/Photofest © Warner Bros*

Baxter, much the way he had with Jane Wyman during the production of *Stage Fright*. Only Malden seemed comfortable working with both Hitchcock and Clift, having gotten used to working with temperamental actors because of his time running rehearsals for Elia Kazan.[13]

As difficult as the film was, however, Hitchcock felt it worthwhile because of the introspective, thoughtful performance Clift gave and the physicality he naturally brought to the role. He particularly noted the walk he employed as the priest, claiming, "It's a forward motion that shapes the whole film. It also solidifies the concept of his integrity."[14] Critics, however, disagreed, finding the casting of Clift generally problematic. *Tribune* critic Mae Tinee wrote that "while Montgomery Clift is very likable, his performance seems a little too wooden under the circumstances. Anne Baxter still has a lovely voice and obvious ability, but I don't think her bleached hair any asset. Karl Malden is, as usual, solid and satisfying as a detective with a one track mind."[15] Another critic went even further, claiming casting Clift was a clear attempt by Hitchcock and Warner Bros. to appeal to box-office trends rather than artistic integrity, writing, "Even the casting reflects lack of grasp of the subject, and the desire for box-office at any price. Montgomery Clift, as a priest, looks like a matinee idol dressed for a masquerade. Anne Baxter looks like a retired chorus girl."[16]

Part of this complaint came from the box-office success of the film. While Hitchcock had selected Clift for artistic merit, he was also very aware of the impact a star can have. To be a star in a film meant a certain responsibility, to be strong enough to carry the movie and to take ownership of a film's success or failure. And while Clift's participation did guarantee box-office success, even if he garnered weak reviews for his work, Hitchcock had no desire to repeat the experience working with him or other method actors again soon.

16

Dial M for Murder

For modern audiences *Dial M for Murder* will always be known first and foremost as the movie that began one of the great screen collaborations between director and actress of all time: Alfred Hitchcock and Grace Kelly. Her performances and screen presence were certainly the most memorable of Hitchcock's women, including her performance in their first film together, *Dial M for Murder*. And while it seems impossible to imagine another actress in the role, she was not Hitchcock's first choice. When first purchasing the property of the stage play, Hitchcock wanted to cast the most elegant and beloved actress of the time: Audrey Hepburn.[1]

Instead, Hitchcock had to settle for an actress whose image he could create: Grace Kelly. She had often played homely girls, often with dark hair, plain clothing, and very little makeup to emphasize her plainness. Stanley Kramer had cast her as the good Quaker wife of Gary Cooper in *High Noon*. It was that role for which she was best known in films when Hitchcock was looking for an actress to play the sophisticated, unfaithful wife at the center of *Dial M for Murder*. She was better known as a memorable television actress in many of the live anthologies on TV at the time (*Kraft Theater*, *Philco-Goodyear*, *Lux*, and *Studio One* to name a few). However, after watching a prerelease print of her next film, *Mogambo*, a film unlikely to do much for her career,[2] and aware that she had received a majority of her training by working in television, Hitchcock hired her for (and to be) his next project, embracing the opportunity to focus his attention on elevating her image.

Dial M for Murder, however, was a project especially suited as a vehicle to both create a new star and challenge the image of another, Ray Milland, as the villain of the film. *Dial M for Murder* also happens to be a picture that offered two lesser-known character actors the opportunity to shine: the Tony Award winner John Williams (who won for playing the same role on Broadway) and respected character actor Tony Dawson. The only actor who isn't given a significant moment in the well-made film is the film's romantic "hero," Robert Cummings, who is shockingly passive in the film, his character only the catalyst that will propel the other characters into action. According to Peter Bogdanovich, the casting of Cummings and Milland was intentionally subversive: a romantic lead who seems bland, especially compared to the villain's charming, engaging character. While Hitchcock once criticized Cummings for failing to be the charismatic star he needed in *Saboteur*, in *Dial M for Murder*, he uses that same quality in Cummings to focus audience attention on a charismatic villain.

Although a star like Audrey Hepburn would have been an undeniable box-office draw for audiences, she would have also been the biggest star in the movie, and in 1952, it would have been shocking for Hitchcock to kill her off halfway through the movie. With the then lesser-known Kelly as the unfaithful wife, Tony Dawson's attempt to kill her was not only possible but genuinely terrifying. The unlikely casting of Kelly, and television actor Robert Cummings as the romantic hero, makes the villain by default our star, drawing our attention to him from the very start of the film. Milland was a movie star at the time, having just won an Oscar for best actor for the film *The Lost Weekend*.

Hitchcock enjoyed casting against type, and the role of a man trying to get away with having his wife murdered (and having her framed) was surprising for Milland in light of the sensitive performance he gave as a man overcome by his alcohol addiction in *The Lost Weekend*. His performance in *The Lost Weekend* was big and sympathetic, while his performance in *Dial M for Murder* was reserved and sleek. To now see him relishing in evil without a hint of remorse made the film thrilling, and adds a dark humor for the way he speaks of murder like a business proposition.

Milland is especially good when working with formidable talents Tony Dawson and John Williams. Dawson, the tall, thin English actor, could, like Milland, play extremely likable, funny characters. Even today, critics call

Oscar winner of *The Lost Weekend* Ray Milland played against type as the precise, cool villain trying to murder his wife in *Dial M for Murder* (1954). *Warner Bros/ Photofest © Warner Bros*

attention to the extended scene between Dawson and Milland planning out the murder as one of the great delights of the film, watching Milland show his precision and capabilities, while Dawson simply reacts to him, stunned by his cool disposition. As Milland discusses how he reacted to learning of his wife's infidelity and his intent to murder her, the audience listens eagerly, making us complicit in the murder being arranged.

Milland's husband is not a character we like, but there is a fascination that comes from watching a character so cool and composed despite doing something so appalling, doing his crimes with care for the detail; if we have any connection to him, there is a begrudging reverence. However, the audience does have sympathy for Tony Dawson, who seems to be resistant to carrying out his job. He is the second hit man in a Hitchcock film (along with Edmund Gwenn's Rowley in *Foreign Correspondent*) whose temperament does not match the act he is committing. When he is killed by Grace Kelly, we feel badly for his loss, not for Kelly, a character we barely know and have only seen in relation to her affair with Cummings.

It isn't until Milland begins to manipulate and frame her for murder that our alliance completely shifts to her favor, and our concern grows sympathetic to her. It is no wonder Hitchcock chose not to show the trial and instead simply shows her trial and conviction in an artistic, time-shifting close-up of her desperate, frightened face (remarkably similar to the close-ups Hitchcock films when Bergman learns of the murder in *Spellbound*). We aren't simply concerned for her; there is guilt in knowing the truth of circumstances that she can't prove, still unaware of her husband's role in her imprisonment and imminent execution. Our only relief comes from seeing her return home, seeing her plain, tired, frightened face after weeks in prison. Kelly arrives at

Hitchcock changed Grace Kelly's homely good girl image established in films such as *High Noon* into the embodiment of Hollywood sophistication when casting her as the unfaithful wife in *Dial M for Murder* (1954). *Warner Bros/Photofest © Warner Bros*

the house, overwhelmed at seeing her love Robert Cummings and confused to see that John Williams's detective is her savior. When we finally see her pained expression when Milland confirms his role in her imprisonment and the attempt he made on her life, Kelly breaks the audience's hearts; and her transformation to beloved movie star is complete.

Grace Kelly's evolution as an actress and her association with Alfred Hitchcock will always be what *Dial M for Murder* is known for first and foremost. It would be the relationship least often mentioned in regard to their collaborations, perhaps because it features the now beloved Kelly as both a scandalous woman (similar to Bergman's character in *Notorious*) and in grave danger. However, to disregard the performance Kelly gave in *Dial M for Murder* is unfair to an actress who created a compelling yet likable character who can change the audience's opinion of her during a rather short film or without any grand emotional scenes, without seeming quick or unnatural. And Kelly would become known as Hitchcock's favorite actress, one Hitchcock would hold up for example to all his future blondes. Always prepared, even-tempered, and able to take direction while still maintaining her emotional hold on the character, Hitchcock himself (along with her costars) quickly fell in love with the woman.

Kelly and Hitchcock's collaborations were fruitful, for both, creating a timeless classic with *Rear Window*, and two lesser, but still beloved films with *Dial M for Murder* and *To Catch a Thief*. The image of Grace Kelly will forever be linked to the image of the feminine ideal Hitchcock created: the elegant blonde with complex, real emotions hiding beneath the cool exterior, adding shades to her characters. When Kelly's name is brought up, it is the image of her in the films of Hitchcock that comes to mind. But her relationship with Hitchcock also created an image of Hitchcock as Svengali—one who can create a star in the image he personally desires—and the actress whose image he constantly tried to re-create in other women.

17

Rear Window

Although Grace Kelly's public personality had changed dramatically with her role in *Dial M for Murder,* her iconic image as the quintessential of the Hitchcock blonde would be secured with her role as Lisa in *Rear Window.* Considered the most romantic of Hitchcock's films since *Notorious,* it is also one of his funniest and most enjoyable. Hitchcock seemed convinced that the appeal of the film, the aspect that appealed most to the target audience of voyeurs, was the same thing that delighted Jimmy Stewart's character Jeffries: the pleasure of gazing upon the beauty of Hitchcock's Grace Kelly. Her iconic introduction on-screen, a close-up on her beautiful face finally coming into focus, certainly makes Hitchcock's, and by extension Jeffries's, opinion of Kelly as the ideal clear to the audience from the first frame in which she appears.

After Grace Kelly's memorable performance in *Dial M for Murder,* she was offered the coveted role of Edie in *On the Waterfront,* the plain, virginal neighborhood girl in love with Marlon Brando. The press even mentioned her being cast when the film production was announced. However, that role would eventually be recast with Eva Marie Saint when Hitchcock offered Kelly the light but glamorous role in *Rear Window.*[1] Saint would win the Oscar for her performance, but it was as Lisa that Kelly truly became a movie star, in a role created specifically for her by Hitchcock, who requested screenwriter John Michael Hayes rewrite the role of the girlfriend not only with her in mind, but as a star vehicle for her.

James Stewart, despite his less than successful experience with Hitchcock on *Rope*, was delighted to be working on *Rear Window*, considering the script and character perfectly suited to his particular image, especially in recent years as he transitioned to more complex characters. Since returning from service during World War II, Stewart had gradually begun to add darker shades to his pedestrian images, largely credited to his collaborations with Anthony Mann and getting out from under the control of studio moguls. Although still the everyman in *Rear Window*, there is a dark side hinted at (rather than overtly stated as it had been in *Rope*), regarding both his voyeuristic tendencies and fears of marriage. It is this aspect of the film that makes the casting of Kelly so brilliant; to resist marriage to Lisa makes Stewart's Jeffries almost unlikable and far less expressive than strong-willed Kelly. As Kelly experienced with Ray Milland, who was supposedly so in love with Kelly he considered leaving his wife against Kelly's wishes, Stewart immediately found himself enchanted by Kelly. Not only was she beautiful, but he found her kind, warm, and unas-

Grace Kelly emerged as a Hollywood icon with her role as Lisa in *Rear Window* (1954). *Paramount Pictures/Photofest © Paramount Pictures*

suming. Only she could create the reaction from men that her character in *Rear Window* does.

Critics, while they liked Stewart and were impressed that he conveys as much as he does from the limitations of a wheelchair, gave Kelly the most praise, delighted by the way the embodiment of the polished woman joins in the spy games, keeping her beautiful looks and temperament intact while climbing fences and sneaking into Raymond Burr's home in an attempt to win favor from her love. Hitchcock himself described it as the height of her career as an actress, stating, "Grace hadn't achieved the final—not in my book. She was just getting started. She showed potential in *Dial M for Murder* but *Rear Window* was the first picture that really brought her out. She had just begun to get somewhere when she quit."[2] As Lisa, Grace Kelly found a character that suggested the beauty was exterior to the "Girl Friday": a funny, cheeky girl willing to be on a man's arm but always one step ahead. The simple wave she gives while breaking into Burr's apartment makes Stewart smile for the same reason it makes the audience smile. We don't expect a woman of Kelly's refinement to be so daring.

While tonally different, playing more like a sophisticated romantic comedy than drama, there are similarities between *Rear Window* and *Notorious*: the pleasure Hitchcock gives to his audience by presenting a regular, approachable, but deeply flawed, character played by Jimmy Stewart, with Kelly who projected almost an ethereal quality in her films. Hitchcock understood that in order to allow audiences to share in the delight of a romance on-screen, there had to be a relatable character to represent the audience, as well as the fantasy to represent movie magic. Like *Notorious*, in which natural Bergman is consumed by her romance with Hollywood's most wanted man, Cary Grant, in *Rear Window* everyman Stewart lives out the desires of those in the audience: not only to have a relationship with Lisa, but to be aggressively pursued by the great beauty and ultimately be the chivalrous hero.

There was, however, a major difference between the two fantasies Hitchcock offered his audiences. Cary Grant's persona was years in the making, long before he appeared in a Hitchcock film, and while Hitchcock utilized this image, it was one Grant brought to his films with Hitchcock, and more importantly, one he owned away from Hitchcock and brought to every "Cary Grant movie." Kelly's persona was so closely tied to her relationship with Hitchcock; although she would use the new image in non-Hitchcock films,

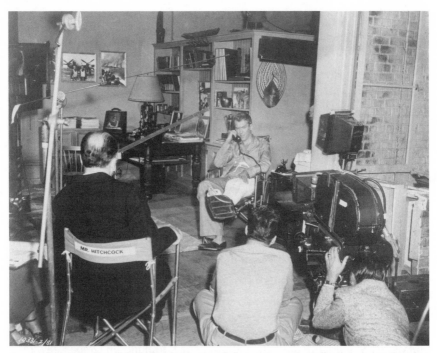

James Stewart returned to Hitchcock after *Rope* with a very different physical acting challenge, forced to act entirely from a wheelchair in *Rear Window* (1955). *Paramount Pictures/Photofest © Paramount Pictures*

the star known as Grace Kelly seemed to exist in a vacuum. Her television and early film work became disconnected from this glamorous new image as the embodiment of "grace" and sophistication in the last days of Hollywood glamour. Ironically, Kelly's last film for Hitchcock, *To Catch a Thief*, would add an independent spirit to the image of Grace Kelly—and hint at the changes coming to Hollywood.

To Catch a Thief

I'd like to point out that it's generally the woman who had the final say on which picture a couple is going to see. In fact, it's generally the woman who will decide, later on, whether it was a good or a bad picture. On condition that it's not displayed by a person of their own sex, women will not object to vulgarity on the screen. Anyway, to build up Grace Kelly, in each picture between *Dial M for Murder* and *To Catch a Thief* we made her role a more interesting one.[1]

Without her performances in the films of Hitchcock, Grace Kelly would not have been cast in films such as *High Society* (the musical version of *The Philadelphia Story*) or the royal comedy *The Swan*. But the complex, earnest performance she gave for Hitchcock suggested the depth to which the under-rated actress could go but had never had the opportunity to as an actress. Between *Rear Window* and *To Catch a Thief* she won her best actress Oscar, not for her collaborations with Hitchcock but for the George Seaton drama *A Country Girl*. But without the opportunities she had been given to grow as an actress and step forward as a leading lady, it's unlikely that the Academy would have taken notice of the range she showed in *A Country Girl*.

After her sudden rise to stardom, her reteaming with Hitchcock on the comedy *To Catch a Thief* placed her in a very different position than when Hitchcock was creating her screen persona. Grace Kelly now owned her image and used it in other films away from her Svengali. And understandably, her name meant something very different than it had in other films. She was now a box-office name, one responsible for some of the success of her films, just like Hitchcock's and Cary Grant's names. The teaming of all three makes *To Catch a Thief* perhaps the most stacked film in Hitchcock's career, and perhaps a bit too top heavy to sustain itself.

Unlike *Rear Window*, in which the image of Kelly as fantasy contrasted Stewart's average guy, there is no earthly connection for the audience to latch onto with two such idealized stars. Grant and Kelly were of equal star stature when making *To Catch a Thief*, though she was (as so often happened with female stars) given a lower credit; ironic, considering the audience's delight in watching classy Kelly dominate Cary Grant.

Despite it being a less beloved film than *Rear Window*, *To Catch a Thief* may be Kelly's best performance in her rather brief career, as she embraces

Grace Kelly's final film, *To Catch a Thief* (1955), showed the most forceful version of her graceful screen persona as the wealthy playgirl Francie. *Paramount Pictures/ Photofest © Paramount Pictures*

the vivacious forcefulness hiding underneath the character's sophisticated, ladylike reserve, almost a shameless version of Bergman's Alicia in *Notorious*. She is hiding behind sunglasses when we first see her, then photographed for an extended period from the back (as Grant was filmed in *Notorious*), and the anticipation building to her first full appearance in the film is undeniable, suggesting she is the predator. His is the focus of the thriller plotline, but she will drive the romance. And just as audiences, and Jeffries, delighted in her willingness to get her hands dirty in the spy games of *Rear Window*, the excitement Kelly has regarding catching a jewel thief like Robbie is shared by the audience. From the glee she has when informing Grant that she's "never caught a jewel thief," we know she enjoys the life she leads without guilt. As written, Grace could have been interpreted as the spoiled little rich girl; however, audiences delighted in her character largely because of their affection for Grace Kelly.

Despite appearing in a film that seems so light and fantastical, from its costuming to its setting and especially casting, and despite being idealized, Kelly and Grant could easily connect to an audience on an emotional level, even if they did not connect to them through transference. Grant noticed this quality in Kelly, seeing the calm serenity she brought to roles, and like all her costars before fell in love with Kelly, declaring her his favorite costar during an interview (and even after both had left Hollywood), stating:

> I think the most memorable and honest actress I've ever worked with was Grace Kelly. Don't misunderstand. I appreciated Ingrid Bergman, Audrey Hepburn, Deborah Kerr, Irene Dunne, Kate Hepburn, and all the women I worked with. Grace had a kind of serenity, a calmness, that I hadn't arrived at at that point in my life—and perhaps never will, for all I know. She was so relaxed in front of the camera that she made it look simple. She made acting look as easy as Frank Sinatra made singing appear. Everyone thinks they can sing after an evening at the theater listening to Frank, but to create that sense of ease takes a tremendous amount of knowledge and experience and talent. Grace was astonishing. When you played a scene with her, she really listened. She was right there with you. She was Buddha-like in her concentration. She was like Garbo in that respect.[2]

Although Grant claimed he didn't project such ease on-screen, it was the naturalism he brought to the "character" of Cary Grant that Hitchcock found so exciting and wanted to show in a new light to audiences, insisting "one doesn't direct Cary Grant, one simply puts him in front of a camera. He enables the audience to identify with the main character. He represents a man we know is not a stranger. He is like our brother."[3] It was the same quality that had first attracted Hitchcock to working with Grant in 1941 on *Suspicion*. Robbie isn't simply a character played by Grant; his character is created to suggest the menace that may be hiding behind the comic sensibilities that had always existed in Grant's 1930s and 1940s screwball comedies (often full of sexual innuendo). By this time in Grant's career, his comedies were far from edgy (*The Bachelor and the Bobby-Soxers*, *Monkey Business*, and *Mr. Blandings Builds His Dream House*), and he had made the decision to retire from acting when Hitchcock brought him back for *To Catch a Thief*.

Cary Grant returned to films after a brief retirement, to star in Hitchcock's *To Catch a Thief* (1955) opposite Grace Kelly, whom he would describe as his favorite leading lady. *Photofest*

When we are introduced to Cary Grant as Robbie, he is happily retired, downright domestic in his gardening pursuits, and possibly has become a bit boring. It isn't until he's dragged back to play the dashing role of a cat burglar to clear his name that we begin to see the dashing fantasy we know as Cary Grant from the golden age of Hollywood still resides in this older man. But like a time travel movie, Cary Grant seems somewhat out of step in this new place where he meets two women far more dominant and dynamic than Robbie knew in his heyday, or than Grant was paired with in the classic comedies that *To Catch a Thief* is reminiscent of. Grant was reentering a new version of Hollywood just as Robbie was meeting a new kind of criminal, and his ability to adapt to the fish-out-of-water scenario is both what makes Grant an enjoyable actor but also informs the audience that he will never become the everyman like Jimmy Stewart but will always be the ideal male.

The star power of both Grant and Kelly are why the underappreciated performance by Bridget Auber as Danielle is of such vital importance to the film. She was a true ingénue of the film, an actress unfamiliar to English-speaking audiences making her debut in a Hollywood film. Hitchcock simply selected her from a French film when casting the part, saying, "Bridgette Auber played that role. I had seen a Julien Duvivier picture called *Sous le Ciel de Paris* in which she played a country girl who'd come to live in the city."[4] Not only was she an acrobat (perfect for her scenes as the cat burglar), but the girlish quality she brings to the role adds a level of sympathy to a role that could seem intrusive in Grant's life. With little acting experience, it is a surprise to see Auber play the character with such tenacity, immediately differentiating herself from Kelly, despite both being vivacious female characters. Much like Hitchcock did with his other love triangles pitting two men against one another, each woman appealed to the man (and audience) they were pursuing.

Auber's spirited young woman suggests the changes that were coming about in society and arising in Hollywood as the star system officially ended. The tenacious Auber suggests certain unrest with the system of Hollywood, which mirrored the upcoming unrest among the younger generation with the status quo. The youngsters wouldn't be held back anymore, even if they had to force themselves onto the world, including in Hollywood.

The Trouble with Harry

Nothing amuses me as much as understatement.[1]

The fact that Hitchcock would follow up the romantic comedy *To Catch a Thief* with another dialogue-heavy romantic comedy is an odd choice for a director who relished the ability to show range and evolution. To differentiate the two, however, one only needs to see the tonal differences he establishes. *To Catch a Thief* was fantastical and energetic in its approach to romance, happily speaking in innuendo and using visual cues such as fireworks to show sexual tension and costuming characters in the most expensive designer clothing, as they explore the most exclusive vacation spot in the world. By comparison, the characters in *The Trouble with Harry* live small, slow, unexciting lives in a small New England town, free of tourists, and their romantic scenes feature characters speaking bluntly about their desires in drawling, disaffected voices as if nothing could possibly shake them. It also happens to feature one of the most interesting heroines in a Hitchcock film: Shirley Mac-Laine's Jennifer, the New England housewife and mother. The embodiment of Hitchcock's philosophy that "an English girl, looking like a school teacher, is apt to get into a cab with you and, to your surprise, she'll probably pull a man's pants open."[2] Jennifer is the good, composed type, but one so disaffected by life, nothing seems to be able to rattle her, even when learning her husband is dead or what needs to be done about it.

This made the initial announcement that Hitchcock wanted sultry sex kit-ten Kim Novak for the role of Jennifer a puzzling notion.[3] Novak would have certainly appealed to male audiences who found the voluptuous lavender blonde extremely appealing. And there is a certain quality to Jennifer, her down-on-her-luck lack of sentimentality, which made such a casting idea log-ical, if obvious. Yet when considering the character of Jennifer as she appears on-screen, the casting seems ridiculous and suggests the uninspired laziness of studio interference Hitchcock was known to criticize. The desperation Jennifer has to leave her husband, and her desire to be with local painter Sam Marlow, is in the film, played as all charm and light humor. But with Novak in the role, considerably more worldly and mature than MacLaine's Jennifer, one can imagine the character with a bit more seediness than girlishness, and the sweet romance would be lost. Fortunately, the aspects that would have made Novak a poor choice to play Jennifer made her the ideal casting choice for her own Hitchcock film just three years later.

For obvious reasons therefore, Jennifer, an unhappily married woman who hits her husband on the head and may have accidentally killed him, was a difficult role to cast. Hitchcock insisted that the role of Jennifer be cast with an unknown (much like *Rebecca*), as he didn't want the film sold around the promise of star power (another way to differentiate *The Trouble with Harry* from the superstar-powered *To Catch a Thief*). Countless Hollywood ingé-nues were considered, but none of them hit the right balance of sweetness, resourcefulness, and pragmatic practicality. Fortunately, the long casting pro-cess brought Shirley MacLaine to the attention of Hitchcock by chance when she stepped into the lead of the musical *The Pajama Game*, as the understudy for Carol Haney.

Producer Hal B. Wallis saw her in the production and auditioned her for the role of Jennifer, an audition that also earned her a Paramount contract she would eventually sue to have terminated, one of the landmark cases lead-ing to the eventual end of the star system. There were always questions over whether Wallis or Hitchcock took responsibility for her being cast, but Mac-Laine was an inspired choice regardless, a breath of fresh air in Hollywood for the unique ladylike style and general oddness she showed to the public. The female answer to the neurotic rebel males[4] arriving on screens, MacLaine was the type of female the public was not familiar with in the 1950s:

Succeeding the vamp of the twenties, the sweater girl of the thirties and the girl next door of the forties, a new kind of female is emerging as one of the dominant screen types of the late fifties—that of the offbeat character, for want of a better label. Shirley MacLaine is the prototype for this new Hollywood mold . . . off screen, too, she represents a noteworthy departure from the old norms of fashion plate glamour. She doesn't hide her elbows or walk with an erect carriage. She doesn't stare at you from within the dark reserve of female mystery. In contrast to the enameled gleam of the usual star, she had the prettiness of a hand-tinted teacup, with her blue eyes and coppery, ash-colored hair framing with full bangs a face as American as a sunflower.[5]

Although she had an appearance that somewhat resembled Audrey Hepburn, even physically she had a unique quality unusual in Hollywood—her compact movements (familiar of Bob Fosse dancers), mischievous grin, and unmistakable, high, nasal speaking voice. The press was especially taken with her spirited nuttiness, refusing to wear glamour girl gowns and usually seen in pants and plain, fitted dresses. She quickly became a favorite interviewee of the press, with her refreshing, un-Hollywood sensibility. For example, when asked the typical question regarding her fashion sense, she responded:

> I have no problems with Edith Head. She recognized immediately the kind of clothes that were right for me. I have no fashion sense at all. But I love to be comfortable. We both agreed that I was the casual type and should stay away from anything fussy. I never wear full skirts and frills around my neck or anything that is sophisticated. I live at the beach. At home I wear toreador pants all the time but I don't like pedal pushers. They strike my leg at an unbecoming place. I don't think being casual means you can't be chic. It is good taste and scrupulous grooming that makes a person well dressed.[6]

But more important for the role of Jennifer, though slightly green, even at that point in her life and career MacLaine had a resilient, independent nature that hid just under the giddy surface smile she projected. When asked how Hollywood tried to improve her, she responded with a passionate yet thoughtful statement that suggests a woman with considerable self-awareness and maturity far beyond her tender age of twenty:

> It wasn't that I felt I was so great, I couldn't be improved, but when they made my test I asked them to let me do it without a make-up man because I didn't

want to look like anyone else. And they bought me the way I was. So why should I change? I wouldn't go so far as to say be glad you aren't beautiful, but I am an offbeat type and I feel I might as well make the most of it. I think it is very important to be yourself and I have never been comfortable around people when I couldn't be. That is one of the things I love so much about my husband. He let me be what I am. When I was in school I had a huge crush on a boy and I was his girl until I hit a home run in a game and all he could hit was a single. Fortunately, my husband does everything better than I do and there are no problems. But if he didn't I wouldn't want to have to pretend.[7]

That maturity and self-reliance were vital not only to make the charac- ter of Jennifer both likable and comfortable to laugh with; it also made her May–December romance with John Forsythe acceptable to audiences despite their considerable age difference. When casting to such an extreme age dif- ference, the youthfulness of the man and maturity of the female is vital to avoid a sinister feeling of the romance being incestuous and the man seeming more father figure than love interest. MacLaine joined the likes of Lauren Bacall and Grace Kelly, who could easily play against men considerably their senior because of their levelheaded, practical sophistication. But while Bacall and Kelly seemed mature for their relatively young ages, MacLaine brought a youthful quality to her older costars.

John Forsythe was, like MacLaine, an inspired bit of casting for an actor who had star potential but had never risen to notable heights. In a role that traditionally would have been better suited for a younger, bohemian-type ac- tor, Forsythe's casting as the artist was an inspired choice. Lovable, paternal, with a homespun sophistication, he had an easy hand playing comedy in the plays *Mister Roberts* and *The Teahouse of the August Moon* (from which he took an eight-week leave of absence to film *The Trouble with Harry*). Accord- ing to MacLaine, it was Forsythe who took a leadership role on set, a paternal figure to the cast who had a temperament that seemed to allow nothing to bother him. It was this quality that made it especially easy for MacLaine to play the love scenes that terrified her and gave the film the light, whimsical quality they, and Hitchcock, wanted for the breezy comedy, which was not as dark as the press suggested.[8]

That was also true of the casting of beloved Edmund Gwenn, who was the first and only choice of Hitchcock's to play the amusing Captain Albert Wiles.

In her film debut, Shirley MacLaine credited John Forsythe with giving her the security to play their love scenes in *The Trouble with Harry* (1955). *Paramount Pictures/ Photofest © Paramount Pictures*

Gwenn's gentle, old man quality earned him an Oscar for playing Santa in *Miracle on 34th Street* just seven years earlier (and seven years after appearing in *Foreign Correspondent*). The biggest name in the cast, Gwenn once again plays a character very close to the lovable Cockney old man, which made him famous in the play *The Wookey*. As if playing an older, retired version of that same character, Hitchcock even dressed him in almost the exact same costume he wore in the play. A grandfatherly, lovable old captain who chatters away, winning over women old and young with his little-boy-in-man's-body sensibility, he easily delighted audiences.

It was especially good casting to hire character actress Mildred Natwick (who played Miss Ivy Gravely), who like Gwenn, was almost playing a version of her first film characters, specifically the Cockney prostitute character she played in John Ford's *The Long Voyage Home* and her landlady in *The Enchanted Cottage*. A favorite to play mature women in John Ford's films, Hitchcock took the proper qualities she was known for in those films and allowed her to finally get some laughs as a respected older woman who

Hitchcock created the role of the Captain in *The Trouble with Harry* (1955) specifically for veteran actor Edmund Gwenn. *Paramount Pictures/Photofest © Paramount Pictures*

accidentally commits murder in a film about first love for both a young and old couple.

Although the film was poorly reviewed when first released, MacLaine received positive notice, mentioning her as a classic screwball actress and even rewarding her with a Golden Globe.[9] Critic Rod Nordell wrote that MacLaine "shows a flair for comedy in an apparently guileless, straight-faced style that is thoroughly her own."[10] Another critic wrote, "MacLaine is a new refreshing personality and does herself well."[11] As the reviews suggest, part of the pleasure of seeing MacLaine in the film was the sense that audiences who saw the film would not only be seeing something different, but making a discovery of someone they would see in the future. By casting an unknown, Hitchcock also offered audiences something rarely considered—the opportunity to find a new star. While the studios have an undeniable amount of power in the creation of a star, the sudden appearance of a new star, allowing the audience to feel as if they have been part of that discovery, is a pleasure, and one those who saw *The Trouble With Harry* had the opportunity to experience when "discovering Shirley MacLaine."

20

The Man Who Knew Too Much

Despite the similarities, they're really quite different from each other. In *The Man Who Knew Too Much*, James Stewart portrayed an earnest and quiet man. Cary Grant couldn't have done it that way. If I'd used him in the picture, the character would have been altogether different.[1]

Because *The Man Who Knew Too Much* was a remake of his early British film, the casting of this American version was largely differentiated by the casting of Hollywood stars. The 1934 film "starred" theater stars Edna Hove and Leslie Banks as the ordinary parents whose child is kidnapped. However the "star" of the film was the villain Peter Lorre, who was already a star for his role in *M* and would work with Hitchcock in the 1936 film *The Secret Agent*. When Hitchcock chose to remake the film, he refocused the film's attention on the role of the ordinary parents put in the impossible position, which represents the fears of every mother and father.

Jimmy Stewart and Doris Day were two of the biggest stars of their day, and their personas included being quintessential "American" stars. Unlike the very British original *The Man Who Knew Too Much*, the Americanisms of Stewart and Day were played up to draw dramatic contrast to the British couple who kidnap their child, reserved and proper in their outer appearance. The popular French actor Daniel Gelin made his English-language debut in *The Man Who Knew Too Much*, but was only familiar to American moviegoers who saw French films in more urban and artsy theaters in the 1950s.

And the difference between American urban and rural characters is one of the major conflicts between the couple at the heart of the film. Jimmy Stewart's character is a rural, suburban, and somewhat conservative character that takes many opportunities to show his domination over his wife as the "head of the household." Stewart is like a darker version of his George Bailey from *It's a Wonderful Life*, who finally takes trips to faraway places. Turning our expectations that Stewart and Day would be the ideal American couple, the first time we see them, they are bickering.[2] One of the ongoing tensions in their marriage is that Stewart's Benjamin McKenna takes many an opportunity to reinforce, publicly, that Doris Day's Jo is not actress/singer Josephine Conway but his wife, as the lesser part of Dr. and Mrs. McKenna.

Despite the frequent reading of Doris Day's Jo as an image of Hitchcock's cinema of "dominating women" (partially based on readings of feminist film

Doris Day was nervous throughout filming *The Man Who Knew Too Much* (1956) because of Hitchcock's lack of communication. *Paramount Pictures/Photofest © Paramount Pictures*

theorist Molly Haskell's reading of the film in the book *From Reverence to Rape*), she is a far more complicated female character in a Hitchcock film. And similarly, *The Man Who Knew Too Much* shows the traditional domestic man in a bad light, threatened by a wife's demand for equality and attempting to forcibly keep her in a secondary position. As played by Doris Day, Jo is one of the few female characters in a Hitchcock film who shows a liberal, feminist approach to a character, partially because of the image of Day as an independent woman.

Day holds a special place in the feminist movement, representing women just ahead of the social concern. In *The Man Who Knew Too Much*, her frustration connects with an inability to accept that being tied down to home, rather than pursuing her own career as a actress, has led her to an unhappy home life, itself affecting her home life and child. Her panic that was usually played as hysterically comic in *My Dream Is Yours*, *Pillow Talk*, and *That Touch of Mink* takes on a very different focus. With *The Man Who Knew Too Much*, however, that hyper focus showed a darker side of women's frustrations in the 1950s.[3]

Day was considered the most popular female star of her time, whose persona was far more complicated than history has made it appear. Like Stewart, Day had an "everywoman" quality and was easy for audiences to identify and sympathize with. Today she is considered too good or optimistic for the times; her films, including the romantic comedies such as *That Touch of Mink* and *Calamity Jane*, showed her as a brassy, confident, and independent woman—who plays second banana to no man. In the press she was outgoing, composed, and opinionated, qualities that could have hurt her appeal during the baby boom but made her stand out even more as new girls became transformed by the rigid control of the studio system that wanted cookie-cutter actresses who could be the next "someone." Day was far from that, and even Hitchcock didn't have interest in transforming her unique star qualities, even if she didn't closely resemble any of his other "blondes," only showing a more serious part of her personality, a more dramatic one, which would also resonate with the baby-boomer culture of many a young woman who found independence during the war effort only to give it up to have a "proper" family life.

Hitchcock's work with male and female stars was always perceived differently. Day was the highest-profile leading lady Hitchcock had ever worked with, and yet she is rarely cited as one of Hitchcock's women because her part in *The Man Who Knew Too Much* is closer to the "hero," usually designated as the male's role in a Hitchcock film. The Hitchcock leading lady was so often first shown in a certain, new (often glamorous) light, their introduction to audiences became closely tied to Hitchcock, even those who brought a very specific quality to their characters. Day's image was already set in stone, and with *The Man Who Knew Too Much*, Hitchcock simply placed Day in an un-comfortable, new setting and let the audience watch her react as Day might. But there was never an attempt to disguise her as anyone but Doris Day, just as there was never an attempt to disguise Jimmy Stewart as himself; the famil-iarity and identification audiences have with these actors are what creates our empathy and immediate sympathy for them and their situations, as well as the sense of disturbance that runs throughout the film, seeing two such exteriorly perfect individuals constantly bicker in a troubled marriage.

Hitchcock brought out the dark side of postwar domesticity by casting everyman James Stewart in films such as *The Man Who Knew Too Much* (1956), *Rear Window*, and *Vertigo*. *Paramount Pictures/Photofest © Paramount Pictures*

Part of what appealed to Hitchcock about casting Day was her anxiety and how tightly wound she was, despite her attempts to hide this part of her personality behind comedy.[4] Day was extremely nervous about making the film due to fear of air travel and dislike of the political-social atmosphere of Marrakech (where they filmed) and found Hitchcock's lack of communication challenging. Day and Stewart had to work out their scenes and performance by themselves and rehearsed without the input from Hitchcock, and Day feared Hitchcock did not like her interpretation because he did not indicate verbally his thoughts on her performance. Hitchcock claimed he didn't want to interrupt her.[5] Hitchcock had little patience for insecure actors, perhaps the reason he so often referred to actors as children. Actors, like anyone working on his film, were expected to give a good performance (as they were hired to do), and if they were failing to do this, he would have told them and made corrections. Doris Day was one actress who did not take notice of this tendency, and throughout the making of *The Man That Knew Too Much*, she was convinced that she was selected only because she could sing and that if she could have been cast, Hitchcock would have preferred Grace Kelly in the role of Stewart's wife.[6]

Ironically, all of Hitchcock's "wrong man films" reflect the iconic image of their leading man. And everyman hero Stewart is perfectly suited to play the role of a homespun Midwestern doctor and family man. While Stewart is so often mentioned as representing warmth, the postwar persona of Stewart was far darker and edgier than contemporary audiences remember. It was that precise quality Hitchcock so wanted to capture in his collaborations with Stewart. Although Stewart resisted this attempt in *Rope*, a role audiences would not accept him in either, Hitchcock's last three roles with Stewart gradually bring forward the dark side of his characters (his voyeurism in *Rear Window*), and the mistreatment, jealousy, and domination of Day in *The Man Who Knew Too Much* is disturbing to see; such as when he forces her to take sedative pills and refuses to share the misguided investigation he is performing, almost always going in the wrong direction when on his own. Day's insistence that she be involved (proved right by all her previous instincts and her claims that she has the right to read the note because "she is his wife") shows signs of the dark side of relationships and domestic life, which Stewart would represent in his final collaboration with Hitchcock, *Vertigo*.

The Wrong Man

Although both James Stewart and Henry Fonda represented the everyman in Hollywood, their images were far from interchangeable. Stewart's everyman qualities were always rooted with the reminder of being "the Hollywood version" of the everyman. By the time Fonda made *The Wrong Man*, he had taken a more realistic persona of that representation. And likewise, while Stewart played his wrong man character in *The Man Who Knew Too Much* with real emotion, audiences always have the protection that this is only a movie. Fonda's terror not only seems more realistic, but also less assured of a Hollywood outcome.

The Wrong Man is Hitchcock's most naturalistic movie ever made in Hollywood and suggests influences of Italian neorealism and gritty "kitchen sink" realism he previously considered less than cinematic. Hitchcock wanted the film to feel less like a cinematic escape and more an exposé on possible "problems of the American justice system," one anyone could and should connect to on a visceral level. Hitchcock chose to return to filming in black-and-white photography (after the Technicolor extravaganzas of *Rear Window* and *To Catch a Thief*), forwent his cinematic cameo to provide an introduction, and took a far more lax approach to directing, allowing the actors more freedom to move on camera than he ever was willing to in the past.

However, whenever you cast a star, even one as good and natural as Henry Fonda, there is a general break in the attempt for realism Hitchcock so wanted. It is perhaps the film that benefits least from the inclusion of a star, especially considering the subject being a case of mistaken identity. Because of the attempt made, by both Hitchcock's film and the other actors, it is almost ridiculous that Fonda could enter a bank and appear both menacing and also be mistaken for the individual we will eventually learn is the wrong man. For a period during the film, the general recognition characters have to Henry Fonda makes sense and is almost humorous: Who wouldn't know the face of Henry Fonda? But when Hitchcock shows the face of the man who turns out to be the robber, the mistakes made call the entire film into question. Fonda looked very little like Richard Robber, and because of our own recollection of Fonda's face, the bizarre confusion caused by so many characters seems ridiculous—especially characters we believe have no personal menace. There is no doubt that Hitchcock made a mistake showing the face of the robber, but to have cast a star like Fonda may have been the fatal error in Hitchcock's attempt for realism.

But the benefit of casting an actor like Fonda is in the performance he gives, one of the most emotionally rich from any Hitchcock film. When playing characters seeking justice and righteousness in the system, Fonda excelled beyond all his peers. When we see him humiliated by the system, watching him be processed in jail and prison and withstanding the trail, the audience's sympathy, and outcry for the humiliation, is remarkable. When one year later he would play the justice-seeking juror in *12 Angry Men*, his outrage and empathy reminded audiences of the experience "he" had in *The Wrong Man*. In a way, his role in *The Wrong Man* expands and enriches his role in *12 Angry Men*, securing his image as the ultimate hero of the people to the point that just one year later he would have been too big a star to play the role in *The Wrong Man*. For a director who insisted movement was what made a film dramatic, he depended a great deal on the power of Henry Fonda's eyes to convey the emotional impact the events in the film were having on him, as Philip Scheuer wrote in the review: "Henry Fonda portrays Manny. He does no acting as such, going to his lighting death, white-faced but outwardly stoical. The agony is all in his expression, voice, and hearing."[1]

The other great benefit of the casting of star Fonda was the chemistry Hitchcock was able to capture between Vera Miles and Fonda as husband and wife. In just a few brief scenes together, Miles and Fonda evoke a loving married couple and close family, so much so that the decisive cruelty of the

Hitchcock's two everyman stars, Henry Fonda and James Stewart, on the set of *The Wrong Man* (1956). *Warner Bros/Photofest © Warner Bros*

officers arresting Fonda is their refusal to simply let him inform his wife of his whereabouts. And Miles's breakdown, tortured that she suddenly doubts her husband, is the great tragedy of the film's ending. Like Fonda, the stillness of her performance is what makes the film so emotional for viewers that it is a difficult film to watch, the *New York Post* calling her "a fragile dynamo" for the power of such a strong, yet vulnerable performance.[2] Bosley Crowther was especially moved by her performance, writing that she "conveys a poignantly pitiful sense of fear of the appalling situation into which they have been cast."[3]

Miles was notoriously discovered as the actress to "replace" Grace Kelly; therefore it is ironic that the first film Hitchcock would cast her in would be so unglamorous a role. While Kelly represented the embodiment of grace and elegance, the naturally beautiful Miles had a wholesome plainness to her appearance in *The Wrong Man*. Hitchcock, often acting more like a manager than director/producer, insisted on her dressing well and wearing makeup in public, often made up to look like Grace Kelly in photographs. And like Teresa Wright, Miles had a clause in her contracts (because of the insistence of Hitchcock of how he wanted her seen by the public) to appear in no "cheesecake images" and to "only be photographed in black, white or grey," "leg art is verboten," and "her curves must be buried in drapery."[4] These restrictions led to a legal battle between producers of the Bob Hope comedy *Beau James*, who argued in court that "Hitchcock's restriction against photographing Miss Miles in any revealing poses, or in anything except white, black or grey dresses, imperils the promotional campaign."[5] Dressed in plain dresses, plain shoes, and very little makeup (almost no color on her lips, similar to the makeup Kelly wears at the end of *Dial M for Murder*), she is far from the glamorous fantasy Kelly represented. On the subject of being cast to be "the next Grace Kelly," Miles stated:

It is true, I suppose, that Hitchcock had a bit of Pygmalion complex. He wanted to make me into a superstar, but I just wasn't interested. It was soon after he'd lost Grace Kelly to Prince Rainer, who met her when she was working on *To Catch a Thief*. Hitchcock found he'd priced her out of the market—or at least his market—when she married Rainer and became the Queen of the May. So when we first met in New York for *The Wrong Man*, he may have wanted to create another Grace Kelly out of me. He assigned me the job of entering society on the jet-set level. I have nothing against society, but it just wasn't me.

I was a working mother, busy raising my children, and my private life has never been discussable.[6]

Named the "polished blonde" by Atra Baer,[7] Miles was (or would) resist such direct comparisons to Kelly,[8] despite Hitchcock's noticeable involvement in shaping not only her career but image: "I feel the same way directing Vera that I did with Grace. She has a style, an intelligence and a quality of understatement."[9] Hedda Hoper noted that behind the glamour of her photographs and stylish clothing was a "star with both feet on the ground"[10] with a family (two children and recent marriage to second husband Gordon Scott) and a focus on her career and building up the craft of acting. After having been dropped by two studios that had no idea how to use the unusual but talented actress, Miles had transitioned to television work (including *Alfred Hitchcock Presents*). Miles's television work included so many roles as psychos that an article appeared stating, "Vera Miles Won Fame Playing Psychotic Gals."[11] When signed by Hitchcock to a five-year, three-picture-a-year contract, she was also signed to a three-year, one-picture-a-year contract to John Ford.[12] But the appeal, according to Miles, of such contracts was the freedom her contracts afforded, compared to the stricter studio contracts she had dealt with years earlier.[13] It offered her the opportunity to work with two of the great directors of the time, both of whom saw in Miles something studio heads hadn't had the vision to take note of. By 1956, with two contracts in hand, Vera Miles was "the hottest player on the Paramount lot these days with producers bidding for her the way they're fighting for Tony Perkins."[14]

Miles, gracious, unassuming, but hardly one to be manipulated according to all who worked and interviewed her, all of whom note in their interviews how articulate a woman she was, never discussed in detail what made her a star, insisting she was just a Midwesterner who rid herself of a regional accent (much like Grace Kelly, although taking less of an upper-class Eastern affectation).[15] She also claimed she never understood what it was about her that Hitchcock noticed, insisting he never told her such a thing: "He never complimented me, or even told me why he signed me," though Hitchcock told the press that his admiration for her was due to her being "an attractive, intelligent, and sexy woman. That about rolls it up."[16] Despite difficulties, it

Vera Miles was promoted as Hitchcock's next Grace Kelly, despite casting her in the very unglamorous role of Fonda's wife in *The Wrong Man* (1956). *Warner Bros/ Photofest © Warner Bros*

was ironically Miles who stepped forward to dispel claims made in Donald Spoto's biography of Hitchcock, *The Dark Side of Genius*, insisting:

> What he, Spoto, said about the making of *The Wrong Man* and *Psycho* is all wrong. It's the kind of book in which the author waits until a famous man dies and then hits him with what can only be guesses. . . . Anyone who knows me knows I would never put up with that sort of thing. There was always a great deal of respect between Hitchcock and me. Spoto says he [Hitchcock] rehearsed me for nine hours a day on *The Wrong Man* which is nonsense. He expected people to be good, and never rehearsed them at all. When you signed a contract with Hitchcock, it stipulated the number of hours a day you would work. And as for playing casting couch to get the role, I'd have told him to go to hell. Neither of us had time for that kind of thing.[17]

22

Vertigo

Vertigo was a project largely based around Hitchcock's desire to cast Vera Miles in the role of his everyman's ideal. Like a contemporary take on the Frankenstein story, Hitchcock would use his creature to seduce and ultimately destroy Hollywood's everyman, Jimmy Stewart. Casting Vera Miles was always his intention, from the point that he first began considering the film's production, even running screen tests of her dressed as the character(s) of Judy and Madeleine. But Miles became pregnant and was unable to do the film, a fact which seemed to derail their relationship during Miles's five-year contract.

However, Miles thought there was a more complex reason for why her career with Hitchcock didn't move forward as had been anticipated. She said during an interview that "over the span of years, he's had one type of woman in his films, Ingrid Bergman, Grace Kelly and so on. Before that, it was Madeleine Carroll. I'm not their type and never have been. I tried to please him, but I couldn't. They are all sexy women, but mine is an entirely different approach."[1] Miles's thoughts on both her image and what Hitchcock would need for the roles were entirely accurate. For while she may have personally fit the role of socialite "Madeleine," that is purely a role played by lower-class Judy, a woman willing to change her entire identity to please men, and for money. The character of Judy required an almost "trashy" quality to the character, and for that character to play Madeleine as a performance. Miles

Vera Miles made costume tests for *Vertigo* (1958) before leaving the project after becoming pregnant and was ultimately replaced by Kim Novak (who wore many of the same costumes). *Paramount Pictures/Photofest © Paramount Pictures*

was anything but sexy or trashy and, despite being an exceptional actress, always provoked a wholesome, honest quality, far from what was needed for *Vertigo*.

Just as the story of *Vertigo* dictates of Scotty, if Hitchcock couldn't have the beautiful blonde, he would create his own, which made the casting of Kim Novak a bit of meta-brilliance. Referred to as "the Lavender Blonde" (for the unnatural-looking dyed blonde hair she had) and "Miss Deepfreeze," as much a comment of her tendency to look somewhat cool as it was to her history as an appliance model, she was the definition of the "detached blonde" that has become synonymous with Hitchcock. Unlike Kelly, who had warmth and sex appeal, and Miles, who was natural and wholesome, Novak was closer to the dangerous woman played by Marlene Dietrich in *Stage Fright* or icy Madeleine Carroll, precisely the quality Hitchcock needed from an actress in *Vertigo*. As *Time Magazine* wrote in their profile of Novak titled "A Star Is Made," "Kim Novak herself was virtually invented, the first top-flight star ever made strictly to order for delivery when needed."[2]

Novak had catlike eyes and often wore clothing that showed her bare shoulders, suggesting she was nude in fan magazines. Even with her hair pinned up and dressed up, she always seemed somewhat uneasy with projecting elegance or class, unlike Grace Kelly who seemed born to make anything look expensive. In 1955 Novak appeared in a provocative photo for *Look Magazine* with the headline "How Much Do You Know About Women," posed to look close to naked.[3] Novak was treated especially cruelly by journalists who seemed to delight in discussing her lack of intelligence and "minor acting abilities," comments that would never have been made about actresses such as Doris Day, Grace Kelly, or Vera Miles. Yet Novak was treated like a foolish pet, writers embracing claims that producer/manager Harry Cohn had "invented her."

Harry Cohn seemed to control every step of Novak's career and life (including who she would date). Novak recalled their relationship, one she described (as Tippi Hedren would recall years later) as emotionally abusive: "I was treated as if I were nothing more than a blonde fluff, a figment of Harry Cohn's imagination—a fabrication built out of press releases and lies. I don't think I'd have lasted a day if I hadn't had outlets for my feelings—poetry and painting. At the studio, the person wasn't cared about. Feelings? What were they? If they couldn't be packaged and sold, who cared? I did!"[4]

Novak had to petition for the role in *Vertigo*, despite being one of the biggest box-office draws of the time. Reading the script, Novak closely identified with the split world of the two women: Judy, the real woman, and Madeleine, the idealized woman she played: "It was everything I felt when I came to Hollywood as a young girl. The studio was trying to make me something I was not, all the time. It was me saying, 'Please see who I am. Fall in love with me, not fantasy.'"[5] But it was the negotiations between Alfred Hitchcock and Harry Cohn (and approval needed from Jimmy Stewart) that would finally secure her fate in the role.[6]

But winning over the role did not mean allowing Novak to interpret the role as she saw it. Hitchcock took even more interest in controlling and crafting the performance. He insisted on approving every piece of clothing (many matching those from the screen test performed by Vera Miles) and refused to accept Novak's input. Novak hated black shoes, finding they were unbecoming on her, but Hitchcock (after listening to her) told her to simply use that discomfort for the role as Madeleine.

> Miss Novak arrived on the set with all sorts of preconceived notions that I couldn't possibly go along with. You know, I don't like to argue with a performer on the set; there's no reason to bring the electricians in on our troubles. I went to Kim Novak's dressing room and told her about the dresses and hairdos that I had been planning for several months. I also explained that the story was of less importance to me than the overall visual impact on the screen, once the picture is completed.[7]

It was all part of Hitchcock's latest opinion that actors should be "treated like children," most of them spoiled rotten.[8] Hitchcock took great pride in the "performance" he found in Novak, stating, "I showed her that what she thought about acting and her own methods were so much rubbish that had to be cleared away. She didn't know what was good for her. Once she had lost her aggressions and misapprehensions I was able to control her characterization. I call it psychology. It's a new word for Svengali."[9] Truffaut felt that was the key to the character (and ultimately film):

> *Vertigo* was undoubtedly a film in which the leading lady was cast as a substitute for the one Hitchcock had in mind initially. The actress we see on the screen is a substitute, and the change enhances the appeal of the movie, since

this substitution is the main theme of the picture. A man who is still in love with a woman he believes to be dead attempts to re-create the image of the dead woman when he meets up with a girl who is her look-alike. . . . I realized that *Vertigo* was even more intriguing in light of the fact that the director had compelled a substitute to imitate the actress he had initially chosen for the role.[10]

It's of little surprise that Hitchcock's unnatural control of his "female" leads was becoming unsettling to some, especially when he made comments suggesting such dominant control and seemingly disparaging of their talents when, even if he took a similarly active role in controlling his male actor, he rarely spoke of it with the press. But Hitchcock was right that Novak's performance is exceptional, and despite lukewarm reviews for the film overall, praise was heaped on Novak. Marjory Adams praised her work, writing, "Probably the most extraordinary part of the situation is that she gives her

Kim Novak's performance in *Vertigo* (1958) was extremely autobiographical for an actress whose public image was supposedly created by Harry Cohn. *Paramount Pictures/Photofest © Paramount Pictures*

best performance to date, without losing any of that sex appeal which has put her into the Marilyn Monroe class with Male America."[11] Other reviewers thought she stole the show, outacting "dependable" Stewart, although Bosley Crowther wrote that he "manages to act awfully tense in a casual way, and Miss Novak is really quite amazing."[12]

Even Truffaut, in discussion with Hitchcock, pointed to the fact that "very few American actresses are quite as carnal on the screen. When you see Judy walking on the street, the tawny hair and make-up convey an animal-like sensuality. That quality is accentuated, I suppose, by the fact that she wears no brassiere [a fact regarding which Hitchcock made the disparaging comment that 'as a matter of fact, she's particularly proud of that']."[13] As with nearly every film that was a disappointment, the blame was given to his stars (Stewart and Novak were both disparaged for their performances in *Vertigo*). While promoting the film, Hitchcock joked that "I was more intolerant in the days when I said actors were cattle and the director was the herder. Today I prefer to say actors are children and the wise director treats them that way."[14]

Stewart was a surprise, especially considering he was not only the biggest name in the film but had reached the point that, like Cary Grant, he had approval on both his costars and script. Although Stewart insisted that he asked to appear in the film, he asked for revisions to the script before he would sign on.[15] It was because of this clause in fact that Barbara Bel Geddes appeared as Midge, a role created because of problems Stewart felt existed in the script with his character of Scotty.[16] Barbara Bel Geddes is good but at times her character seems unimportant, the last-minute addition it is. But like Novak, she found Hitchcock to have an especially heavy hand with her performance, instructing every turn of the head. *Vertigo*'s notoriety and respect came about after his death when the seedy details of his life were becoming better known—particularly the obsessions and often cruel treatment he gave to women. The gaps were filled in by the story of Hitchcock.

Novak, although she needed to be approved by Stewart, found Stewart to be extremely easy to play off of and, like Doris Day, found he put her at ease on set, stating, "I still felt intimidated by nearly everything in those days, especially the big stars alongside me. But Jimmy made me feel like I belonged. He had a wonderful way of making you feel that he'd never met anybody like you before. In the weeks ahead, he looked after me. He was like the boy next door, my father, and the brother I wished I had had."[17] It was that sweetness

Novak believed made Stewart a strong leading man, stating, "He [Stewart] was sexy, a term overused then as now; but I tell you that he was the sexiest man who played opposite me in thirty years. And if you ask me why, I'll tell you it was the boyish charm, that enchanting innocence."[18] Stewart gave praise to Novak, but made a point to give credit primarily to Hitchcock, stating during interviews:

> He did a great job with Kim Novak, who was extremely self-conscious when the picture started. He gave her confidence and I think for the first time in her life she was put at her ease. Then he is able to explain to her what he wanted her to do. She has never been so good. I honestly don't think she had much of the right kind of direction prior to this picture.[19]

Hitchcock came to the opinion that Stewart was, despite being a good actor, limited by the persona that had made him so likable in *Rear Window* and *The Man Who Knew Too Much*, the dimensional but decent Hollywood everyman. Push that image too far in a different direction, and audiences would pull away. Although Stewart wanted to star in his next feature, *North by Northwest*, which like *Rear Window* would have been a lighter film of his collaborations with Hitchcock, Hitchcock refused the request, having created the role specifically for Cary Grant, a man very different from Stewart. Although both Hitchcock and Stewart were gradually expanding the image of Stewart from saintly Boy Scout to a more nuanced, darker character, he was a hero in *Rear Window* and *The Man Who Knew Too Much*. When cast as the villain, as in *Rope*, audiences rejected the thought and refused to give in to the suggestion. In *Vertigo*, although a nuanced performance of a normal man who becomes obsessed, he is not the protagonist or even an antihero, but becomes the antagonist.

23

North by Northwest

Cary Grant is never used by Hitchcock in quite this way: he may lie to and manipulate women [*Suspicion*], but he doesn't try directly to dominate them. When he is given something like the Stewart dominating image, Hitchcock plays the effect for comedy, as in the celebrated invert shot near the beginning of *Notorious* where he is seen from Ingrid Bergman's point of view as she lies in bed. As Andrew Britton has suggested in his marvelous monograph on Grant, the image typically carries connotations of gender-role ambiguity so that he becomes, among other things, the perfect medium for Hawks's play on sexual role reversal. The Hitchcock films with Grant move toward equalized male/female relations. Stewart, on the other hand, embodies for Hitchcock the desperate and hopeless drive to dominate—to assert an ideologically constructed "masculinity" that always sits uneasily on the Stewart persona and, in *Vertigo,* provokes the film's catastrophe. *Rear Window*, of course, is built entirely on Stewart's physical inability to assume the position of domination, and his desperate drive to compensate for this via the potency of the look.[1]

Truffaut noted that "it might seem as if Cary Grant and James Stewart were interchangeable in your work, but you actually use each one in a different way. With Cary Grant the picture is more humorous, and with James Stewart the emphasis is on emotion."[2] Grant was an asset because of the carefree humor he brought to films, and Hitchcock had already learned that miscasting (*Suspicion* and *Rope*) could have errors that would be impossible to repair.

Part of the plot and humor of *North by Northwest* comes from seeing Cary Grant, master at adapting to situations with ease, attempting to make sense of the situation he finds himself in throughout this wrong man story. The polar opposite of Henry Fonda in *The Wrong Man*, the audience is never especially worried that he won't survive or come out on top over these situations, so Hitchcock and his writer were able to make them outlandish and humorous. The character Grant plays came out of a conversation regarding the film Hitchcock had with Grant, who remembered that "Hitch and I sat down one day and worked out a certain character which became the basis of all the comedies I played in after that. In the films I made with Hitchcock, the humor relieved the suspense. People laugh in the theater because what's on the screen is not happening to them. I played my role as though it wasn't happening to me. And I think that's how I got the audience on my side."[3]

Despite all his appearances in films, several considered classics, there may be no film that is more synonymous with Cary Grant than *North by Northwest*. The quintessential thriller comedy is, like *Suspicion*, dependent on the audience being familiar with the actor's persona. The comedy of many scenes is far more referential than actual punch lines. As one critic, Richard Griffith of the *Los Angeles Times*, wrote, "Cary Grant, a veteran member of the Hitchcock acting varsity, was never more at home than in this role. He handles the grimaces; the surprised look, the quick smile and all the derring-do with professional aplomb and grace."[4]

But with the familiarity of Grant and general lack of suspense regarding his character, only the curiosity of how the clever character will avoid disaster remained. The thrills involving characters were primarily dependent on the casting of the villains and leading lady, one who would be unexpected and with an air of mystery.

Rather than cast an actress with an established glamorous image or undetermined persona, Hitchcock further reinforced Grant's persona as part of the character by casting against type with an actress known for her homely, virginal characters, selecting Grace Kelly's replacement for *On the Waterfront*, Eva Marie Saint. The beautiful doe-eyed blonde had played many characters of harsh circumstances victimized by realities, most notably in Kazan's *On the Waterfront* and the family drama *A Hatful of Rain*, as the wife of a drug addict in love with her brother-in-law. But Eve Kendall is about as far from those characters as any she had played before. Glamorous, mysterious, heroic, and

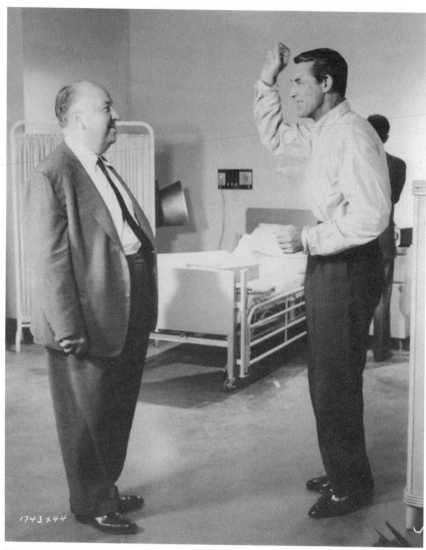

Hitchcock cast Cary Grant in *North by Northwest* (1959) specifically with the intention of the star playing a version of himself. *Metro-Goldwyn-Mayer/Photofest © Metro-Goldwyn-Mayer*

self-reliant, she is one of Hitchcock's most active female characters, who, like Grace Kelly in *To Catch a Thief*, played a far greater role in moving the story and characters than the more passive character played by Grant.

Grant and Saint essentially switch gender roles from Grant's earlier Hitchcock feature, *Notorious*, which makes the initial reports of casting the role of Eve Kendall such a remarkable subject. For a time there were rumors that the role of Eve Kendall was intended for Grace Kelly, which would have furthered her evolution from passive female to active. In the press, the name of Elizabeth Taylor was frequently batted about, a younger and more sexual actress than Kelly or Saint.[5] Cary Grant, who like Jimmy Stewart had authority over both script and casting approval, suggested Hitchcock cast the actress he was obsessed with (and with whom he had a brief affair), Sophia Loren. This aspect of Grant, both on-screen and in his real life, shows the dramatic difference between Hitchcock's two leading men, Stewart and Grant. Stewart's affection for costars was always described as friendly and almost brotherly, never in terms of sexual obsession or even affairs, which made his obsession in *Vertigo* seem especially uncharacteristic. But audiences had come to expect and delight in seeing Cary Grant as a carefree playboy whose affairs and multiple marriages did nothing to hurt his public image. Even his obsessions were accepted as romantic pursuits of lucky women, rather than the inappropriate sexual harassment they would be seen as today (and later would be spoken of in regard to Hitchcock's obsessions).

Despite Grant's insistence, Loren was not selected, and instead Hitchcock selected Saint, hoping, as he had delighted in doing with Kelly and Miles, to find an actress whose sophistication and elegance had gone untapped and he could uncover for the audience. He selected Saint, cut her hair, and selected clothing from the mannequins of Bergdorf Goodman (for her public appearances and the film), all to give her an exotic, glamorous appearance of "kept woman" (the character Eva plays) but also a woman who is "smart, simple, subtle, and quiet" (Eve's own personality as the spy). Although Saint insisted that Hitchcock worked with her extensively, including insisting she lower her voice and giving similar technical directions, Eva Marie Saint gives one of her best performances.

Like Kim Novak, playing two characters, the woman she is and woman her character is playing, Eve Kendall plays a multitude of roles, all making perfect sense and never giving away or winking at the camera. Seducing Grant on the train, she possesses Grant, convincing everyone that she is in love, but hinting that there is far more to the character than is suggested. When it is finally revealed that she is associated with the villains, the audience accepts her sudden shift as logical, but never completely turns against her, always anticipating either a reversal of character or additional information.

Saint was praised by critics, who delighted in the multiple layers she plays as Eve Kendall. Cyrus Durgin took note of the remarkable range she showed in the role, writing, "Eva Marie is bewitching in hairdo and makeup and manner as a girl well-mannered Eve. Those plain roles and plain facades are forgotten in this luxuriant blooming of active femininity";[6] and A. H. Weiler wrote, "In casting Eva Marie Saint as [Cary Grant's] romantic vis-a-vis, Mr. Hitchcock has plumbed some talents not shown by the actress heretofore. Although she is seemingly a hard, designing type, she also emerges both the sweet heroine and a glamorous charmer."[7] Even Hitchcock, happy with the unexpected and layered performance she had given, praised her, though as usual based largely on image rather than character, telling her, "I don't want you to do a sink-to-sink movie again, ever. You've done these black-and-white movies like *On the Waterfront*. It's drab in that tenement house. Women go to the movies, and they've just left the sink at home. They don't want to see you at the sink."[8]

Saint did not take this advice, insisting as Vera Miles had that part of the profession of acting included taking on a range of characters and types of roles. She did, however, enjoy working with her costars, James Mason and Grant, whose image was more than secured by audience expectation, and delighted in the lightness of the film, suggesting that "you don't have to cry in a movie to have a good time. Just kick up your heels and have fun."[9] It was good advice but showed the difference between carefree Grant and the more serious Mason, differences magnified in the film.

Mason had to, like *Notorious*'s Claude Raines, have an attractiveness that was considerably different from Grant. As written by Ernest Lehman, the character of Vandamm had to walk with distinction of "about forty, professional in manner but definitely sexually attractive [to women] and only slightly sinister,"[10] not to mention a wit that more than matched Cary Grant's sense of humor. What Mason provided, significantly different from Grant, was the element of surprising the audience, used to seeing him as "losers" (such as his role in *A Star Is Born*) and having just recently seen him in *Larger than Life*. While as confident as he would be in *North by Northwest*,

One of the most important aspects of casting *North by Northwest* (1959) was casting an actor (James Mason) who was attractive and charismatic enough to rival Cary Grant for Eva Marie Saint's affection. *Metro-Goldwyn-Mayer/Photofest © Metro-Goldwyn-Mayer*

this confidence manifests in an out-of-control rage brought on by illness. The difference between Mason in the two films is similar to the range Ray Milland showed in his signature role in *The Lost Weekend* and as the cool, skillful villain in *Dial M for Murder*. No wonder no such otherwise ordinary-looking men could convincingly be with such desirable women as Grace Kelly and Eva Marie Saint.

One of the elements frequently overlooked is the need for, even if only briefly, James Mason's villain must plausibly have the affections of Eva Marie Saint. Hitchcock insisted Mason play the role as "smooth and distinguished" but still threatening.[11] Just as Claude Raines had to have enough chemistry with Ingrid Bergman for the audience to believe they would marry without raising eyebrows, Mason and Saint had to appear to have a similar relationship, as to not hint at the truth of Saint's real mission, giving away the truth to the audience too soon. And for part of the film, before we know the truth about Saint, we have to believe that she would be torn between these two men—which James Mason, despite all his villainy, did with ease.

Saint's Eve Kendall is very similar to Bergman's Alicia, daring the audience to see the virginal angel in a different light. And yet, Grant is a combination of *Suspicion*'s carefree Johnnie (at the beginning) and responsible, complex man (at the end). From selfish to selfless is his journey. And it was a journey Grant had gone on many times in film in both comedies (*Philadelphia Story*) and dramas (*Penny Serenade, None But the Lonely-hearted*).

24

Psycho

You will have to see the picture to understand what I mean when I say
Perkins gives a remarkable performance. However, it won't exactly further
his career. Does Hitchcock still hate actors?[1]

If *Psycho* was, as Truffaut claimed, the last masterpiece of Hitchcock, it gave
Hitchcock the opportunity to test his theories of casting stars in a multitude
of ways. The film would also be one of the defining moments in the end of the
studio system. According to Leo Braudy, "Hitchcock achieved his ultimate
goal of making the irresponsible audience, already conditioned by Hollywood
(including some of Hitchcock's own films) to expect certain things of their
stars so Hitchcock could gleefully defeat our expectations."[2]

After having to deal with the prohibitive price tags of his stars of both
Vertigo and *North by Northwest* (Cary Grant's salary alone was considered
excessive), Hitchcock was eager to work with actors who would demand far
less and approach the opportunity to work on a Hitchcock film as proper
compensation. It was an opinion one of *Psycho*'s stars, Vera Miles, voiced
when discussing her career (and one reminiscent of Teresa Wright): "What I
can't understand is an actor asking a million dollars per picture. It's snobbery
in a way. But our industry made it that way, or let's say the agents have done
it, and the industry has let them get away with it."[3]

Ironically, in only her second film for Hitchcock, this would be Vera
Miles's last performance, as Lila, the older sister of Janet Leigh. Once high on

147

the actress as the next Grace Kelly, Hitchcock's delight had become boredom with the actress after she was unable to take on the role of Judy/Madeleine in *Vertigo*, pregnant with her first son of her second husband. Hitchcock's sudden coldness toward Miles he explained being due to her having to leave the project he was inspired to do because of her, telling Truffaut, "She became pregnant just before the part that was going to turn her into a star. After that I lost interest; I couldn't get the rhythm going with her again."[4] And as if to further show his disinterest in Miles, Lila was not only a secondary character in *Psycho*, but positioned as a rather frumpy and uninteresting character. Miles is good in the film but given a dull character to play, which makes the character more frustrating to watch than anything else.

Donald Spoto recalled that even Miles's clothes, once stylish and beautifully selected to please Hitchcock, were far less flattering and she was given an unbecoming wig. The wig, however, was due to a role she had played in the gritty war drama *5 Branded Women*, edgier than any film Hitchcock (or John Ford) would have permitted if she were under exclusive contract. As a Yugoslavian woman forced into a sexual relationship with a Nazi, she gives one of her best performances. And like Bergman, who had essentially left Hitchcock a decade earlier for the experimental European films, Miles wanted to stretch as an actress far more than Hitchcock wanted from a muse. Miles was no longer the wet clay who could be shaped into a new statue, but an independent actress with her own goals. She would never complain or justify claims that she had been abused by Hitchcock the way Tippi Hedren did. But she did admit to being unable to fill the void she felt she had been hired to:

> Over the span of years, he's had one type of woman in his films, Ingrid Bergman, Grace Kelly and so on. Before that, it was Madeleine Carroll. I'm not their type and never have been. I tried to please him, but I couldn't. They are all sexy women, but mine is an entirely different approach.[5]

As unflattering as Miles was as Lila, her matronly good sister provided a nice juxtaposition to the new, risqué image Janet Leigh presented as Marion Crane. In 1960, Janet Leigh was the quintessential good girl of Hollywood. Perky, sweet, and seemingly blessed with a very happy (and very public) family life, she was also a much stronger actress than many of the golden girls being brought to Hollywood at the time. Similar to actresses such as Vera Ellen or Debbie Reynolds, she often appeared in comedies and musicals (such as *My Sister Eileen* and *Holiday Affair*); she was excited to, much like Miles, stretch as an actress. In 1958 she appeared as the kidnapped rape victim in *Touch of Evil* for Orson Welles.

But there was a big difference between casting innocent Leigh as a woman in danger and making it appear as if she had been corrupted as her character of Marion has been. Introduced in the midst of an affair, she has been corrupted by her lover, to the point that she would steal from her boss just to be

Hitchcock delighted in working with stars Anthony Perkins and Janet Leigh while filming *Psycho* (1960), and even encouraged Perkins to interpret and add to his Norman's dialogue and mannerisms. *Universal Pictures/Photofest © Universal Pictures*

with him. After failing to show a woman corrupted with Bergman in *Under Capricorn* or Valli in *The Paradise Case*, Hitchcock finally convincingly shows a woman corrupted with Leigh's performance as Marion.

Leigh was the red herring of *Psycho*, the example of a star being cast against type, which was so common in Hitchcock films. It was unexpected to see a good girl like Leigh with short hair and in her bra and underwear, committing robbery and trying to escape. Hitchcock even films the usually beautiful Leigh in a harsh yet voyeuristic manner. Even in scenes of an overt sexual nature with Leigh, including scenes of her lying on a bed with her boyfriend in her underwear, she is never presented as an object of desire in *Psycho*, but as a real (and potentially dangerous) woman we feel we are spying on, as Hitchcock immediately forces his audience to become voyeurs. She is even lit in a harsh manner to evoke the impression of reality and magnify any lines on her face.[6] Her usually freshly scrubbed face and blond hair (often pulled back in a ponytail or falling on her shoulders) is short and slightly darker (almost dirty blond).

The opportunity to play against her good girl image in the role of Marion, and the challenges presented to her with working with Hitchcock, more than delighted Leigh. When first meeting with Hitchcock, he took the time to explain his specific technical instruction of actors and that he would only interfere to make a correction (a bit of information about himself he rarely shared). Leigh understood that he would give precise instructions of how to move, look, and position her body, but that finding the character was up to her. Leigh embraced the challenge of playing a character so physically restricted and Hitchcock found her to be a cooperative, professional actress. With Leigh he found he could even use her to motivate other actors in scenes, specifically love interest John Gavin, whom Hitchcock referred to as "The Stiff."

Gavin was the quintessential beefcake actor, discovered and promoted to stardom by agent Henry Wilson primarily because of his physical similarities to actor Rock Hudson. He would star in several films for Douglas Sirk (who frequently worked with Hudson) such as the forgettable *A Time to Love and a Time to Die* and was asked to perform "stud service" in his women's picture *Imitation of Life*. He was a pretty boy, whom even critics disparaged, claiming: "The actors act, and those who cannot, like Gavin, look beautiful."[7]

When announced as a leading man in the Douglas Sirk film *A Time to Love and A Time to Die*, Universal promoted him as the "$5,000,000 Gamble"[8] and the "Non-Neurotic Newcomer" in 1958 and declared him to be "the normal

Gregory Peck, rather than the neurotic James Dean school of actors."[9] Ironically, Paramount had already used similar wordage to promoted their biggest
star in 1956, declaring Anthony Perkins "the $15,000,000 gamble" (in reference
to the most lucrative principal contract every signed).[10] Perkins had been promoted as a neurotic, and costar Karl Malden made similar comparisons to acting predecessors, announcing, "Tony's a combination of Marlon Brando and
Jimmy Dean, with maybe a little Gregory Peck. That's quite a combination"[11]

By casting hunk Gavin, Hitchcock was immediately calling attention to
their different "types." Gavin was conservative in his appeal and was promoted as a throwback to the "classic leading men" of yesterday. Perkins was
part of the new Hollywood emerging, considered the heir apparent to the
popularity Montgomery Clift and James Dean once had. And those differences were applied to their characters. Despite seeing Leigh and Gavin in
bed, half naked, there is very little chemistry, sexual or romantic, between

When compared to John Gavin's beefy but dull screen image, Perkins's likable and
fascinating Norman Bates in *Psycho* (1960) was the definition of a likable Hitchcock
villain. *Universal Pictures/Photofest © Universal Pictures*

them. Every moment on-screen together, Gavin seems uncomfortable and cold toward Leigh. Leigh's interactions with Perkins are far more natural and easy, suggesting the cause of her corruption was Mitch and Norman will save her. Even the theme of sandwiches is used to compare the two men: Mitch prevented her from eating her sandwich and Norman is the one who brings her one.

Much the way Gavin had been introduced in connection to another actor from the "golden age of cinema," Perkins was introduced to the world on the cover of *Life Magazine* with the headline "24 Year Old Copy of Cooper."[12] The article was in reference to his Oscar-nominated role as Gary Cooper's son in the drama about Quakers during the Civil War, *Friendly Persuasions*. The film was a huge, star-making hit for Perkins, and his public image rose so high, Hollywood considered him the most likely heir to James Dean's popularity. After the teen idol's death, Perkins was given two of the icon's next starring roles, *Fear Strikes Out* and *This Angry Age*. He had played sensitive, passive young men in films such as *On the Beach*, *Tin Star*, and *The Tall Story*, and often juvenile love interests in films such as *The Matchmaker*, *Desire under the Elms*, and *Green Mansions*.

He had been described as the next Gregory Peck, Henry Fonda, and James Stewart (Samuel Goldwyn claimed "that boy has seen too many Jimmy Stewart movies"). He was very much the link between two generations of actors: the golden age of studio system and new method actors (although he refused to study method),[13] and appealed to both fractions of the audience, a quality Bill Tusher described as "gentle, yet urgent. Females from eight to eighty from coast to coast get his message. . . . Perkins doesn't ride motorcycles, beat bongo drums, insult interviewers, or drive at breakneck speed, but he has a charming collection of eccentricities of his own."[14] Perkins had, like his predecessors, a neurotic dark side in many of his films and his persona, but while other actors displayed such darkness and rage for public view, Perkins kept his hidden beneath the surface, adding a mysterious depth to performances. His performance in *Fear Strikes Out* caught the attention of the public, including Truffaut who claimed Perkins was the link between "the simplicity of the young stars of an older generation, Jimmy Stewart and Gary Cooper, with the physical modernity of the Brandos and James Deans, without ever resorting to trickiness or exhibitionism."[15]

It was that quality, the misunderstood neurosis, the outwardly well-disaffected youth, that excited both Hitchcock (who referred to Perkins as the "bobbysoxers' dreamboat" with a brain) and screenwriter Joseph Stefano to reimagine the character of Norman for him. Stefano said in an interview that after Hitchcock's casting of Perkins, "I suddenly saw a tender, vulnerable young man you could feel incredibly sorry for."[16] Stefano eventually wrote the character description of Norman Bates with the image of Perkins in mind: "somewhere in his late twenties, thin and tall, soft-spoken and hesitant . . . [with] something sadly touching in his manner."[17]

Perhaps because the role had been written for him, Perkins had more freedom in the role of Norman Bates than any other actor who had worked with Hitchcock in Hollywood. He was permitted to improvise lines and suggest his own physicality and even asked Hitchcock if he could not scream in the climactic scene when Bates finds Vera Miles in the cellar. Although he had agreed to loop the scene later (when he was not working on the Broadway musical *Green Willow*), Hitchcock simply chose to use the scene as it was. And even today, Perkins's performance is considered by many to be not only the greatest performance Hitchcock ever captured on-screen, but one of the best and most natural performances in cinematic history.

Although Norman Bates would typecast Perkins in Hollywood, the role in this film (and René Clément's *This Angry Age*) would make Perkins such a big star in Europe that the next year he would win best actor honors at Cannes, the David di Donatello Award, and second place at the BAMBI Awards (German honors) for the romantic drama *Goodbye Again*, as the shiftless playboy son of Jessie Royce Landis (Cary Grant's mother in *North by Northwest*) in love with the much older Ingrid Bergman. For the next seven years he would exclusively work in Europe (living a majority of his time in Paris) as one of the most popular American stars overseas.

Perhaps it is should be expected that Perkins would become a star in Europe, as *Psycho* seemed to signify the end of the Hollywood star system. François Truffaut wrote that "*Psycho* is the film which showed the ability for Hitchcock to have mass success with a small film"[18] and, as a student of auteur theory, credited largely "Hitchcock" overlooking the thrill of seeing good girl Leigh in a role often given to a sex kitten and reframing the image of one of the most popular leading men of the time as the most dangerous character. And yet Hitchcock seemed to overlook the vital importance stars had had on his films.

25

The Birds

Grace hadn't achieved the final—not in my book. She was just getting started. She showed potential in *Dial M for Murder* but *Rear Window* was the first picture that really brought her out. She had just begun to get somewhere when she quit. . . . Tippi stands entirely on her own. She doesn't relate to Grace at all. She has her own individuality, her own style, her own personality, and the American public is going to be very grateful we gave her to it. She has to be accepted for what she has herself. After all there are all types of blondes. Jean Harlow was a blond, Marilyn Monroe was blond, and Grace is a blond, but each is quite different. When Mary Pickford was a great star, the studios were always introducing some new actress as another Mary Pickford. But they didn't get away with it because there was only one Mary Pickford.[1]

Once delighted by the very idea of getting his hands on stars, Hitchcock seemed at best frustrated by the stars and at worst outright hostile. The financial considerations connected to hiring the biggest names in Hollywood were no longer affordable because of their studio contracts. For example, had he been able to afford him, Hitchcock would have liked to have had a masculine star the likes of Cary Grant as the hero in his next film, *The Birds*.[2] But by 1963, Grant was working less and less and his price tag was far larger than Hitchcock was willing to pay for any actor.

Instead, Hitchcock insisted that what he really needed for *The Birds* were no-names, to make the birds the true stars. With this insistence, he selected the model Tippi Hedren. Tippi was a print and television model with no professional experiences as an actress and barely any training. Although she had taken a few classes in voice and speech, Hedren was an untrained beauty whose primary interest to Hitchcock seemed to be her similarities to the iconic Hitchcock blonde and her raw, untrained quality. As Hitchcock delighted in explaining to the press, "Beginners have an enormous advantage over those with experience, for the most obvious of reasons . . . they have nothing to unlearn."[3]

After she signed to a personal contract with Hitchcock, he was certain she could be turned into his next muse. Hitchcock began testing her in scenes from some of his best-known films (*Rebecca, Notorious, To Catch a Thief*) in the roles of some of his most beloved and memorable leading ladies (Joan Fontaine, Ingrid Bergman, and Grace Kelly). She was dressed in beautiful clothing by Edith Head and did a reasonable job impersonating these iconic performers. But from the very beginning (despite Hitchcock's insistence that she would be a star for her individuality), Hedren was hired to be a version of these memorable, undeniably unique actresses—with no image or personality of her own through which the audiences could build affection. She was, even more than Kim Novak or Vera Miles, the real-life version of the women from *Vertigo*: a re-creation of the ideal Hitchcock had lost.

While focusing on the technical aspects of *The Birds*, Hitchcock approached "creating" a star in Hedren with the same detail and focus he took preparing his films. When introducing Hedren to the press, as she sat next to him, he detailed how he was going to cultivate her image and turn her into a star:

It's going to be tough because I can't give her repeated exposure the way we did with young players years ago when studios were making 50 and 60 films a year. But what I plan to do is to promote Tippi in "big pictures," films of quality that compel attention, rather than "slot machines" [cheap B movies]. . . . If I can get this girl to give outstanding performance in two or three films, so that we start a favorable word-of-mouth campaign, if I can build her up as a young actress and beauty, dignity and mystery, a gracious, high-style lady—some like a young Grace Kelly, Myrna Loy, Irene Dunne, Greer Garson, Claudette Colbert, then I think we've got a chance of making a new star, because I think that's the type of star a hungry public wants, not the girl with the big, bold, brazen, top heavy front. . . . The thing to do is to cloak Tippi with a veil of mystery, keep her out of

Star of *The Birds* (1963) Tippi Hedren was asked to impersonate Hitchcock's classic heroines, more than create her own public persona. *Universal Pictures/ Photofest* © *Universal Pictures*

the gossip columns. I don't want phony items planted about her such as "Troy Donahue's new love is Tippi Hedren" or "Cary Grant's latest heartthrob is Tippi Hedren." That's worthless. I want Tippi to get a publicity build-up away from the movie pages, and I want it to be gradual and dignified.[4]

The hubris on display from Hitchcock, believing he could select and create any actor to become a star, is startling considering the way he once spoke of stars. When he first arrived in Hollywood, Hitchcock had respect for stars with a unique, ethereal individuality that represented something personal and special about them, which led the public to make them stars. Thirty years earlier, he sided with the stars against the publicity machines, insisting:

If the public had seen, as I have done, the reverse of the picture, those bitter struggles to stardom—the disappointments, the sheer hard work, the poverty often coupled with starvation at the beginning, the courage and pluck and determination to win through, I do not think they would grudge them the electric lights. Stardom is not won easily. I know people whisper about the power of the publicity drum, but no amount of publicity can create something which is not there, and a star who is only a child of publicity will not last.[5]

Now Hitchcock rather than the public would choose the stars . . . and Hitchcock chose Hedren as a star. When *Look Magazine* finally introduced her to the world on the cover of their magazine (in profile with a bird over the photograph), it ran with the headline "Hitchcock's New Grace Kelly." Considering the way he seemed to only talk to or about his stars when he had complaints or wanted to make corrections, Hitchcock went to extra effort to make Hedren a "name," explaining to *Look Magazine* that "Grace is an easy-going, elegant woman, who moves with a benign dignity. Tippi has a faster tempo, city glibness, and more humor." Hitchcock's comments about Hedren were rarely what we could consider "praise of her," especially as his contempt for actors seemed to escalate. In the same article, which focused far more on Hitchcock than Hedren, he joked, "I took on two almost impossibly difficult tasks at once—a picture in which I had to train birds and a new girl."[6]

With a new actress in the lead, a role that would become the predecessor of the horror female (*Halloween* or *Nightmare on Elm Street*), he chose not to select a name actor to balance the film (as he would have done earlier in his career) but selected supporting actors who were barely recognizable to filmgoers. Costume designer Rita Riggs recalled that had the price been lower, Hitchcock would have certainly tried to convince Cary Grant to take the role of Mitch. But Hitchcock wanted to keep the cost of his cast down and considered Chuck Connors (a big name in television because of his role in *The Rifleman* but with minimal film experience) and the Australian-born actor Rod Taylor, described as "the rough, B Cary Grant" (along with comparisons to being the next Rock Hudson and Errol Flynn), who was best known for his work in TV westerns and a muscular build. Taylor was promoted as being a rugged man among the new soft American men ("People are getting soft here and they eat all those beautiful desserts that waiters press on you") and claimed to have no intention of being "the next anything"[7] or even being a star, a system he felt was on its way out. "Stars went out with Clark Gable, Spencer Tracy and Jean Harlow. I know a lot of gas station attendants who have landed in television and now are being called 'stars.' Leading actors maybe, but stars they aren't. The term star doesn't mean anything anymore."[8]

Hitchcock seemed to agree with Taylor's statements about modern stardom and his own image, describing him to Truffaut as a competent actor who "lacked charisma."[9] But unlike the unknown Hedren, Hitchcock was uninterested in promoting Taylor's image to the press. When discussing the decision to hire two nonstars in the leading roles, Hitchcock claimed it was purely for artistic motives: "I felt that one should have anonymous people because the subject matter was not as facetious as some of my other films. Anyway, the stars of the film were the birds; anyone else was secondary."[10] That lack of charisma and sparkling star quality is noticeable throughout *The Birds*, particularly in the scenes between Hedren and the rugged but slightly uninteresting Taylor. For a film with such an interesting concept, the underdeveloped and vapid leading characters bring down the film's enjoyment considerably as there is very little empathy for the individual characters.

Yet there are scenes with Taylor that pop out to audiences as special and memorable, especially those with Jessica Tandy, as his mother. Unlike Taylor and Hedren, who were replacements for the script's inspiration of Grace Kelly and Cary Grant, the role of the mother was written with the actress in mind, and the size of the role was ultimately expanded and further developed based on the notes provided by husband Hume Cronyn (who was well aware that she topped the list of actresses for the role) for Hitchcock.[11]

Not only is her character one of the most complex and sympathetic of Hitchcock's traditional mother characters, but there are also passing allusions to the Broadway role she had originated and made famous, Blanche in *A Streetcar Named Desire*. Sympathetic in its suggestion that she feels completely alone since the death of her husband, there is a disturbing quality to her dependence on her grown son that adds far more depth to the film than as purely written. The tensions brought about by the birds are obvious, but the unsettling quality and tension that is rising before the birds begin attacking in number is hinted at more by these two actors. Critics took notice, with Crowther writing, "Rod Taylor is stolid and sturdy as the mother-smothered son. Jessica Tandy is querulous as the mother and pretty Suzanne Pleshette is pleasant but vaguely sinister as the old girlfriend."[12]

Like Tandy, actress Suzanne Pleshette added far more to the film than the underwritten role of the schoolteacher may have had with a lesser actress. Ironically, for a film about a playgirl with a reputation, the actress who would have fit the role of Melanie better would have been New Yorker Pleshette. The daughter of a club owner, the husky-voiced actress often appeared in gossip columns, noted as a hip conversationalist who frequently dated men twice her age (and, as if Hitchcock's comment was directed at her, a relationship with Troy Donahue).[13] But when asked to audition for *The Birds*, Pleshette was revitalizing her image. Her bombshell style was replaced with what the press called "sophisticated mod,"[14] and her flirtatious style was replaced with a composed, independent woman with poise dubbed "Good Girl in Town Manhattan."[15] Although it would be another decade before she found a role that elevated her to a true star (as Emily in *The Bob Newhart Show*), she spent the next ten years establishing herself as a classy, modern, independent career women.[16] Her turning point in her career was also in 1961, when she replaced Ann Bancroft in *The Miracle Worker* on Broadway.

When brought in for the small role as a schoolteacher for *The Birds*, Pleshette thought the original role was simply too small. Hitchcock liked Pleshette for the role and had it rewritten for the twenty-six-year-old, though Pleshette joked that "I'd have played one of The Birds, just to be in a Hitchcock picture, but he just liked me, so he rewrote everything."[17] Even with the slightly fleshed-out role, Pleshette was truly given one of the most thankless roles in a Hitchcock film. She is a strong, sexual actress (very different from Hedren) whose husky voice and far more solid frame suggest an independent

Hitchcock instructing Rod Taylor and Suzanne Pleshette in one of the few scenes that does not include Hedren's Melanie in *The Birds* (1963). *Universal Pictures/Photofest © Universal Pictures*

spirit at play. While she is given little in terms of character development or even arc, her single speech, about her history with Taylor's character, is far better than any other bit of acting in the film. While the premise of *The Birds* remains engaging, the characters' story, told by Tandy, Taylor, and Pleshette, as being in the past, is far more interesting than what we are shown between Hedren and Taylor.

Hitchcock almost replaced Pleshette in the cast because he feared her presence would take away from Hedren's star buildup.[18] Yet, to appease Hitchcock and his preoccupation with promoting Hedren to a star, the usually sophisticated Pleshette was refashioned as an "earthy broad." The unflattering image Hitchcock photographed her at is almost acceptable. In fact, despite Hitchcock's acknowledgment that his preoccupation was on the technical aspects of the birds, the other actors noticed that any attention Hitchcock gave to actors was focused almost exclusively on Hedren. Taylor claims they were given remarkably little direction, but could sense a growing contempt from the director toward the actors. During an interview, Taylor told the press that Hitchcock referred to actors as sheep and they could sense his dislike for them and their demands on the set.[19]

Yet the disproportionate amount of attention given to Hedren left the actress uncomfortable and exhausted by the constant preoccupation with her every move and aspect of her appearance. Rita Riggs, who costumed Hedren, noticed that "towards the end of *The Birds*, Tippi was getting tired of the hot house system where everything was carefully controlled. Everything was so carefully manipulated with Peggy Robertson and Suzie Gauthier. It was a whole system and we all recognized it and followed it."[20] Riggs recalled that even the importance he placed on her hair color seemed obsessive.

Many critics took notice of her lack of acting abilities and made it a specific point in their reviews, even while praising *The Birds*. Brendan Gill sniped in his review for *The New Yorker* that "Miss Hedren is so new a newcomer that Universal has boasted in print of her having no previous acting experience whatever. Not everything about this picture is hard to believe."[21] Similarly, Bosley Crowther gave only faint praise to Hedren, writing, "Tippi Hedren is pretty, bland and wholesome as the disruptive girl."[22] But according to Camille Paglia, there are no positive assessments of her performance and the critical opinion of her work frequently leans toward a fateful opinion of her (often comparing her unfavorably to Grace Kelly) with little blame given to Hitchcock who controlled her every move and variation as an actress.[23]

When promoting the film, Hitchcock changed his demeanor from choosing to be a Svengali to appearing resentful that he had to take on such an active role in crafting her performance, stating:

> There is no question that all actors are children. Some are good children; some are bad; many are stupid children. Because of this childlike quality, actors and actresses should never get married. An actress, for example, attains the blissful state of matrimony and almost immediately goes to work in a picture with a new leading man. She plays a love scene with him so strongly that after three weeks on the pictures, she comes home to her husbands and says, idiotically, "Darling, I want a divorce."' During her love scenes at the studio, she has heard people say, "Look, it's real," and she now thinks it's real, too. They are children who never mature emotionally. It's a tragedy.[24]

For such a singular performance, one is struck upon repeated viewing by how isolated the character of Melanie (and ultimately Hedren) is. If Hitchcock was ultimately dissatisfied with Hedren's performance, a great deal of the responsibility falls on Hitchcock, and he could place none of the blame on his stars, as he had done with Bergman, Wyman, and Novak before.

It is part of the reason critiquing Hedren's performance is increasingly difficult because her contributions as an actress are unknown. When she does less as an actress in *The Birds* is when she is the most fascinating to watch, especially compared to the clipped way of speaking she used in both *The Birds* and *Marnie*, which is remarkably unnatural. Hitchcock's opinion of Hedren, despite the buildup and investment of her as his next great star, seemed remarkably low. Unlike Fontaine and Kelly, it showed an elevated sense of himself rather than his belief in his new muse. While always controlling of these new "creatures," there was a sense that they became better actresses with his guidance and control. But by the time Hitchcock had discovered Hedren, she was merely his version of a Galatea whom he could turn into an actress. Hitchcock believed he could make anyone with a pretty face, a good body, and complete obedience to him into a star.

26

Marnie

I'm surprised he went ahead with *Marnie*, because it was an undertaking, more of an acting challenge, and I think he felt he could get things out of people as a director and he believed in himself as a director.[1]

When looking at Marnie in regard to its place in Hitchcock's filmography, there is darkness behind the scenes of that picture. Although it seems like the flip side of both *Notorious* and *Vertigo*, it focuses on contemporary themes Hitchcock would only allude to in other films. He referred to it as a sex thriller, which may have been the biggest mistake he made; for to contemporary audiences the film is far from sexy, due to the scenes of psychological trauma, rape, and child abuse.

There seemed to be a disconnection between what Hitchcock wanted and what he knew the audience would connect to; surprising for a director considered such a showman who made pictures primarily to please his audiences. While promoting the film, Hitchcock made statements that would leave his once loyal audiences with a chill, such as:

Marnie is symptomatic of the America female; she is basically frigid. There is a vast amount of difference between appearance and actuality in the American woman. She is schooled from childhood by magazines and advertisements to make herself seem alluring and sexy. But alas, her inhibitions are too great. There is in this country a long tradition of puritanism. There is also a lack of sophistication. That is why there is so much divorce in America. When a wife suspects that her husband is having an affair, she immediately summons a lawyer. A European wife is more sophisticated. She says, "Let him have his fling; he will come back to me." And he generally does.[2]

How could the same director who once understood so well that women in the audience had far more say than the studios previously assumed; that even the most fantastical women should appeal to both men and women (the reason for the lasting appeal of Grace Kelly), now speak of women with such venom? Why was a film with one of the great women's roles turned in a fetish film?

The film did not start out under such dark circumstances, but rather a film "lovingly conceived for one actress, and finally enacted by another,"[3] as a love letter of sorts to Grace Kelly. After the performance she had given as the thrill-loving girl aroused by the idea of being with a criminal in *To Catch a Thief*, Hitchcock next wanted to cast her as a disturbed thief. This was obvious development of her image from fantasy to identifiable character. It could give Kelly the opportunity to act and reach acting heights never before seen on film. Joseph Stephano, after working on *Psycho* in 1959, was asked to adapt the book into a film scenario with Kelly in mind for the leading role of Marnie. Stephano had already written a female thief (Marion) and psychologically tortured lead (Norman) in *Psycho*. Marnie would combine both qualities without the murders.

He also knew how to write psychological ideas into films relatively well and wrote three male supporting characters: a psychologist, a husband, and the husband's business partner. Remembering the classic love triangles from Hitchcock's previous films (*Dial M for Murder, Notorious, Under Capricorn, The Paradine Case*, and even *Psycho*), Stephano approached the character not as someone likable, as Grace Kelly always was, but whose appeal could potentially destroy men: "Marnie was a strange, unlikeable character. By which I mean men might not like her but they would fall in love with her."[4] The idea of casting Kelly as unlikable seemed an impossible challenge, but like James Stewart and Cary Grant, she wanted to take the chance to grow and test her acting abilities.

And there was the other fact that Cary Grant, once so insistent on only being the leading man, enjoyed working with Kelly so much, he offered himself to Hitchcock with a comment in *Variety*. Not only would there now be two stars returning for a Hitchcock film, but to cast Grant as the controlling and often cruel Mark would finally allow Hitchcock to test how dark audiences would allow their Cary Grant to be before turning against him (an experiment started more than twenty years earlier with *Suspicion*). The reunion of Hitchcock with Grant and Kelly was anticipated until the day Kelly wired that she could not appear in the film because of obligations to Monaco, the country of which she was now princess.

On losing yet another actress to domestic obligation (as he had with Bergman's affair with Rossellini and Vera Miles's pregnancy), Hitchcock was forgiving of the beloved actress but also quite bitter, as when he wrote, in production notes for the film, "There is no question that all actors are children. Some are good children, some are bad children, and many are stupid children. Because of this childlike quality, actors and actresses should never get married."[5]

With Kelly gone, Hitchcock also lost Cary Grant, whose primary interest in the role was the opportunity to work with Kelly again. And the awareness the public had of Hitchcock's plans to reunite them for the anticipated *Marnie* made it difficult for critics not to compare Hedren and Sean Connery to Kelly and Grant, as Eugene Archer wrote: "Hitchcock has taken a pair of attractive and promising young players, Miss Hedren and Mr. Connery, and forced them into roles that cry for the talents of Grace Kelly and Cary Grant. Both work commendably and well—but their inexperience shows."[6]

Part of the reason for the difficulty of recasting the role of Marnie (and Mark) was that the character had similarities to Kelly's own public life, which made the film seem like a dark take on the Cinderella fairy tale Kelly experienced in her own life (like *Rebecca*). A common Philadelphian (as Kelly was), Marnie pretends to be upper class and sophisticated, which "wins" her a prince who holds her captive in marriage. It was the reason that Mark's Philadelphia businessman has hints of being part of a fictional American aristocracy. Without the ironic personal-professional connection Kelly would have brought to the role, the public's awareness of her journey from Philadelphia girl to Hollywood icon and real-life princess, Hitchcock needed a man to play the dark side of Prince Charming to suggest any of the themes that attracted Hitchcock to the story.

Which makes the casting of Sean Connery appear, at least at first glance, a logical development. Having just completed the first James Bond film,

Hitchcock was well aware that the role of Bond had been developed in the image of Cary Grant (and certainly some of the dashing spy films he had directed the actor in). But Bond stories were darker and more violent stories than his, a quality Connery embraced as an actor. Connery's biographer, who wrote well of Hitchcock's brilliance in casting, wrote:

> Instead of casting him against type, Hitchcock seems to have been using him in order to dissect and analyze the make-up of the chilling, sex-charged monster that was his Bond. On the strength of Connery's performance in *Dr. No*, that is, Hitchcock had seen through the glitz and glamour of Saltzman and Broccoli's technocratic hero to the barely socialized psychopath underneath. Like so many of the Bond audience, Hitchcock had thrilled to the animal grace of Connery's Bond. Unlike them, he had thought what fun it would be to put that kind of wild, self-regarded behavior under the microscope. He only half got his way.[7]

Alfred Hitchcock filming the controversial rape scene in *Marnie* (1964) with stars Sean Connery and Tippi Hedren. *Universal Pictures/Photofest © Universal Pictures*

Yet Connery's performance of Mark is oddly undefined by both Connery and Hitchcock. Is he the antihero or a sexual predator? Even the writers were unsure of this, as voiced when attempting to write the still controversial rape scene in the film. Evan Hunter, who had written *The Birds* (also with Cary Grant in mind), told Hitchcock he did not want to write the scene (and went so far as to write one version of the script without it) because "I would have a hell of time recovering the character."[8] Hitchcock instead fired Hunter and hired playwright Jay Presson Allen (the writer of the scandalous *The Prime of Miss Jean Brodie*), who claimed she didn't even feel the scene was a rape scene: "When you think about a rape scene, you think of a woman being grabbed by a stranger in the park. This was just a trying marital situation. I did not define it as rape, and Hitch never used the word *rape*."[9] Indeed, Hitchcock found it to be an erotic scene of a powerful European man taking control of a temperamental woman, all part of the difference of how Europeans saw sex differently from Americans. As Presson Allen told Hunter, "The only reason he wanted to do that movie was for that scene."[10]

Hitchcock many have been able to film a rape scene without question, if he hadn't attempted to keep the audience's identification with the character of Mark. Prescott felt that simply casting a star like Connery was enough (as it had been a few years earlier in *Notorious*) to allow the audience to forgive his behavior, joking, "How you redeem it is through the actor's charisma. They're not stars for nothing. And you forgive him."[11] But Mark never has a redemptive moment when he amends for the violent action. Instead, as Connery's biographer wrote:

> The trouble is that Connery's putative gentleman publisher; fascinated though he may himself be with predators, can't help but come across as the movie's big beast. . . . It is simply the case that by dint of his panther-like gait and mocking feline face, Connery cannot help but be the movie's wildest animal.[12]

Ironically, Sean Connery may be one of the few actors to collectively bridge the sexual power of Cary Grant *(To Catch a Thief* and *North by Northwest)* and domestic impotence of James Stewart's frustrated Hitchcock characters (in *The Man Who Knew Too Much* and *Vertigo*), suggesting that if everyman James Stewart had the magnetism and sex appeal of Grant, the characters would have been the "most in charge of situations, most complete master of himself and his environment, most decisive and active and purposive."[13] Even critics admitted to being rather confused by the average-male approach Connery and Hitchcock took to the character.[14] Walter J. Carroll wrote in his review of the film for *The Village Voice*, "Similarly, it is hard to really understand what Sean Connery finds so interesting about Miss Hedren, and why he bothers to marry her in the first place, and then to be locked out of the bedroom. He is so identified with the character of James Bond by now, that the least one expects is that he asserts himself somewhat more persuasively."[15] Had they perhaps delved into, or even hinted at, the aspects of Mark's life that make him so attracted, and obsessed, with Marnie, the character would have been far more compelling and seem less as if Connery was simply attempting to play a hero when there was none on the page.

Connery was, by all accounts, well liked by all on set and, according to Hitchcock's secretary, quickly became a personal favorite of Hitchcock's actors because of his sense of humor.[16] Yet part of that certainly also had to do with Hitchcock's attempt to, as he had on *Rebecca* before, manipulate his cast into living out their characters on set just as they would on-screen. Connery was, as is Mark, the golden boy given more freedom than anyone else on the set.[17] Hitchcock not only comparatively controlled Diane Baker and Hedren, but also attempted to pit them against each other.

When Grace Kelly had to leave *Marnie*, Hitchcock was excited to have his latest muse waiting on the sidelines. Hedren was given the novel to read and sat in on meetings conducted by Hitchcock during preproduction (while still in production on *The Birds*), listening as they described the character. But during production on *The Birds*, with Hitchcock's obsessive hand "directing" every aspect of her performance, their relationship became volatile and, as documented by Donald Spoto, outright abusive (particularly with the scene when Hedren is attacked by the birds). After the high-pressure experience on *The Birds*, the promotional tour, and going into production on *Marnie*, the exhaustion set in. When discussing her experience as Hitchcock's new star with columnist Wanda Hale (of the *Daily News*), there was almost a *Stepford Wives* quality in Hedren's reserved response:

> I feel wonderful. Completely relaxed. I don't even have to think for myself. They do it for me. They called and said get ready to go east—New York, Washington, Chicago, and Detroit—to say a few words for *Marnie*. They sent a couple out to

the house to pack for me. Filled five traveling bags with my things, three more than I would have brought if it had been left to me. But I won't complain as long as they pay the overweight. So here I am, without a care in the world.[18]

The interview strikes a reader as tongue and cheek, Hedren subversively voicing her thought on the total (and obsessive) control Hitchcock had over her career and hiding the truth of the mistreatment she experienced at the hands of Hitchcock (and Universal), who demanded she be an unthinking, untrained, and undereducated ingénue, existing simply to keep her director happy. The stories of Hitchcock's mistreatment of Tippi Hedren have become part of Hollywood history; so much that the performances are rarely considered. And while his treatment of Hedren certainly had an effect, the three key performances are arguably unrated, especially the work of Diane Baker.

Supposedly described by Hitchcock (and wife Alma) as reminding them of a young Grace Kelly, Baker was far from another woman who could be molded into one of Hitchcock's ideal women—more Vera Miles than another Grace Kelly. Baker was fiercely independent, both personally (being on her own at the age of eighteen to pursue her acting career) and professionally (often voicing her opinion as to how she was used during her seven-year contract at Fox). Baker had bought out her contract with Fox two years earlier, frustrated playing dithery young women after cutting her teeth in the memorable (and beloved) feature film version of the play *The Diary of Anne Frank*. Freed from the studio's hold, she immediately bought her own properties, hoping to find interesting projects of her own. Even in publicity she, like Shirley MacLaine and Teresa Wright, insisted on having control of her public image, choosing how she would wear her hair and makeup.[19]

When brought to the attention of Mr. Hitchcock, she was under no studio contract and refused to sign one with either Universal or Hitchcock. Years later she would say she simply didn't want to be under others' control: "I didn't like being under anyone's thumb. I didn't like the idea of being the next Grace Kelly, or anyone else but myself. I told Hitchcock this clearly one day before we finished the film."[20] For that, it seems that Baker's role was significantly cut, to the point that critics questioned her very purpose, writing, "Diane Baker, as a girl in fruitless pursuit, has a winsome smile to match his but it radiates in a vacuum."[21]

Indeed, while a striking beauty, Baker was far from the traditional Hitchcock woman in appearance. With almond-shaped eyes, porcelain skin, and dark (almost black hair), she, like raven-haired Suzanne Pleshette, created an instant visual contrast to Hedren. But unlike Pleshette, who's sturdy, working-girl qualities were a strong contrast to Hedren's playgirl, Baker was not given a character sufficiently unique from Hedren's. Marnie was a thief pretending to be prim and proper (the English schoolteacher Hitchcock mentioned so often), and Baker was Lil, the playgirl reminiscent of Hedren's Melanie in *The Birds*.

She was neither a movie star lending credibility or prestige to a role, nor an ingénue allowing Hitchcock to build a performance with her. Baker was a new, self-reliant actress, and it shows in her performance, which is far better and deeper than the script would call for. Her walk is a bit faster, less mod-

Pictured are Hedren and Hitchcock while filming the fox hunt scene in *Marnie* (1964), when she kills her horse. *Universal Pictures/Photofest © Universal Pictures*

elesque than his classic blondes, and her speech pattern is uniquely her own. And unlike Hedren, asked to take instructions passively, Baker looked for ways in which his technical instruction could improve her screen acting in the future. Hitchcock's frustrations with Hedren's failure to become the star he promoted her as led to him ignoring and gossiping about her, often directing his attention to Baker. Baker took notice of this behavior and in an attempt to avoid Hitchcock, she informed him that she had no intention of becoming one of his women.[22]

With Baker admitting to having compassion for the troubles Hedren had while working on *Marnie*, there is an undercurrent that lies beneath the performance of Baker and Hedren that can't be attributed to Hitchcock. He had made every effort to create the animosity between the two actresses, similar to the mood he encouraged between Judith Anderson and Joan Fontaine on the set of *Rebecca*. There was even to be a scene in which Baker explains her character Lil's animosity toward Marnie, which Baker felt rounded out her character, and she was disappointed when the scene didn't appear. However, the most memorable scene between the two is Lil's attempt to convince broken Marnie not to shoot her own horse.

If Hitchcock meant for the scene to play cold and suggest female hostility, he fails, as Baker shows a compassion for Marnie and Hedren a level of pain that makes the often overly formulistic film show some of the true, human emotion—not from Hitchcock but from the camaraderie between two actresses. It is one of the few scenes in which the humanity of Hedren's performance shines through and she is more than a clone of Hitchcock's heroines, but it isn't enough to add real depth to the feature. Baker was similarly controlled at times, with Hitchcock once even physically fixing her face (the scene of her in the window). But she already had the grasp of acting, how to find the emotions behind the character, so there always seems to be a real person behind the rigid physicality.

Even critics admitted that Hedren may have perhaps improved, but not enough for the size and complexity of the role, writing, "Miss Hedren has improved considerably since her unfortunate debut in *The Birds* and she looks like the typical Hitchcock heroine—fashionable, blonde, slender, sophisticated. However, she is still not sufficiently accomplished to give depth in a character study that demands deeper."[23] Yet the fault in Hedren's limited performance seems directed toward Hitchcock.

Hedren, however, has a vacancy, which was especially evident with the film *Marnie*. While in *The Birds* she is an empty vessel for the audience to attach themselves to, Marnie is perhaps the most complex female character of any Hitchcock film, a woman who has to play one version of herself on top of the other. And Hedren may have simply not been up to such a task at that stage in her career, partially because of the lack of training she had been given by Hitchcock, who wanted to keep her untrained, despite the experience she should have gotten on the set of *The Birds*. Despite all the promises Hitchcock made regarding the casting of his ingénue, claiming, "She's like a seemingly quiescent volcano—one whose molten lava we know will one day erupt with coruscating splendor,"[24] Hedren's limitations are magnified in *Marnie*, which calls for as psychological a performance as Gregory Peck in *Spellbound*, Jimmy Stewart in *Vertigo*, or Anthony Perkins in *Psycho*.

Hedren was never given the tools necessary to capture the emotions and psychological truth of the character, and was forced by Hitchcock to make no effort to find these skills within. As Louis Chaplin noted, "Miss Hedren is an obedient and glamorous façade for Mr. Hitchcock's directorial purposes. Of her own [skills] we are shown very little."[25] It is perhaps the great tragedy of *Marnie*, and Hedren's falling out with Hitchcock, that we didn't have the opportunity to see the kind of development Hitchcock allowed other actresses such as Vera Miles, Grace Kelly, or Joan Fontaine to reach under his guidance. In a role far beyond her skills, she blows in the wind, stretching in her hysterical scenes and vacant when being deceptive.[26] Only when Marnie is in a trance, detached when standing with Sean Connery or driven to steal, does she seem to fully understand the role and bring something from within to the screen. Had she been given a bit more instruction and technical skills, who knows if she would have developed into a fine actress? But ultimately, Hedren's career never recovered from Hitchcock's abuse and disregard of her, an experience that didn't even leave her with a new set of skills.

Hedren may be the prime example of why Hitchcock's insistence on absolute directorial control of his actresses was his downfall; they outgrew the paternal control he desired. He could have easily hired lesser or untrained actresses for his film who would have submitted to his control. However, their performances would have been shallow and lacking the depth he found from skilled actresses, bringing originality to their roles, adding to what was on the page. However, having their individualism meant they would ultimately outgrow the control he wanted to have on their career, like Hedren had to outgrow the gilded cage he had placed her in for *The Birds* in order to play Marnie. Hitchcock may have established the image of these women, and crafted their great performances, but eventually, they had to break away from his control.

27

Torn Curtain

Because of our mass psychology, we will always need stars. In reality, however, you realize that in recent years the biggest stars have disappointing records at the box office. The star is no better than the story. In the right picture, the star will be as big as ever; put him in the wrong picture and you're no better off than if you used an unknown.[1]

While on promotional tour for *Marnie*, Hitchcock made this provocative statement about the current state of the powerful and highly paid stars. As Hollywood was experiencing a major change in its economic structure, Hitchcock's feelings toward stars—whom he had once been "eager to get his hands on"—had soured. His comments, insisting that he could create stars from the unknown and untrained, signaled the change in thinking, markedly different from his previous belief that there was not only a purpose to stars, but that stardom could not simply be created from thin air and publicity machines ("No amount of publicity can create something which is not there, and a star who is only a child of publicity will not last"[2]). Despite his new belief in the alternative, he did not have the power to create stars the public didn't want. Yet his comments on the power of a star was also telling, considering the experience he would have on his next feature, the Cold War thriller *Torn Curtain*.

Despite the high paychecks they demanded, Universal believed it completely worth the money to hire two of the biggest box-office names, Paul Newman and Julie Andrews, despite Hitchcock's belief that their casting was no guarantee of a good movie or a profitable movie. While Hitchcock was correct in his estimation that the miscast actors would lead to a poorly reviewed film (the film is considered one of the worst in Hitchcock's filmography), Hitchcock misjudged the public's taste, making *Torn Curtain* Hitchcock's biggest box-office hit. *Torn Curtain* was the highest-grossing film (upon initial theatrical release) in Hitchcock's career, making more than four times the budget of three million dollars—and leaving Hitchcock so disillusioned by the star system, he would walk away from Hollywood for nearly a decade.

Initially, Hitchcock considered *Torn Curtain* a possible bookend to his collaboration with Cary Grant, as a suitable pairing of their other spy films: *Notorious* and *North by Northwest*. The concept would have been inspired and could have elevated the minor narrative of *Torn Curtain* to another of Grant's films about sexual politics. Grant, however, had no desire to step away from the self-imposed retirement he began that same year.

Instead of commenting on Grant's image, Hitchcock then conceived *Torn Curtain* as another film dependent on tricking his irresponsible audience and considered casting Eva Marie Saint and Anthony Perkins.[3] However, the failure of *Marnie* at the box office and critical disregard for the psychological film made it impossible for him to have the kind of casting authority he previously had, and unproven box-office stars like Saint and Perkins were no match for the international box office movie stars Paul Newman and Julie Andrews promised.

But Hitchcock's initial casting ideas for the film would have added a considerable level of suspense to the relatively bland characters. Saint was still a highly respected actress, but the captivating, glamorous image she had cultivated in *North by Northwest* as Eve Kendall remained her iconic image. To return to a Hitchcock film with that memory, in another Cold War thriller, would excite audiences expecting her to play a variation on her Eve Kendall and leave audiences guessing whether she was the sweet innocent she played so often or the reincarnation of mysterious Eve; rather than have audiences believe all at face value, as they did with Julie Andrews in the role. Likewise, the audience's assumption that Norman Bates cannot be trusted would have added intrigue regarding what the viewer can and cannot trust. However, Universal insisted bigger names were needed to ensure box-office success and selected Newman and Andrews as Michael and his bride-to-be, who pretends to defect in order to infiltrate the Russian government.

Andrews was an undeniable box-office star and popular actress in 1966, having won an Oscar for Disney's *Mary Poppins* and leading the international smash *The Sound of Music*. But Julie Andrews possessed none of the sultry, double-crossing qualities Eva Marie Saint would have brought with her from her association to *North by Northwest*. But worst was the fact that Hitchcock saw none of the darkness hiding beneath Andrews's beautiful, smiling face that had inspired him to cast her predecessors such as Doris Day, Janet Leigh, or Saint and show a new side to them. Hitchcock doesn't even give Andrews the kind of transformative makeover he had given to Hedren, Saint, or Novak to suggest to the audience that one should not expect "the typical Andrews" from this film; she looks just as the public knew her and she plays Sarah as just another "Julie Andrews role."

The apparent miscasting of Andrews falls to both Hitchcock's inability to adapt to the studio interference in casting and animosity he felt toward his

Julie Andrews was considered simply too sweet and pure to play Sarah in the Cold War thriller *Torn Curtain* (1967). *Universal Pictures/Photofest © Universal Pictures*

actors because of this, and Andrews's inability to find and develop the character without the guidance of a director. To suspect Andrews of any villainy would have arguably added far more power to *Torn Curtain* than the film's specific narrative. But Andrews did not stretch as far as she needed to and Hitchcock did not motivate her and her character always appears pure as the driven snow.

Perhaps the greatest problem with the casting of Andrews was the utter lack of sexual chemistry between her and Paul Newman. Despite the narrative's concern that the character of Sarah is overpowered by her love for Paul Newman's Michael, Andrews and Newman never project the obsessive love, or even sexual connection, such characters would have. Andrews lacked sex appeal; one critic wrote seeing her in bed with Newman was as appealing as seeing "Shirley Temple kick a cat." While not cold, she seems incapable or unwilling to embrace the sultry idea of that scene—a scene and character that should be as memorable as the scandal of Janet Leigh in bed with John Gavin in *Psycho*.

Part of the failure of their scene in bed certainly goes to Andrews's simple lack of sensuality. But Hitchcock also seems incapable of filming the scene in a way to suggest the scandalous romantic nature of this scene. In a similar scene, in *Notorious*, Hitchcock filmed Grant and Bergman's kisses in such extreme close-up, the audience feels an almost intrusive intimacy with the couple. Or the kiss between Saint and Grant in *North by Northwest* when Saint's face melts into a smile as they embrace and the camera moves with them across the screen during their long embrace on the train. In *Torn Curtain*, Hitchcock's camera seems remarkably neutral and bored in what should be a key scene. Similarly, perhaps the worst scene in the film, Newman's confession to Andrews in the park, is similarly uncinematic and dispassionate, robbing the film of any romantic intimacy between the two intended characters.

But while Hitchcock was uninspired by the casting of Andrews, he had a strong dislike for Paul Newman. Ironically, Newman was the biggest rival to Anthony Perkins for roles at the time of James Dean's death and, like Perkins, had taken over roles originally intended for Dean (at the same time that Perkins took over the role in *Fear Strikes Out*, Newman was given the lead in *Someone Up There Likes Me*). They even shared the Golden Globe Star of Tomorrow honors in 1956. But Newman was a method actor, like Montgomery Clift, which Hitchcock always found difficult to work with.

Hitchcock and Newman first began having problems during preproduction, when Hitchcock received a three-page memo from the actor with notes on how to improve the script. Hitchcock was admittedly well aware of the numerous problems with the script, which he was working on up to and during production. Yet, Hitchcock found it disrespectful for an actor, who had a very clear set of responsibilities in his mind, to interject on the writing process. Hitchcock took the break in decorum personally, calling it unprofessional, and became leery of working with Newman, who he said "was an actor who liked to do things his way." To Hitchcock, Newman wanted considerably more control than the average leading man (certainly average Hitchcock leading man). He began voicing his opinions on everything from cameras to editing. Newman, who believed in actors having a collaborative spirit on sets, explained that the memo was justifiable and any problems Hitchcock may have had were projections on him due to frustrations with the script: "I think I could have hit it off better with Hitchcock if the script had been better. It was not a lack of communication or a lack of respect. The only thing that constantly stood in our way was the script."[4]

But Newman's other sin (along with an irksome habit of constantly chewing gum, which became an annoyance to Hitchcock) was the fact that he was a method actor, like previous frustrating leading men Montgomery Clift and Gregory Peck. On his general dislike of "method actors," Hitchcock quipped that they would constantly ask questions that he had no interest in answering. It was the actor whose job he thought it was to develop their own character motivations within the restrictions he gave them:

Method actors say, "I don't know what I might do there; I have to feel it." They're not very helpful in this business. They may be fine in the theater. But they're taught to improvise, which, to me, is very risky. "Well, I went to such and such a school, and I was told to improvise," and I said to him [Newman], "That's not improvising; that's writing."[5]

Paul Newman was a faithful student of that school of acting and could not be convinced to abandon his approach despite Hitchcock's insistence that it did not work for his style of filmmaking. Hitchcock told Truffaut:

I wasn't too happy with the way Paul Newman played it. As you know, he's a method actor, and he found it hard to just give me one of those neutral

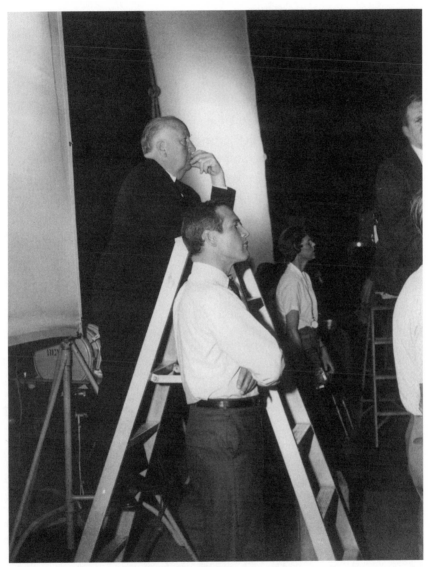

Hitchcock came to generally dislike method actor Paul Newman, whom he considered unprofessional, while filming *Torn Curtain* (1967). *Universal Pictures/ Photofest © Universal Pictures*

looks. I needed to cut from his point of view. Instead of simply looking toward Gromek's brother, toward the knife or the sausage, he played the scene in the "method" style, with emotion, and he was always turning away.[6]

In fact this critique of Newman may be the greatest flaw of *Torn Curtain*, the inability of Newman to even suggest he could be a traitor. He shows too much of his inner workings during the film, pursing his lips, mumbling his words, seeming to squirm during scenes when he should be composed. His desire for realism hurts the only suspense the film has and turns what should be a spy thriller into a humorless procedural.

Similarly, Newman was incapable of playing the dashing "young Cary Grant" Hitchcock wanted for the role, which as written should be a more dashing, James Bond-esque spy than hard-boiled detective, as Newman plays him. Even in perfectly fitted suits, Newman's lack of polish makes him appear remarkably casual, and it recalls the fact that Newman's biggest successes came playing gritty antiheroes rather than dashing romantics; not to mention that absence of chemistry he had with Julie Andrews whom he seemed at best apathetic toward.

Critics expressed their disappointment, most mentioning the miscasting of Andrews and Newman, such as Bosley Crowther, who wrote an especially negative piece on their performances:

> She [Lila Kedrova] is more inventive, more expressive in this one little bit [the farmhouse murder] than Mr. Newman or Miss Andrews are throughout the film. They seem to have no sense whatsoever of the fancifulness of the piece, no ability or willingness to play it strictly with tongue in cheek. Mr. Newman goes at it really as though he meant to pick a German scientist's brain, and Miss Andrews is like an English nanny who means to see that no harm comes to him. The scene of the two under covers at the beginning of the film—a scene as harmless as it is now notorious, is a fraud. They never get that close again.[7]

During the promotional tour, Newman claimed Hitchcock behaved as a total gentleman on set, never suggesting to them that they were doing a poor job. Hitchcock, who came close to dismissing the film completely, publicly placed some of the film's problems on having to cast Andrews and Newman, who he felt lacked chemistry and were overpaid, and claimed Andrews lacked the grace and elegance of his best leading ladies. Hitchcock's decision to discuss their miscasting publicly did not sit well with his stars who found it ungentlemanly of him, considering they were cast specifically to bring their loyal audiences into theaters, which they did. Hitchcock had previously insisted that while not one for praise, he would speak up to correct a performance; a courtesy Newman and Andrews felt had not been afforded them by the noticeably frustrated director.

28

Family Plot

By the time Hitchcock announced plans to direct the film *Family Plot*, it was apparent that matching or even living up to the success he had previously experienced in the heyday of the studio system would be close to impossible. *Marnie* and *Torn Curtain* were both considerable disappointments to Hitchcock, and while *The Birds* pleased many audiences, the lackluster reviewers focused on the fact that the outlandish premise was limited by the underwritten characters and uninspired acting. *Psycho* would remain his final classic, and even that had not been a favorite among critics when initially released.

However, this was also a time of transition in Hollywood. The studio system that kept stars under restrictive contracts (either for a specific number of years or dictating a number of pictures) was nearly at an end. The stars were now free agents, going from one project to the other, and those directors able to make films with little risk to the studios were given far more editorial control over their films. Hitchcock had been in this desirable position for some time, but even he had been forced to give up control (including over casting) by the time he returned from his time filming in Europe. Hitchcock essentially returned as the grandfather to a new Hollywood, still respected but somewhat out of step.

Torn Curtain, and the obligation to hire box-office stars, had turned Hitchcock away from the stars system that once excited him. When making *Topaz* (his last film for Universal and one of Hitchcock's least known films), he refused to use Hollywood stars and selected an international ensemble, actors who were reasonably well known in their countries but far from box-office names. Along with the star of *The Trouble with Harry*, John Forsythe, Hitchcock hired one of the ingénues of the French New Wave (of which he was also a pioneer), Claude Jade. Truffaut noted that Jade, the actress who a year earlier had starred in his film *Stolen Kisses*, was reminiscent of Hitchcock's Grace Kelly.[1] She was far from a leading lady, in France or Hollywood, and Hitchcock had to argue with the studio to cast her. Ironically, while critics had been noticeably frustrated with the miscasting of Paul Newman and Julie Andrews, Hitchcock's decision to use no stars in *Topaz* was also a disappointment to critics. They found Hitchcock's innovated and stylish use of stars to be part of the pleasure in watching his films.

Although Hitchcock considered it a benefit to no longer have to concern himself with the wishes and temperaments of stars, Truffaut, one of his greatest and most loyal protégés, was in agreement with critics who felt Hitchcock films were better when featuring stars, writing:

> Hitchcock needed them [stars] more than other directors because his cinema was based not on characters but on situations. He hated useless scenes, the kind that can easily be dropped during the editing because they do not serve to move the action forward. He was not a man for digressions, or for those petty details that "ring true." In his films, one never sees an actor attempt a superfluous gesture, like smoothing down his hair or sneezing. If the actor is framed in a full shot, his silhouette must be impeccable; if he is filmed from the waist up, his hands will not appear at the bottom of the frame. Because of this, the life-like impact of a Hitchcock movie is based on a personality previously acquired by the actor in films by other directors. James Stewart brought the warmth of a John Ford to Hitchcock films, and Cary Grant brings to them the charm he displays in his comedies on marital infidelity.[2]

But instead of returning to Hollywood to make another picture, Hitchcock chose to cast from a pool of respected English actors for his next film, *Frenzy*. Jon Finch and Alec McCowen were best known as theater actors, and Barry Foster was known primarily for his work in television. In many ways, *Frenzy* mixes the murder story of *Psycho* and the classic wrong man scenario. However, without the star power of either film, the movie at times seems to embrace the explicit violence gaining popularity in the late 1960s and 1970s, when the antihero was key to a film's success. *Frenzy* was a moderate success when released (the thirty-third-highest grossing film of that year).

Hitchcock didn't return to Hollywood filmmaking until a decade after *Torn Curtain*, with the crime-comedy *Family Plot*, one of the few pure comedies in Hitchcock's filmography, like *Mr. and Mrs. Smith* or *The Trouble with Harry*. But unlike these other films, there was a contemporary-meta quality, which adds new energy to an old-fashioned premise. *North by Northwest* scribe Ernest Lehman had made his own step toward working in new Hollywood with the screenplay for Mike Nichols's *Who's Afraid of Virginia Woolf* and had even directed his adaptation of the Philip Roth youth-in-revolt novel *Portnoy's Complaint*. He was hired by Hitchcock to adapt Victor Canning's forgotten novel *The Rainbird Pattern* and asked not only to make it a suspense film in the style of *North by Northwest* but also to add an element of comedy.

Cinematically, the film would mix contemporary anti-stars as the heroes, with a parody of the classic Hitchcock characters. Initially, Hitchcock wanted to hire one of the two actors who were the definition of the antihero, Al Pacino or Jack Nicholson, but with their high price tags, he once again had to settle on lesser-known members of the new generation of actors; this time selecting Bruce Dern, whom he had directed previously in the flashback scene of *Marnie*. Comic actress Goldie Hawn was similarly considered for the heroine Blanche, as she was known as a star of throwback screwball comedies (such as *Cactus Flower* and *Butterflies Are Free*), but Hitchcock ended up casting theater actress Barbara Harris. But the two roles he had the greatest difficulties casting were characters that were parodies of iconic characters: villain Arthur Adamson and iconic cool blonde Fran.

Hitchcock initially selected character actor William Devane for the role of Adamson, the charming jewel thief willing to murder to keep the con up. Hitchcock wanted the role to not only be a reminder of some of the clever villains of his classic films (Joseph Cotton in *Shadow of a Doubt*, Ray Milland in *Dial M for Murder*, Otto Kruger in *Saboteur*), but also pay homage to William Powell's iconic personality. Devane was known as a talented impressionist as well as an actor, and Hitchcock was well aware of an impression he had mastered of Powell's signature style. Yet Devane was unavailable and Hitchcock would have to settle for another.

After Burt Reynolds and Roy Scheider were suggested and rejected, Hitchcock agreed to cast television actor Roy Thinnes, known for the series *The*

The cast of *Family Plot* (1976) celebrating Hitchcock receiving a statue; pictured is Roy Thinnes, who was subsequently fired from the picture when William Devane became available to do the picture. *Universal Pictures/Photofest © Universal Pictures*

Invaders. Thinnes was a talented actor, whose own style did resemble some of the iconic stars of the past, but he was not one to do true impressions. Despite filming several scenes with Thinnes, all of which were considered well acted, Hitchcock couldn't resist replacing him with first choice Devane when his schedule changed and he was suddenly available. Hitchcock unceremoniously fired Roy Thinnes and reshot scenes with William Devane at considerable expense.

If the character of Adamson was, as Hitchcock insisted, homage to the Powell persona, Devane is exceptional at capturing the sly, whip-smart quality and masters Powell's memorable voice. Yet, as an actor, it must have been frustrating for Devane to be cast in one of his first starring roles and be judged merely by how well he could impersonate another actor. Devane was skilled as an improviser and wanted to showcase more of his abilities and interpret the character himself. But Hitchcock would keep insisting, in his only directorial instruction, "More William Powell."

Karen Black was similarly frustrated with her role as Fran, which required her to play a comic version of the Hitchcock blonde, only wearing a blonde wig and stylish clothing when kidnapping and the rest of the time playing a bland, underwritten girlfriend. Originally intending the role for Faye Dunaway, who personally did capture the iconic cool blonde Hitchcock had created, Black is far quirkier than the role she was asked to play and seems miscast and unused. As so often happened when Hitchcock could not cast a specific actor in a role, he deemed the alternative as a B version, which Devane and Black both felt they had been deemed, and treated them with brisk, impersonal instructions.[3]

Hitchcock gave blunt, cold instructions to character actors Karen Black and William Devane (pictured) while filming *Family Plot* (1976), but played favorites with Barbara Harris and Bruce Dern, whom he let improvise and add to their characters. *Universal Pictures/Photofest © Universal Pictures*

His disinterest in developing the performances of his villains beyond mere superficial impressions was not the way he approached his hero couple, who were playing characters very different from any other Hitchcock couple. By the mid-1970s, the antiheroes were king, and there was a growing trend of preferring unique and unprepossessing character actors in leading roles. Rather than take the old-fashioned approach, Hitchcock embraced this new style and cast two unlikely leads, Barbara Harris and Bruce Dern. And rather than give strict directions to mold their performance, he stepped back to allow his leads to bring their own spirit to the roles. All Hitchcock asked of them was that they keep him entertained.

At the time, Dern was known for his motorcycle B movies (*Bloody Mama, The Cycle Savages,* and *The Wild Angels*), many guest appearances on television, and murdering John Wayne in *The Cowboys.* His attempts to play lighter roles, such as the hippie botanist in *Silent Running* and a delusional beauty queen judge in *Smile,* did little business at the box office. But he had a habit of giving energetic and unexpected performances, as he did in *The Great Gatsby* as Tom Buchanan (which costarred Karen Black as Myrtle), pointing him out as the highpoint of the disappointing film.

It was a quality Hitchcock had seen in Dern when casting him in his television show in the episodes "Night Caller" and "Lonely Place," the latter of which was considered one of the high-water marks of *The Alfred Hitchcock Hour* for the performance of both Dern and Teresa Wright. It took twelve years for Dern to be cast in another Hitchcock project after *Marnie,* but the role was not only well suited to Dern, but elevated the position he currently held in Hollywood. Dern was a dependable working man in Hollywood but usually asked to play characters that were unhinged or hard. Even his performance in the applauded *The King of Marvin Gardens* played into that sense of mania. The character of George Lumley, the hero of *Family Plot,* is far from the typical Dern role, as he is funny, calm, and analytical. And Dern was given the remarkable honor of being permitted to perform the role as he saw fit. An honor rarely given to Hitchcock actors, it was not only offered to both Dern and Harris but encouraged.

With *Family Plot,* the characters of Lumley and Tyler were worth seeing only if Dern and Harris could bring something captivating to their role, which hadn't been seen in a Hitchcock film before. Dern claims Hitchcock referred to him as his golden calf (in reference to the comment that Hitchcock called his actors cattle). Of his work on the picture, Hitchcock told Patrick McGilligan, "Some of them [actors] are extremely efficient. They can take direction very easily. 'Slow down, speed up, make this point.' I have an actor like Bruce, and you see a tempo. You say, 'Speed it up there, and don't make that pause so long.'"[4]

Like Bruce Dern, Barbara Harris was also a Midwesterner (both Chicagoans) and theater trained. She brought far more of her unique personality to her roles than any of Hitchcock's recent leading ladies. Harris was a mysterious star, rarely offering interviews but the subject of many profiles by theater critics, enchanted by her fearless sense of humor, capable of disarming and challenging any man. Often mentioned as reminding critics of Hitchcock actress Shirley MacLaine[5] due to her quirky sense of self and musical comedy talents, Lerner and Rogers were so delighted by the actress they wrote their first musical collaboration specifically for her to star in on Broadway.

Harris, like Dern, was also not a film star at the time, though wanted for many starring roles, which she turned down. Her first film, *A Thousand Clowns*, was a departure for the Second City girl, playing opposite Jason Robards in the warmhearted melodrama in the spirit of *The Champ* and *Kramer vs Kramer*. She also had her signature daffy roles in odd comedies such as *Oh Dad, Poor Dad, Mamma's Hung You in the Closet and I'm Feelin' So Sad* (a darker play on *The Trouble with Harry* plot) and *Who Is Harry Kellerman and Why Is He Saying Those Terrible Things About Me?* (with Dustin Hoffman). But when she was asked to appear in *Family Plot*, she was best known for playing opposite Walter Matthau in *Plaza Suite* and her go-for-broke performance as a country singer in *Nashville*, one of the most liberated female performances of the 1970s. Hitchcock approached the initially resistant actress and spent considerable time attempting to convince her to take the role of Blanche.

As if commenting on claims that Hitchcock was a misogynist who used women to fulfill masculine fantasies, he not only hired a fiercely independent female lead, but one very vocal as a feminist and supporter of women's liberation. Two years before her casting in *Family Plot*, Harris told the *New York Times* of her support of the cause, explaining:

> Women's lib is a fabulous thing, although it's probably broken up a lot of marriages. I always assumed my needs were very secondary; I acquiesced to a kind

of servitude. Men are spoiled by women, beginning with their mothers. That's not saying a lot of women aren't spoiled too. But that's an act of retarding, of making a woman a passive princess. It puts a woman in a kind of prison, in a role in which the man is the manipulator. Now I consider myself of equal value. I don't walk around in Levis and boots and I haven't stopped using a deodorant. I'm not into the reverse image.[6]

The pairing of Harris and Dern as George and Blanche is the unlikely bookend to the domestic thrillers of *The Man Who Knew Too Much* and *North by Northwest*. From unhappy nuclear family to equal cohabitants, George and Blanche are the unexpected, yet truly in love romantic couple in this Hitchcock film. To see a character like George cooking for his girlfriend, as she makes plans for their next con, is delightful because it was written by the team behind *North by Northwest*.

Critics were equally delighted by what they saw from Harris and Dern's performance:

As performed by Miss Harris and Mr. Dern, they are two of the most appealing would-be rascals that Hitchcock has ever given us. For that matter, so are Adamson and Fran (she has no last name, which leaves her matrimonial state in old world, gentlemanly doubt). Though Adamson is portrayed as being perfectly winging to murder, when cornered, he never succeeds, and Fran is the kind of kidnapper who prepares gourmet meals for her involuntary guests.[7]

In fact while the majority of critical praise was offered to Dern and Harris, the performances were generally considered the bright spot of Hitchcock's last, lightweight feature. Edward L. Blank wrote:

Miss Harris impresses as the slightly daffy heroine as does Devane as the debonair heavy. Miss Black, billed first, has comparatively little to do. The cast's main delight is Dern, usually cast as a villain or as a general unsympathetic leading man. He's different here as the put-upon boyfriend bearing white sox and a pipe. Quite a switch from Hitchcock's normally urbane leading men.[8]

Similarly, Norman Dresser wrote:

Dern is immensely likable as a Los Angeles cabbie, an absurd but appealing would-be actor who is at once vague, tender, and tough. Miss Harris is utterly captivating as a phony psychic who cons with great charms. Hitchcock always has been great in creating villains of great resourcefulness and raffishness. Devane as Adamson, the jeweler who adds to his stock with gems paid as ransom, is suave and sinister. Ms. Black is perfect as his confederate who doesn't mind a career of crime but finally balks at murder.[9]

Ironically, Dane Lanken wrote high praise for the actors in reference to Hitchcock's infamous "actors are cattle" statements, writing, "The performances are perfect. They say Hitchcock says actors are cattle and he only needs them to work out the mechanics of his story. But for whatever purpose, Hitchcock gets his stars to deliver memorable roles. The actors are, after all, all he has to make us believe enough of some yarn long enough so that we'll swallow the suspense."[10]

Conclusion:
Hitchcock's Influence

In February of 1973, the *Washington Post* published an editorial titled, "Director Hitchcock Is Really Star of His Own Films." It was in the midst of promoting *Frenzy*, a starless feature with all the cinematic elements of a Hitchcock film, but not on the inspired casting choices that had made Hitchcock's work so thrilling.[1] The critics who claimed part of the allure of Hitchcock movies was to see the top stars of their time in new and provocative ways were dismissed by a director no longer interested in discussing how he would use a star. Hitchcock's contempt for actors was a gradual and puzzling change that occurred during the trajectory of his career, which seemed to correlate to the rise of his own notoriety, when the greatest star of a Hitchcock movie was Hitchcock the man. As his status rose, his willingness to collaborate decreased.

By 1973, Hitchcock was as close to worshipped as any director could be, the symbol of auteurs theory, the belief that a film is first and foremost a reflection of the director's vision and the best work seeks to show that personal creative vision to the screen without interference. Hitchcock's first protégé, François Truffaut, believed and spread this belief in his writings for French publications (such as *Cashiers du Cinema*) and in his own work, many paying direct and indirect homage to his mentor. Truffaut noted, however, that despite the brilliance of Hitchcock, he may have been wrong for dismissing stars' vital aspects to his film's success, as he wrote in the epilogue of his book of interviews, "Hitchcock needed them [stars] more than other directors because his cinema was based not on characters but on situations."[2]

Hitchcock utilization of the star system was precise, applying a star's persona to elevate the character development he otherwise would not have had time to establish on his own, and showed the brilliance of Hitchcock's casting when thoughtful and provocative. The casting of Cary Grant or James Stewart brings a wealth of historical and cultural knowledge that would not have occurred with unknown stars in the same roles. One only needs to look at Robert Cummings's character in *Saboteur* or Rod Taylor in *The Birds* to see how a character can seem shallow because the minimal character development is not fleshed out through the actor's history with the audience and established persona.

It is no wonder that the performers who were unknowns when Hitchcock "discovered" them were also in roles that offered more backstory and depth than those which used established stars. Joan Fontaine's characters in *Rebecca* and *Suspicion* would establish the Joan Fontaine persona for the remainder of her career, as Shirley MacLaine's performance in *The Trouble with Harry* hinted at the character she would be capable of playing in *The Apartment* or *Some Came Running*. He found the glamour in Grace Kelly, Kim Novak, and Eva Marie Saint, and the dark side of former good guys like Jimmy Stewart, Cary Grant, and Anthony Perkins.

Christopher Bray, the author of Sean Connery's biography, noted that even more than the technological innovations Hitchcock made in cinema, it was casting that was Hitchcock's "lasting contribution to the craft of movies."

> No director, it seems fair to say, has ever been quite so alert to the reef of meanings the mere presence of a given actor can bring to a given picture. Anyone going to see *Notorious* in expectation of another Cary Grant light comedy, for instance, was in for a shock. And though it was Anthony Mann who, in a series of triumphantly tragic westerns first exposed the neurotic sociopath simmering beneath the seemingly relaxed hick of so many Jimmy Stewart characters, it was Hitchcock who refined and polished this image of degradation by bringing the character up-to-date in the Eisenhower years of post-Freudian America. No movie subverts the Stewart persona of down-to-earth self-possession like Hitchcock's *Vertigo*. A couple of years later, Hitchcock took the technique even further, casting Anthony "apple-pie/boy-next door" Perkins as the momma-fixated serial killer in *Psycho*.[3]

But did his contributions elevate casting, or was he ultimately one of the individuals to destroy the star system? By 1960, claims were made that Hitchcock had "proved" with the casting of *Psycho* that one doesn't need big names to sell a movie. While it was true that the younger cast of *Psycho* was far from the name value of his previous two films, *Psycho* was not cast with unknowns. If Marion had been played by an unknown, the press and audience would have never been shocked by the decision to "kill off their star" halfway through the movie. Janet Leigh was a star, and to kill her throughout the movie was shocking because she was a star.

The difference with *Psycho* and *The Birds* was the fact that while we have a leading character, we have none of the alliance or trust in Hitchcock that he would not do the very same to the character of Melanie. She was not a star that the audience would latch onto, and as introduced as having some value to the story (which is never paid off), Suzanne Pleshette could have just as easily become the lead, or Melanie could have been killed at the film's conclusion.

Part of the downfall in the provocative casting Hitchcock was able to utilize was the growing influence of casting departments. As casting directing became a job in the 1950s and 1960s, there was a stronger push toward performance rather than personality. This isn't to claim one is mutually exclusive to the other. No one would deny that a majority of Hitchcock's biggest stars were also some of the best actors of their generation. But they and the public had an awareness and appreciation of the persona they brought to films. The casting of personalities in such roles by the time casting director was king was considered passé and part of the outdated studio system.

New actors were given opportunities to emerge as stars, but with that came a new shift in power. Not only were younger directors looking to cast from this pool of talent, but actors were also testing their own power. Young actors and actresses were buying rights to films they wished to produce, writing their own scripts, and even directing. Men like Dustin Hoffman, Paul Newman, and Robert Redford were all finding properties that they not only felt they could play, but offered new acting opportunities. To play into a marketed image was superficial and anti-film-as-art.

The performances in new Hollywood may have offered audiences better acting or richer performances, but it also robbed audiences and directors of the chance to use persona, with the exception of comedians and action stars. Action heroes (Arnold Schwarzenegger, Bruce Willis, Mel Gibson, Sylvester

Stallone, Tom Cruise) were marketed for the personality and charisma they brought to action scenes. Likewise, comedians (Bill Murray, Chevy Chase, Gene Wilder, John Candy, Steve Martin) would establish a type through which they could build loose story structure around their comic personalities. One only needs to watch the "Hitchcock-inspired thriller" *The Spanish Prisoner* (1997) to see an example of how the "Steve Martin" persona is utilized the same way the James Mason and Herbert Marshall images were used to add suspense for the "irresponsible audience" Hitchcock had mentioned.

We certainly still have stars—George Clooney, Brad Pitt, Leonardo DiCaprio, Johnny Depp—but most of these stars' personas are vague. All buy properties to their own films, produce and hire big-name directors, and cast themselves in desirable roles. It is part of the financial reality of global Hollywood. However, it is becoming rare for Hollywood films to suggest something evocative in casting choices.

There are, as you may note, even fewer women who can be considered true stars, but unlike male stars, their film work tends to, like Hitchcock's great male stars, appeal to the personality of the actress put forth. A Julia Roberts or Sandra Bullock vehicle usually embraces or has comment on their golden girl status, with their other films (usually dramas) attempting to avoid connection to their persona. A character performed by Diane Keaton usually allows her to play "a version" of her public image (and has since *Annie Hall*). However, there are far less of these actresses (and far less longevity for these actresses to be considered movie stars). The fact that the most recognized actress in the history of screen acting, Meryl Streep, actively avoided creating a strong "persona" shows the dramatic difference in the industry, considering the second most honored actress, Katharine Hepburn, had one of the strongest star images in Hollywood history.

However, the influence of Hitchcock and the way he cast films will always be felt because of the imprint it had on his stars. He gave iconic images of movie stars that are burned into our collective memory of popular culture. And however long that Hitchcock's films remain relevant, an impression of these stars will remain strong and ever present.

Notes

INTRODUCTION

1. Digby Diehl, "Q&A Alfred Hitchcock," *Los Angeles Times*, June 25, 1972, W20.

2. Walter Raubicheck and Walter Srebnick, *Scripting Hitchcock:* Psycho, The Birds, *and* Marnie (Urbana: University of Illinois Press, 2011), 2.

3. Danvers J. Williams, "What I'd Do to the Stars," *Film Weekly*, March 4, 1939, 12–13.

4. François Truffaut, Alfred Hitchcock, and Helen G. Scott, *Hitchcock* (Paris: Ramsay, 1983), 140.

5. Truffaut, Hitchcock, and Scott, *Hitchcock*, 92.

6. Truffaut, Hitchcock, and Scott, *Hitchcock*, 94.

CHAPTER 1

1. François Truffaut, Alfred Hitchcock, and Helen G. Scott, *Hitchcock* (New York: Simon & Schuster, 1985), 132.

2. "Selznick Interview: *Rebecca*: A Tribute to Producer's Ingenuity" (*Rebecca* film file, New York Public Library of the Performing Arts at Lincoln Center).

3. Truffaut, Hitchcock, and Scott, *Hitchcock*, 91.

4. "Selznick Interview."

5. Truffaut, Hitchcock, and Scott, *Hitchcock*, 140.

6. Untitled newspaper blurb (*Rebecca* film file, New York Public Library of the Performing Arts at Lincoln Center).

7. Donald Spoto, *Spellbound by Beauty: Alfred Hitchcock and His Leading Ladies* (New York: Harmony Books, 2008), 91.

8. Spoto, *Spellbound*, 91.

9. "How Joan Fontaine Found Her New Personality," unknown fan magazine (Joan Fontaine file, New York Public Library of the Performing Arts at Lincoln Center).

10. Spoto, *Spellbound*, 62.

11. "Selznick Interview."

12. Spoto, *Spellbound*, 64–65.

13. Joan Fontaine, *No Bed of Roses* (New York: Morrow, 1978).

14. Truffaut, Hitchcock, and Scott, *Hitchcock*, 140.

15. Spoto, *Spellbound*, 94.

16. Archer Winsten, "*Rebecca* on Screen at the Music Hall," *New York Post* (*Rebecca* film file, New York Public Library of the Performing Arts at Lincoln Center).

17. David Platt, "*Rebecca* Is Treat for Mystery Film Lovers," *Daily Worker*, February 5, 1940.

18. Review of *Rebecca* (*Rebecca* film file, New York Public Library of the Performing Arts at Lincoln Center).

19. "Selznick Interview."

20. Winsten, "*Rebecca* on Screen."

21. Review of *Rebecca*.

22. Truffaut, Hitchcock, and Scott, *Hitchcock*, 74.

22. Review of *Rebecca*.

23. Review of *Rebecca*.

CHAPTER 2

1. Donald Spoto, *Spellbound by Beauty: Alfred Hitchcock and His Leading Ladies* (New York: Harmony Books, 2008), 100.

2. Spoto, *Spellbound*, 67.

3. François Truffaut, Alfred Hitchcock, and Helen G. Scott, *Hitchcock* (New York: Simon & Schuster, 1985), 133.

4. "Kobal People Will Talk" (Joel McCrea file, New York Public Library of the Performing Arts at Lincoln Center).

5. Judson Hand, "Hollywood's Lovable Cad," *Daily News on Books*, November 11, 1979, 2.

6. *Picturegoer Magazine*, 1937 (Herbert Marshall file, New York Public Library of the Performing Arts at Lincoln Center).

7. Peter B. Flint, "Joel McCrea, Actor, Dies at 84: A Casual, Amiable Leading Man," *The New York Times*, October 21, 1990, 38.

CHAPTER 3

1. Donald Spoto, *Spellbound by Beauty: Alfred Hitchcock and His Leading Ladies* (New York: Harmony Books, 2008), 102.

2. François Truffaut, Alfred Hitchcock, and Helen G. Scott, *Hitchcock* (New York: Simon & Schuster, 1985), 139.

3. Truffaut, Hitchcock, and Scott, *Hitchcock*, 92.

4. Truffaut, Hitchcock, and Scott, *Hitchcock*, 92.

5. "Women Are a Nuisance," *Film Weekly*, September 20, 1935, 10.

6. Hubert Cole, "She Nearly Died Laughing," *Picturegoer and Film Weekly*, December 23, 1939.

7. Spoto, *Spellbound*, 102.

8. "Comedy Needs Serious Touch, Says Hitchcock," *Washington Post*, October 20, 1940, A3.

9. "Comedy Needs Serious Touch."

10. Truffaut, Hitchcock, and Scott, *Hitchcock*, 140.

11. Truffaut, Hitchcock, and Scott, *Hitchcock*, 140.

CHAPTER 4

1. "Surprise: Nigel Bruce Prefers to be Typed in Roxy Picture" (Nigel Bruce file, New York Public Library of the Performing Arts at Lincoln Center).

2. "Crime Doesn't Pay," *Film Weekly*, April 30, 1938, 9.

3. Charles Higham and Roy Moseley, *Cary Grant: The Lonely Heart* (San Diego: Harcourt Brace Jovanovich, 1989), 124.

4. Untitled film review of *Suspicion*, *Atlantic Monthly* (*Suspicion* film file, New York Public Library of the Performing Arts at Lincoln Center).

5. Richard Maltby, *Hollywood Cinema*, 2nd edition (Oxford: Blackwell Publishing, 2003), 386.

6. François Truffaut, Alfred Hitchcock, and Helen G. Scott, *Hitchcock* (New York: Simon & Schuster, 1985), 310–11.

7. Higham and Moseley, *Cary Grant*, 65.

8. Truffaut, Hitchcock, and Scott, *Hitchcock*, 142.

9. "*Suspicion* at Keith Theatre" (*Suspicion* film file, New York Public Library of the Performing Arts at Lincoln Center).

CHAPTER 5

1. "Director's Touches are Numerous," *Schenectady Gazette*, May 25, 1942, 3.

2. François Truffaut, Alfred Hitchcock, and Helen G. Scott, *Hitchcock* (New York: Simon & Schuster, 1985), 145.

3. Truffaut, Hitchcock, and Scott, *Hitchcock*, 146.

4. Truffaut, Hitchcock, and Scott, *Hitchcock*, 146.

5. Truffaut, Hitchcock, and Scott, *Hitchcock*, 147.

6. Archer Winsten, "Hitchcock's *Saboteur* at Radio City Music Hall," *New York Post*, May 3, 1942, 44.

7. Nelson B. Bell, "Hitchcock Finds Drama in Terror of the Times," *Washington Post*, 1942.

CHAPTER 6

1. "What I'd Do to the Stars," *Film Weekly*, March 4, 1939, 12–13.

2. "Crime Doesn't Pay," *Film Weekly*, April 30, 1938, 9.

3. Digby Diehl, "Q&A Alfred Hitchcock," *Los Angeles Times*, June 25, 1972, W20.

4. "*Shadow of a Doubt* a Gripping Film" (*Shadow of a Doubt* film file, New York Public Library of the Performing Arts at Lincoln Center).

5. Alton Cook, "*Shadow of a Doubt* Gives Full Scope to Hitchcock Talent" (*Shadow of a Doubt* film file, New York Public Library of the Performing Arts at Lincoln Center).

6. "*Shadow of a Doubt* Outstanding" (*Shadow of a Doubt* film file, New York Public Library of the Performing Arts at Lincoln Center).

7. Donald Spoto, *Spellbound by Beauty: Alfred Hitchcock and His Leading Ladies* (New York: Harmony Books, 2008), 118.

8. "*Shadow of a Doubt* Outstanding."

9. Untitled review (*Shadow of a Doubt* film file, New York Public Library of the Performing Arts at Lincoln Center).

10. Stephen Talty, "A Genius for Decency," *Film Comment*, October 1990, 18–19.

11. Spoto, *Spellbound*, 118–19.

12. Paul Rosenfield, "Teresa Wright: Enter Teacher, Stage Left," *Los Angeles Times*, January 18, 1982, 6.

13. Ward Morehouse, "Teresa Wright Enchants without Frills" (Teresa Wright file, New York Public Library of the Performing Arts at Lincoln Center).

14. Julia McCarthy, "Serene Tess Wright Astounds Hollywood" (Teresa Wright file, New York Public Library of the Performing Arts at Lincoln Center).

15. "Wright Was Fired for Refusing to Promote Her Movie in New York," *New York Herald Tribune* (Teresa Wright file, New York Public Library of the Performing Arts at Lincoln Center).

16. "Teresa Wright No Sweater, Bathing Roles" (Teresa Wright file, New York Public Library of the Performing Arts at Lincoln Center).

17. François Truffaut, Alfred Hitchcock, and Helen G. Scott, *Hitchcock* (New York: Simon & Schuster, 1985), 154–55.

18. Teresa Wright's interview, *Beyond Doubt: The Making of Hitchcock's Favorite Film*, video documentary, 2000.

19. "How I Choose My Heroines," *Who's Who in Filmland*, 1931, xxi–xxiii.

CHAPTER 7

1. Paul Jones, "Thrills, Suspense Mark *Lifeboat* Fox Feature," *Atlanta Constitution*, February 2, 1944, 13.

2. Abe Hill, "*Lifeboat* Called Good Movie Far by Our Reviewer, Abe Hill," *New York Amsterdam News*, January 29, 1944, 11A.

3. Hedda Hopper, "Manning the Lifeboat," *Washington Post*, December 16, 1943, 19.

CHAPTER 8

1. Robin Wood, "Star and Auteur: Films with Bergman," *Hitchcock's Films Revisited* (New York: Columbia University Press, 2002), 311–12.

2. François Truffaut and Alfred Hitchcock, *Hitchcock* (New York: Simon & Schuster, 1967), 167.

3. Gordon Gow, "Gregory Peck in an Interview with Gordon Gow," *Films and Filming*, June 1974, 32.

4. Gow, "Gregory Peck," 32.

5. Film review (*Spellbound* film file, New York Public Library of the Performing Arts at Lincoln Center).

6. Edwin Schallert, "*Spellbound* Intrigues as Popular Film Event," *Los Angeles Times*, November 10, 1945, A5.

CHAPTER 9

1. "Cary Grant, Ingrid Bergman in *Notorious* at Keith's," *Christian Science Monitor*, September 19, 1946, 5.

2. "New Films Reviewed," *The Sydney Morning Herald*, June 16, 1947, 3.

3. Charles Higham and Roy Moseley, *Cary Grant: The Lonely Heart* (San Diego: Harcourt Brace Jovanovich, 1989), 65.

4. Andrew Britton, "Cary Grant: The Comedy of Male Desire," *Cineaction*, 1987, 7.

5. Dennis Logue, "Hitchcock's 'Notorious' Direction of Film Proves Successful," *Cavalier Daily*, September 25, 1986, 10.

6. "Cary Grant, Ingrid Bergman in *Notorious* at Keith's."

7. François Truffaut, Alfred Hitchcock, and Helen G. Scott, *Hitchcock* (New York: Simon & Schuster, 1985), 261–62.

8. Andre D. Sennwald, "That Invisible Actor," *New York Times*, September 3, 1933.

9. Donald Spoto, *Spellbound by Beauty: Alfred Hitchcock and His Leading Ladies* (New York: Harmony Books, 2008), 149.

10. Nancy Nelson and Cary Grant, *Evenings with Cary Grant: Recollections in His Own Words and By Those Who Knew Him Best* (New York: W. Morrow, 1991), 151.

CHAPTER 10

1. François Truffaut, Alfred Hitchcock, and Helen G. Scott, *Hitchcock* (New York: Simon & Schuster, 1985), 174.

2. Truffaut, Hitchcock, and Scott, *Hitchcock*, 173.

3. Audio Hitchcock interview with Peter Bogdanovich (2008 DVD release of *The Paradine Case*), Twentieth Century Fox Home Entertainment.

4. Truffaut, Hitchcock, and Scott, *Hitchcock*, 177.

5. Audio Hitchcock interview with Peter Bogdanovich.

6. Truffaut, Hitchcock, and Scott, *Hitchcock*, 174.

7. Donald Spoto, *Spellbound by Beauty: Alfred Hitchcock and His Leading Ladies* (New York: Harmony Books, 2008), 163–65.

8. Audio Hitchcock interview with Peter Bogdanovich.

9. Truffaut, Hitchcock, and Scott, *Hitchcock*, 173.

10. Truffaut, Hitchcock, and Scott, *Hitchcock*, 170–71.

11. "Review: *The Paradine Case*," *Variety*, December 31, 1946, online edition: http://variety.com/1946/film/reviews/the-paradine-case-1200414964/#.

12. "Cinema," *Time Magazine*, January 12, 1948, online edition: http://content.time .com/time/magazine/article/0,9171,794154,00.html.

CHAPTER 11

1. "*Rope*," *Films and Filming*, October 1973, B11.

2. Robert L. Pela, "Goldenboy," *The Advocate*, August 20, 1996, 69–71.

3. *North Star* press notes, RKO Radio Pictures publicity materials.

4. "Every Star Should Get Married" (Farley Granger file, New York Public Library of the Performing Arts at Lincoln Center).

5. Judy Richheimer, "Farley Granger: Star of Talley and Son at Circle Repertory," *West Side (NY) Shopper*, November 23–29, 1985, 17.

6. "Out into the World," *Films and Filming*, October 1973, 16.

7. "Out into the World," 16.

8. Laurent Bouzereau, Rope *Unleashed* (documentary, 2001), interview with Arthur Laurents.

9. "Out into the World," 17.

10. Arthur Laurents, *Original Story By: A Memoir of Broadway and Hollywood* (New York: Knopf, 2000), 127.

11. Donald Dewey, *James Stewart: A Biography* (Atlanta: Turner Publications, 1996), 279.

12. Dewey, *James Stewart*, 280.

13. Scott Vernon, "Alfred Hitchcock Skips Mysteries for Travel Books," *Boston Globe*, April 3, 1954.

14. Vincent Canby, "*Rope*: A Stunt to Behold," *New York Times*, June 3, 1984.

15. Laurents, *Original Story By*, 131.

16. "*Rope*," B11.

17. "*Rope*," B11.

CHAPTER 12

1. Audio Hitchcock interview with Peter Bogdanovich (2008 DVD release of *The Paradine Case*), Twentieth Century Fox Home Entertainment.

2. François Truffaut, Alfred Hitchcock, and Helen G. Scott, *Hitchcock* (New York: Simon & Schuster, 1985), 185–86.

3. Truffaut, Hitchcock, and Scott, *Hitchcock*, 187.

4. Truffaut, Hitchcock, and Scott, *Hitchcock*, 187.

5. Edwin Shallert, "Comedy's No Chore for Michael Wilding: Actor to Portray One of His Few Serious Roles," *Los Angeles Times*, April 1, 1951, D3.

6. "New Films on View," *Cue*, September 10, 1949, 16.

7. Roy Kohler, "Hitchcock, Ingrid Team in *Under Capricorn*," *The Pittsburgh Press*, October 15, 1949, 4.

8. Russell Rhodes, "*Under Capricorn* is Music Hall Feature" (*Under Capricorn* film file, New York Public Library of the Performing Arts at Lincoln Center).

9. Ingrid Bergman, "Ingrid Bergman Cables Story of Technique Used in *Under Capricorn*," *Toledo Blade*, August 27, 1949, 15.

10. Truffaut, Hitchcock, and Scott, *Hitchcock*, 187.

11. Truffaut, Hitchcock, and Scott, *Hitchcock*, 189.

12. Robin Wood, *Hitchcock's Films Revisited* (New York: Columbia University Press, 2002), 321.

13. Charlotte Chandler, *It's Only a Movie: Alfred Hitchcock, A Personal Biography* (New York: Simon & Schuster, 2005), 137.

14. Truffaut, Hitchcock, and Scott, *Hitchcock*, 186.

CHAPTER 13

1. François Truffaut, Alfred Hitchcock, and Helen G. Scott, *Hitchcock* (New York: Simon & Schuster, 1985), 190–91.

2. Interview with Michael Wilding, July 11, 1979 (*Stage Fright* film file, New York Public Library of the Performing Arts at Lincoln Center).

3. Philip Scheuer, "Hitchcock Returns to Light Murder," *Los Angeles Times*, April 1, 1950, 14.

4. "Obituary: Michael Wilding," *Daily Variety*, December 9, 1979, 23.

CHAPTER 14

1. François Truffaut, Alfred Hitchcock, and Helen G. Scott, *Hitchcock* (New York: Simon & Schuster, 1985), 199.

2. Beverly Linet, *Star-Crossed: The Story of Robert Walker and Jennifer Jones* (New York: Putnam, 1986), 255.

3. Linet, *Star-Crossed*, 255.

4. "Obituary of Robert Walker," *Daily Variety*, August 25, 1951.

5. James Henaghan, "Robert Walker: Aside from a Few Annoying Habits, He's Simply a Nice Kid from Utah" (Robert Walker file, New York Public Library of the Performing Arts at Lincoln Center).

6. "Fated to Play Cute Boys" (Robert Walker file, New York Public Library of the Performing Arts at Lincoln Center).

7. Anthony Cassa, "Robert Walker: The Man Who Lost Himself," *Hollywood Studio Magazine*, February 1982.

8. "Robert Walker Well Again" (Robert Walker file, New York Public Library of the Performing Arts at Lincoln Center).

9. Hedda Hopper, "Walker Eager To Do Film with Hitchcock," *Los Angeles Times*, October 13, 1950, B10.

10. Bosley Crowther, "Dexterity in Void," *New York Times*, July 3, 1951, 65.

11. Truffaut, Hitchcock, and Scott, *Hitchcock*, 199.

12. Michael Ehrhardt, "Not Just a Pretty Face," *Village Voice*, March 22, 2007, 28.

13. Sidney Skolsky, "Hollywood Is My Beat," *New York Post*, July 15, 1951, M5.

CHAPTER 15

1. François Truffaut, Alfred Hitchcock, and Helen G. Scott, *Hitchcock* (New York: Simon & Schuster, 1985), 204.

2. Hedda Hopper, "Director Still Down on Downbeat Films: Lack of Elegance in Movies Distresses Alfred Hitchcock," *Los Angeles Times*, July 1, 1963, C8.

3. George Kingsley, "Forget the Mystery, Meet the Man—Montgomery Clift," *Photoplay*, December 1954.

4. Patricia Bosworth, *Montgomery Clift: A Biography* (New York: Harcourt Brace Jovanovich, 1978), 189–90.

5. Bosworth, *Montgomery Clift*, 189–90.

6. Bosworth, *Montgomery Clift*, 200–201.

7. Hedda Hopper, "Anne Baxter Selected for Hitchcock Movie," *Los Angeles Times*, August 9, 1952, 8.

8. Hedda Hopper, "Monty Clift to Star with Jennifer Jones," *Los Angeles Times*, October 6, 1952, B8.

9. Donald Spoto, *Spellbound by Beauty: Alfred Hitchcock and His Leading Ladies* (New York: Harmony Books, 2008), 198.

10. Truffaut, Hitchcock, and Scott, *Hitchcock*, 203.

11. Spoto, *Spellbound*, 199.

12. Spoto, *Spellbound*, 199.

13. "Karl Malden's Letter to the *New York Times* from William Fields" (Karl Malden file, New York Public Library of the Performing Arts at Lincoln Center).

14. "Montgomery Clift, The Movie Maverick," *New York Post*, July 15, 1966, 204.

15. Mae Tinee, "New Hitchcock Film Not Quite Up to His Best: *I Confess*," *Chicago Tribune*, March 23, 1953, B6.

16. "New Films," *Hartford Courant*, February 19, 1953, 11.

CHAPTER 16

1. Hedda, Hopper, "Looking at Hollywood: How Hitchcock Helped Shape Grace's Life," *Chicago Tribune*, July 15, 1959, B5.

2. Donald Spoto, *Spellbound by Beauty: Alfred Hitchcock and His Leading Ladies* (New York: Harmony Books, 2008), 203.

CHAPTER 17

1. Newspaper blurb announcing casting change of *On the Waterfront* (Eva Marie Saint file, New York Public Library of the Performing Arts at Lincoln Center).

2. "Princess Grace Role Went to a Second Regal Blonde," *Boston Globe*, April 14, 1963, A55.

CHAPTER 18

1. François Truffaut, Alfred Hitchcock, and Helen G. Scott, *Hitchcock* (New York: Simon & Schuster, 1985), 226.

2. Nancy Nelson and Cary Grant, *Evenings with Cary Grant: Recollections in His Own Words and By Those Who Knew Him Best* (New York: W. Morrow, 1991), 184.

3. Nelson and Grant, *Evenings with Cary Grant*, 124.

4. Truffaut, Hitchcock, and Scott, *Hitchcock*, 224.

CHAPTER 19

1. François Truffaut, Alfred Hitchcock, and Helen G. Scott, *Hitchcock* (New York: Simon & Schuster, 1985), 227.

2. Truffaut, Hitchcock, and Scott, *Hitchcock*, 224.

3. Marc Eliot, *Jimmy Stewart: A Biography* (New York: Harmony Books, 2006), 308.

4. Joan Mellen, *Big Bad Wolves: Masculinity in the American Film* (New York: Pantheon Books, 1977), 198–99.

5. Richard W. Nason, "Offbeat Success Saga," *New York Times*, May 24, 1959, X5.

6. Lydia Lane, "Shirley MacLaine Prefers Her Individuality to Film Glamour," *Los Angeles Times*, November 10, 1957, D10.

7. "Hitchcock's Understated View of Death," *The Listener*, 1989, 39.

8. Shirley MacLaine, *My Lucky Stars: A Hollywood Memoir* (New York: Bantam Books, 1995), 253.

9. Bosley Crowther, "Screen: 'The Trouble with Harry': Whimsical Film from Hitchcock at Paris," *New York Times*, October 18, 1955, 46.

10. Rod Nordell, "'The Trouble with Harry' at Paramount and Fenway," *Christian Science Monitor*, February 3, 1956, 5.

11. *"The Trouble with Harry*: He's Funny and Dead," *The Miami News*, January 5, 1956, 20.

CHAPTER 20

1. François Truffaut, Alfred Hitchcock, and Helen G. Scott, *Hitchcock* (New York: Simon & Schuster, 1985), 228.

2. Tom Santopietro, *Considering Doris Day* (New York: Thomas Dunne Books, 2007), 95.

3. Molly Haskell, *From Reverence to Rape: The Treatment of Women in the Movies*, 2nd edition (Chicago: University of Chicago Press, 1987), 64–65.

4. Santopietro, *Considering Doris Day*, 95.

5. Truffaut, Hitchcock, and Scott, *Hitchcock*, 254.

6. Truffaut, Hitchcock, and Scott, *Hitchcock*, 325.

CHAPTER 21

1. Philip K. Scheuer, "Hitchcock's *Wrong Man* Lifelike But Plodding," *Los Angeles Times*, January 24, 1957, C9.

2. "Film Review," December 6, 1959 (clipping located in Vera Miles clipping file, New York Public Library).

3. Bosley Crowther, *New York Times* (Vera Miles file, New York Public Library of the Performing Arts at Lincoln Center).

4. "Hollywood's Latest: Vera Miles Not To Be Photographed in Shorts," *Daily Defender*, May 14, 1957, 18.

5. "No Cheesecake Rule Stirs Suit by Movie Producers," *New York Herald Tribune* (Vera Miles file, New York Public Library of the Performing Arts at Lincoln Center).

6. Richard Freedman, "Psycho Actress Defends Hitchcock," *The Spokesman-Review*, July 25, 1983, 44.

7. Atra Baer, *Ladies Journal*, May 16, 1956.

8. François Truffaut, Alfred Hitchcock, and Helen G. Scott, *Hitchcock* (New York: Simon & Schuster, 1985), 379.

9. Robert Marks, "Vera Miles—Hitchcock's New Star," *McCall Magazine*, May 1957.

10. Hedda Hopper, "The Star with Both Feet on the Ground," *Boston Globe*, March 29, 1959, 6.

11. Steven Scheuer, "Vera Miles Won Fame Playing Psychotic Gals," *The Hartford Courant*, December 23, 1956, 6F.

12. *Life Magazine* profile of Vera Miles, 1959 (Museum of Modern Art files).

13. Hedda Hopper, "Vera Miles: Farmer's Daughter in Hollywood Blonde Graduate of Miss . . . ," *Chicago Daily Tribune*, March 1, 1959, H24.

14. Hedda Hopper, "Vera Miles' Screen Career Skyrockets," *Los Angeles Times*, September 15, 1956, B8.

15. Hopper, "Vera Miles: Farmer's Daughter," H24.

16. *Look Magazine*, August 7, 1956.

17. Freedman, "Psycho Actress Defends Hitchcock," 44.

CHAPTER 22

1. Donald Spoto, *Spellbound by Beauty: Alfred Hitchcock and His Leading Ladies* (New York: Harmony Books, 2008), 222–23.

2. "A Star Is Made," *Time Magazine*, July 29, 1957, 52.

3. "How Much Do You Know About Women," *Look Magazine*, May 13, 1955.

4. "Kim Novak," *US Magazine*, February 17, 1981.

5. "The Sex Symbol Who Said No," *Daily Telegraph*, April 14, 1997, 13.

6. Lawrence J. Quirk, *James Stewart: Behind the Scenes of a Wonderful Life* (New York: Applause Books, 1997), 240–42.

7. François Truffaut, Alfred Hitchcock, and Helen G. Scott, *Hitchcock* (New York: Simon & Schuster, 1985), 247–48.

8. Marjory Adams, "Alfred Hitchcock Now Says Actors Are Children: Not Cattle," *Boston Globe*, June 19, 1958, 11.

9. Adams, "Not Cattle," 11.

10. Truffaut, Hitchcock, and Scott, *Hitchcock*, 325.

11. Adams, "Not Cattle," 21.

12. Bosley Crowther, "*Vertigo*, Hitchcock's Latest: Melodrama, Arrives at the Capital," *New York Times*, May 29, 1958, 24.

13. Truffaut, Hitchcock, and Scott, *Hitchcock*, 248.

14. Adams, "Not Cattle," 11.

15. Jimmy Stewart, "Together on *Vertigo*: Hitchcock Best, Claims Stewart," *The Deseret News*, June 10, 1958, 5.

16. Walter Raubicheck and Walter Srebnick, *Scripting Hitchcock: Psycho, The Birds, and Marnie* (Urbana: University of Illinois Press, 2011), 7.

17. Starr Smith, *Jimmy Stewart: Bomber Pilot* (St. Paul, MN: Zenith Press, 2005), 265.

18. Smith, *Bomber Pilot*, 264–65.

19. Stewart, "Together on *Vertigo*," 5.

CHAPTER 23

1. Robin Wood, *Hitchcock's Films Revisited* (New York: Columbia University Press, 2002), 364–65.

2. Wood, *Hitchcock's Films Revisited*, 228.

3. Nancy Nelson and Cary Grant, *Evenings with Cary Grant: Recollections in His Own Words and By Those Who Knew Him Best* (New York: W. Morrow, 1991), 124.

4. Richard Griffith, "Eastern Critics Like *North by Northwest*," *Los Angeles Times*, September 1, 1959, 18.

5. Hedda Hopper, "Hitchcock Would Costar Liz," *Los Angeles Times*, July 17, 1958, C8.

6. Blurb announcing casting change, Eva Marie Saint Clipping File, NYPL (believed to be the review from the *Boston Globe*).

7. A. H. Weiler, "Hitchcock Takes Suspenseful Cook's Tour: *North by Northwest* Opens," *New York Times*, August 7, 1959, 28.

8. Greg Garrett, "Hitchcock's Women on Hitchcock," *Literature Film Quarterly* 27, no. 2, 278–89.

9. Interview with Eva Marie Saint, *Destination Hitchcock* (2000 documentary), Warner Home Video (2004 DVD release of *North by Northwest*).

10. Bruce Babington, *British Stars and Stardom: From Alma Taylor to Sean Connery* (Manchester: Manchester University Press, 2001), 118.

11. Babington, *British Stars*, 107.

CHAPTER 24

1. Philip K. Scheuer, "*Psycho* as Brilliant as It Is Disagreeable," *New York Times*, August 11, 1960, B9.

2. Leo Braudy, "Hitchcock, Truffaut, and the Irresponsible Audience," *Film Quarterly* 21, no. 4 (Summer 1968): 23–24.

3. Hedda Hopper, "Vera Miles: Farmer's Daughter in Hollywood Blonde Graduate of Miss . . . ," *Chicago Daily Tribune*, March 1, 1959, H24.

4. François Truffaut, Alfred Hitchcock, and Helen G. Scott, *Hitchcock* (New York: Simon & Schuster, 1985), 248.

5. Donald Spoto, *Spellbound by Beauty: Alfred Hitchcock and His Leading Ladies* (New York: Harmony Books, 2008), 222–23.

6. Richard Dyer and Paul McDonald, *Stars* (London: BFI Publications, 1998), 144.

7. "After Dark," November 1973 (John Gavin file, New York Public Library of the Performing Arts at Lincoln Center).

8. "$5,000,000 Gamble," *New York Mirror*, August 3, 1958 (John Gavin file, New York Public Library of the Performing Arts at Lincoln Center).

9. "Non-Neurotic Newcomer," *Look Magazine*, July 22, 1958, 65.

10. Sheila Graham, *North American Newspaper Alliance Newswire*, Museum of Modern Art Film Department.

11. Jess Zunzer, "Young Star Annoyed," *Cue Magazine*, November 17, 1956, 14.

12. "24 Year Old Copy of Cooper," *Life Magazine*, July 16, 1956, cover (and interior photo spread).

13. Laura Lane, "Little Boy: Tony Perkins," *Photoplay Magazine*, January 1957.

14. Bill Tusher, "That," *New York Daily News* (Anthony Perkins file, New York Public Library of the Performing Arts at Lincoln Center).

15. François Truffaut, *The Films in My Life* (New York: Simon & Schuster, 1978), 136.

16. Robert Philip Kolker, *Alfred Hitchcock's* Psycho: *A Casebook* (New York: Oxford University Press, 2004), 261.

17. Stephen Rebello, *Alfred Hitchcock and the Making of* Psycho (New York: Dembner Books, 1990), 59.

18. Truffaut, Hitchcock, and Scott, *Hitchcock*, 325.

CHAPTER 25

1. "Princess Grace Role Went to a Second Regal Blonde," *Boston Globe*, April 14, 1963, A55.

2. François Truffaut, Alfred Hitchcock, and Helen G. Scott, *Hitchcock* (New York: Simon & Schuster, 1985), 323.

3. Tony Lee Moral, *Hitchcock and the Making of* Marnie (Lanham, MD: Scarecrow Press, 2002), 83.

4. "Tippi Hedren: Can Hollywood Still Make a Star?," *Boston Globe*, December 8, 1963, B22.

5. Alfred Hitchcock, "Are Stars Necessary?," *Picturegoer*, December 16, 1933, 13.

6. "Tippi Hedren: Hitchcock's New Grace Kelly," *Look Magazine*, December 4, 1962.

7. *Newark Evening News*, October 27, 1968 (Rod Taylor, New York Public Library of the Performing Arts at Lincoln Center).

8. Vernon Scott, "'No Such Thing as TV Star': Hong Kong's Rod Taylor," *Telegraph New York*, December 13, 1960.

9. Truffaut, Hitchcock, and Scott, *Hitchcock*, 323.

10. Tony Lee Moral, *The Making of Hitchcock's* The Birds (Harpenden: Kamera Books, 2013), 64.

11. Moral, The Birds, 67.

12. Bosley Crowther, "Hitchcock's Feathered Fiends Are Chilling," *New York Times*, April 1, 1963.

13. Suzanne Pleshette file (New York Public Library of the Performing Arts at Lincoln Center).

14. Sidney Skolsky, "Tintypes . . . Suzanne Pleshette," *New York Post*, May 27, 1967.

15. James Gregory, "Exclusive Interview with Suzanne Pleshette," *Screen*, December 1964, 54.

16. Suzanne Pleshette file.

17. Moral, The Birds, 68.

18. Moral, The Birds, 68.

19. Howard Thompson, "Up the Ladder from Down Under," *New York Times*, July 19, 1964.

20. Moral, The Birds, 202.

21. Brendan Gill, "*The Birds*," *The New Yorker*, April 6, 1963.

22. Crowther, "Feathered Fiends."

23. Mark Sullivan, "Pecking Order Cultural Critic Camille Paglia Calls *The Birds* Tippi Hedren Hitchcock's Ultimate Heroine," *New York Times*, August 21, 1985, 25.

24. "Actors Like Children, Says Hitchcock, 'Birds' Director," *The Deseret News*, March 27, 1963, 55.

CHAPTER 26

1. Tony Lee Moral, *The Making of Hitchcock's* The Birds (Harpenden: Kamera Books, 2013), 202.

2. Bob Thomas, "Still Some Shock is Left," *Kentucky New Era*, November 29, 1963, 32.

3. Donald Spoto, *Spellbound by Beauty: Alfred Hitchcock and His Leading Ladies* (New York: Harmony Books, 2008), 325.

4. Joseph Stephano interview for "The Trouble with *Marnie*" (2000 documentary), Universal Studios Home Entertainment DVD *Marnie*, 2005.

5. Press notes for *Marnie*, Universal Pictures Publicity.

6. Eugene Archer, "Hitchcock's *Marnie*, With Tippi Hedren and Sean Connery," *New York Times*, July 23, 1964, 19.

7. Christopher Bray: *Sean Connery: A Biography* (New York: Pegasus Books, 2011), 99.

8. Evan Hunter interview for "The Trouble with *Marnie*" (2000 documentary), Universal Studios Home Entertainment DVD *Marnie*, 2005.

9. Jay Presson Allen interview for "The Trouble with *Marnie*" (2000 documentary), Universal Studios Home Entertainment DVD *Marnie*, 2005.

10. Presson Allen, interview.

11. Presson Allen, interview.

12. Bray, *Sean Connery*, 99–100.

13. Robin Wood, *Hitchcock's Films Revisited* (New York: Columbia University Press, 2002), 186.

14. Ray Oviatt, "*Marnie* Carries Clear Stamp from Hitchcock," *Toledo Blade*, August 19, 1964, 28.

15. Walter J. Carroll, "Film Reviews," *The Village Voice*, July 2, 1964.

16. Patrick Goldstein, "Ex-Secretary Recalls Memories of Hitchcock," *Los Angeles Times*, November 14, 1983, G1.

17. François Truffaut, Alfred Hitchcock, and Helen G. Scott, *Hitchcock* (New York: Simon & Schuster, 1985), 331.

18. Wanda Hale, "Hollywood Visitor: Tippi Plays It Cool," *Daily News*, July 13, 1964.

19. Arlene Dahl, "Diane Baker Doesn't Like to Use Make-Up: Let's Be Beautiful," *Chicago Tribune*, February 12, 1964, B4.

20. Tony Lee Moral, *Hitchcock and the Making of* Marnie (Lanham, MD: Scarecrow Press, 2002), 103.

21. Louis Chaplin, "With Hitchcock Pulling the Strings," *Christian Science Monitor*, July 27, 1964.

22. Truffaut, Hitchcock, and Scott, *Hitchcock*, 331.

23. Mike McGrady, "Poor Marnie; She's Got Problems," *Newsday*, July 23, 1964, 3C.

24. Press release for *Marnie*, Universal Studios.

25. Chaplin, "Pulling the Strings."

26. Chaplin, "Pulling the Strings."

CHAPTER 27

1. Press notes for *Marnie*, Universal Pictures Publicity.

2. Alfred Hitchcock, "Are Stars Necessary?," *Picturegoer*, December 16, 1933, 13.

3. Interview with Anthony Perkins (1986 program *Shock Corridor* for UK/Channel 4; conducted by Claude Ventura and Philippe Carnier).

4. Joe Morella and Edward Z. Epstein, *Paul & Joanne: A Biography of Paul Newman and Joanne Woodward* (New York: Delacorte, 1988), 112.

5. Patrick McGilligan, *Film Crazy* (New York: St. Martin's Press, 2000), 266.

6. François Truffaut, Alfred Hitchcock, and Helen G. Scott, *Hitchcock* (New York: Simon & Schuster, 1985), 313.

7. Bosley Crowther, "Screen: *Torn Curtain* at 3 Theaters: Sinatra Picture Also Begins Run," *New York Times*, July 28, 1966, 23.

CHAPTER 28

1. François Truffaut, Alfred Hitchcock, and Helen G. Scott, *Hitchcock* (New York: Simon & Schuster, 1985), 233.

2. Truffaut, Hitchcock, and Scott, *Hitchcock*, 325.

3. Patrick McGilligan, *Film Crazy: Interviews with Hollywood Legends* (New York: St. Martin's Press, 2000), 266.

4. McGilligan, *Film Crazy*, 266.

5. Malcolm L. Johnson, "Film: Hitchcock's *Family Plot*," *Hartford Courant*, April 18, 1976, 13F.

6. Mel Gussow, "*Family Plot*," *New York Times*, May 24, 1976, 52.

7. Vincent Canby, "Screen: Hitchcock's 'Family Plot' Bubbles Over," *New York Times*, April 10, 1976, 18.

8. Edward L. Blank, "Hitchcock Adds New Twist to Old Tricks in *Family Plot*," *Pittsburgh Press*, April 9, 1976, 5.

9. Norman Dresser, "*Family Plot* a Superb Thriller," *Toledo Blade*, April 12, 1976, 47.

10. Dane Lanken, "With a Full Dose of Suspense, *Family Plot* Good Hitchcock," *Montreal Gazette*, April 10, 1976, 17.

CONCLUSION

1. "Director Hitchcock Is Really Star of His Own Films," *Washington Post*, February 12, 1973.

2. François Truffaut, Alfred Hitchcock, and Helen G. Scott, *Hitchcock* (Paris: Ramsay, 1983), 325.

3. Christopher Bray, *Sean Connery: A Biography* (New York: Pegasus Books, 2011), 98–99.

Filmography

Rebecca (1940)
United Artists
Director: Alfred Hitchcock
Writers: Robert E. Sherwood and Joan Harrison (scenario by Barbara Keon, adaptation by Philip MacDonald and Michael Hogan), based on the novel by Daphne du Maurier
Producer: David O. Selznick
Primary Cast: Laurence Olivier (as Maxim De Winter), Joan Fontaine (as Mrs. De Winter), George Sanders (as Jack Favell), Judith Anderson (as Mrs. Danvers), Nigel Bruce (as Major Giles Lacy), Gladys Cooper (as Beatrice Lacy)

Foreign Correspondent (1940)
United Artists
Director: Alfred Hitchcock
Writers: Charles Bennett and Joan Harrison
Producer: Walter Wanger
Primary Cast: Joel McCrea (as John Jones), Laraine Day (as Carol Fisher), Herbert Marshall (as Stephen Fisher), George Sanders (as Scott), Albert Basserman (as Van Meer), Robert Benchley (as Stebbins), Edmund Gwenn (as Rowley)

Mr. and Mrs. Smith (1941)
RKO Radio Pictures
Director: Alfred Hitchcock

Writer: Norman Krasna

Producer: Harry E. Edington

Primary Cast: Carol Lombard (as Ann), Robert Montgomery (as David), Gene Raymond (as Jeff), Jack Carson (as Chuck), Philip Mervale (as Mr. Custer), Lucile Watson (as Mrs. Custer), William Tracy (as Sammy)

Suspicion (1941)

RKO Radio Pictures

Director: Alfred Hitchcock

Writers: Alma Reville, Samson Raphaelson, and Joan Harrison, based on the novel *Before the Fact* by Anthony Berkeley (writing as Frances Iles)

Producer: Harry E. Edington

Primary Cast: Cary Grant (as Johnnie), Joan Fontaine (as Lina), Sir Cedric Hardwicke (as General McLaidlaw), Nigel Bruce (as Gordon Cochran), Dame May Whitty (as Mrs. Laidlaw), Isabel Jeans (as Mrs. Newsham)

Saboteur (1942)

Universal Pictures

Director: Alfred Hitchcock

Writers: Peter Viertel, Joan Harrison, Dorothy Parker

Producer: Frank Lloyd

Primary Cast: Priscilla Lane (as Pat), Robert Cummings (as Barry), Otto Kruger (as Tobin), Alan Baxter (as Freeman), Clem Bevans (as Neilson), Norman Lloyd (as Fry), Alma Kruger (as Mrs. Sutton), Vaughan Glaser (as Mr. Miller)

Shadow of a Doubt (1943)

Universal Pictures

Director: Alfred Hitchcock

Writers: Thornton Wilder, Sally Benson, and Alma Reville, based on a story by Gordon McDonell

Producer: Jack H. Skirball

Primary Cast: Teresa Wright (as Young Charlie), Joseph Cotton (as Uncle Charlie), MacDonald Carey (as Jack Graham), Henry Travers (as Joseph Newton), Patricia Collinge (as Emma Newton), Hume Cronyn (as Herbie Hawkins), Wallace Ford (as Fred Saunders), Edna May Wonacott (as Ann Newton), Charles Bates (as Roger Newton)

Lifeboat (1944)

Twentieth Century-Fox Films

Director: Alfred Hitchcock

Writers: John Steinbeck, Jo Swerling, and Alfred Hitchcock
Producer: Kenneth MacGowan
Primary Cast: Tallulah Bankhead (as Constance Porter), William Bendix (as
   Gus Smith), Walter Slezak (as Willi, the German), Mary Anderson (as Alice
   Mackenzie), John Hodiak (as Kovac), Henry Hull (as C. J. "Ritt" Rittenhouse),
   Heather Angel (as Mrs. Higley), Hume Cronyn (as Stanley "Sparks" Garrett),
   Canada Lee (as Joe Spencer)

Spellbound (1945)
United Artists
Director: Alfred Hitchcock
Writer: Ben Hecht (adaptation by Angus Macphail), based on the novel *The House
   of Dr. Edwardes* by Francis Beeding
Producer: David O. Selznick
Primary Cast: Ingrid Bergman (as Dr. Constance Peterson), Gregory Peck (John
   Ballantine), Michael Chekhov (as Dr. Alex Brulov), Leo G. Carroll (as Dr.
   Murchison), Rhonda Fleming (as Mary Carmichael), John Emery (as Dr. Fleurot),
   Norman Lloyd (as Garms)

Notorious (1946)
RKO Radio Pictures, Inc.
Director: Alfred Hitchcock
Writer: Ben Hecht
Producer: Alfred Hitchcock
Primary Cast: Cary Grant (as Devlin), Ingrid Bergman (as Alicia Huberman),
   Claude Rains (as Alexander Sebastian), Louis Calhern (as Paul Prescott), Madame
   Konstantin (as Mme. Sebastian), Reinhold Schunzel (as Dr. Anderson)

The Paradine Case (1948)
Selznick Releasing
Director: Alfred Hitchcock
Writers: David O. Selznick and James Bridle (adaptation of Alma Reville, additional
   dialogue by Ben Hecht), based on the novel by Robert Hichens
Producer: David O. Selznick
Primary Cast: Gregory Peck (as Anthony Keane), Ann Todd (as Gay Keane),
   Charles Laughton (as Lord Thomas Horfield), Charles Coburn (as Sir Simon
   Flaquer), Ethel Barrymore (as Lady Sophy Farrell), Joan Tetzel (Judy Flaquer)

Rope (1948)
Warner Bros. Pictures, Inc.

Director: Alfred Hitchcock

Writer: Arthur Laurents (adaptation of Hume Cronyn), based on the play by Patrick Hamilton

Producer: Alfred Hitchcock

Primary Cast: James Stewart (as Rupert Cadell), John Dall (as Brandon), Farley Granger (as Philip), Edith Evanson (as Mrs. Wilson), Douglas Dick (as Kenneth), Joan Chandler (Janet), Sir Cedric Hardwicks (as Mr. Kentley), Constance Collier (as Mrs. Atwater)

Under Capricorn (1949)

Warner Bros. Pictures, Inc.

Director: Alfred Hitchcock

Writers: James Bridie, John Colton, and Margaret Linden (adaptation of Hume Cronyn), based on the novel by Helen Simpson

Producer: Alfred Hitchcock

Primary Cast: Ingrid Bergman (as Lady Henrietta), Joseph Cotton (as Sam Flusky), Michael Wilding (as Hon Charles Adare), Margaret Leighton (Milly)

Stage Fright (1950)

Warner Bros. Pictures, Inc

Director: Alfred Hitchcock

Writer: Whitfield Cook (adaptation of Alma Reville, additional dialogue by James Bridie), based on the novel by Selwyn Jepson

Producer: Alfred Hitchcock

Primary Cast: Jane Wyman (as Eve Gill), Marlene Dietrich (as Charlotte Inwood), Michael Wilding (as Detective Wilfred), Richard Todd (as Jonathan Cooper), Alistar Sim (as Commodore Gill), Sybil Thorndike (Mrs. Gill), Kay Walsh (Nellie Goode)

Strangers on a Train (1951)

Warner Bros. Pictures, Inc

Director: Alfred Hitchcock

Writers: Raymond Chandler and Czenzi Ormonde (adaptation of Whitfield Cook), based on the novel by Patricia Highsmith

Producer: Alfred Hitchcock

Primary Cast: Farley Granger (as Guy Haines), Ruth Roman (as Anne Morton), Robert Walker (as Bruno Antony), Leo G. Carroll (as Senator Morton), Patricia Hitchcock (as Barbara Morton), Laura Elliott (as Miriam Haines), Marion Lorne (as Mrs. Antony), Jonathan Hale (as Mr. Antony)

I Confess (1953)
Warner Bros. Pictures, Inc
Director: Alfred Hitchcock
Writers: George Tabori and William Archibald, based on the play by Paul Anthelme
Producers: Alfred Hitchcock and Sidney Bernstein
Primary Cast: Montgomery Clift (Father Michael Logan), Anne Baxter (as Ruth
     Grandfort), Karl Malden (as Inspector Larreau), Brian Aherne (as Willie
     Robertson), O. E. Hasse (as Otto Keller), Roger Dann (as Pierre Grandfort), Dolly
     Haas (as Alma Keller), Charles Andre (as Father Millais)

Dial M for Murder (1954)
Warner Bros. Pictures, Inc.
Director: Alfred Hitchcock
Writer: Frederick Knott, based on his play
Producer: Alfred Hitchcock
Primary Cast: Ray Milland (as Tony Wendice), Grace Kelly (as Margot Wendice),
     Robert Cummings (as Mark Halliday), John Williams (as Inspector Hubbard),
     Anthony Dawson (as Cap. Lesgate)

Rear Window (1954)
Paramount Pictures Corp.
Director: Alfred Hitchcock
Writer: John Michael Hayes, based on the short story by Cornel Woolrich
Producer: Alfred Hitchcock
Primary Cast: James Stewart (as L. B. "Jeff" Jeffries), Grace Kelly (as Lisa Carol
     Fremont), Wendell Corey (as Thomas J. Doyle), Thelma Ritter (as Stella),
     Raymond Burr (as Lars Thorwald), Judith Evelyn (as Miss Lonely Hearts)

To Catch a Thief (1955)
Paramount Pictures
Director: Alfred Hitchcock
Writer: John Michael Hayes (contract writer Alec Coppel), based on the novel by
     David Dodge
Producer: Alfred Hitchcock
Primary Cast: Cary Grant (as John Robie), Grace Kelly (as Frances "Francie"
     Stevens), Jessie Royce Landis (as Mrs. Jessie Stevens), John Williams (as H. H.
     Hughson), Charles Vanel (as Bertani)

The Trouble with Harry (1955)
Paramount Pictures

Director: Alfred Hitchcock
Writer: John Michael Hayes, based on the novel by Jack Trevor Story
Producer: Alfred Hitchcock
Primary Cast: Edmund Gwenn (as Albert Wiles), John Forsythe (as Sam Marlowe), Mildred Natwick (as Miss Ivy Graveley), Mildred Dunnock (as Mrs. Wiggs), Jerry Mathers (as Arnie Rogers), Shirley MacLaine (as Jennifer Rogers)

The Man Who Knew Too Much (1956)
Paramount Pictures
Director: Alfred Hitchcock
Writer: John Michael Hayes (contract writer Alec Coppel), based on a story by Charles Bennett and D. B. Wyndham-Lewis
Producer: Alfred Hitchcock
Primary Cast: James Stewart (as Dr. Ben McKenna), Doris Day (as Jo Conway McKenna), Brenda de Banzie (as Mrs. Lucy Drayton), Bernard Miles (as Mr. Drayton), Ralph Truman (as Inspector Buchanan)

The Wrong Man (1957)
Warner Bros. Pictures, Inc.
Director: Alfred Hitchcock
Writers: Maxwell Anderson and Angus MacPhail
Producer: Alfred Hitchcock
Primary Cast: Henry Fonda (as Christopher Emanuel "Manny" Balestrero), Vera Miles (as Rose Balestrero), Anthony Quayle (as Frank D. O'Connor), Harold J. Stone (as Lt. Bowers), Charles Cooper (as Det. Matthews), John Heldabrand (as Tomasini)

Vertigo (1958)
Paramount Pictures
Director: Alfred Hitchcock
Writers: Alec Coppel and Samuel Taylor (contract writer Maxwell Anderson), based on the novel *D'Entre Les Morts* by Pierre Boileau and Thomas Narcejac
Producer: Alfred Hitchcock
Primary Cast: James Stewart (as John "Scottie" Ferguson), Kim Novak (as Madeleine Elster/Judy Barton), Barbara Bel Gegges (as Midge Wood), Tom Helmore (as Gavin Elster)

North by Northwest (1959)
Metro-Goldwyn-Mayer
Director: Alfred Hitchcock

Writer: Ernest Lehman

Producer: Alfred Hitchcock

Primary Cast: Cary Grant (as Roger Thornhill), Eva Marie Saint (as Eve Kendall), James Mason (as Phillip Vandamm), Jessie Royce Landis (as Clara Thornhill), Martin Landau (as Leonard)

Psycho (1960)

Paramount Pictures

Director: Alfred Hitchcock

Writer: Joseph Stefano, based on the novel by Robert Bloch

Producer: Alfred Hitchcock

Primary Cast: Anthony Perkins (as Norman Bates), Vera Miles (as Lila Crane), John Gavin (as Sam Loomis), Martin Balsam (as Milton Arbogast), Janet Leigh (as Marion Crane)

The Birds (1963)

Universal Pictures

Director: Alfred Hitchcock

Writer: Evan Hunter, based on the short story by Daphne du Maurier

Producer: Alfred Hitchcock

Primary Cast: Rod Taylor (as Mitch Brenner), Tippi Hedren (as Melanie Daniels), Jessica Tandy (as Mrs. Brenner), Suzanne Pleshette (Annie Hayworth), Veronica Cartwright (as Cathy Brenner)

Marnie (1964)

Universal Pictures

Director: Alfred Hitchcock

Writer: Jay Presson Allen, based on the novel by Winston Graham

Producer: Alfred Hitchcock

Primary Cast: Tippi Hedren (as Marnie Edgar), Sean Connery (as Mark Rutland), Diane Baker (as Lil Mainwaring), Martin Gabel (as Sidney Strutt), Louis Latham (as Bernice Edgar)

Torn Curtain (1966)

Universal Pictures

Director: Alfred Hitchcock

Writer: Brian Moore

Producer: Alfred Hitchcock

Primary Cast: Paul Newman (as Prof. Armstrong), Julie Andrews (as Sarah Sherman), Lila Kedrova (as Countess Kuchinska), Hansjorg Felmy (as Heinrich Gerhard)

Family Plot (1976)
Universal Pictures
Director: Alfred Hitchcock
Writer: Ernest Lehman, based on novel *The Rainbird Pattern* by Victor Canning
Producer: Alfred Hitchcock
Primary Cast: Karen Black (as Fran), Bruce Dern (as Lumley), Barbara Harris (as
    Blanche), William Devane (as Adamson), Ed Lauter (as Maloney), Cathleen
    Nesbitt (as Julia Rainbird), Katherine Helmond (as Mrs. Maloney)

Index

About the Author

Leslie L. Coffin works as a critic, columnist, and freelance writer for a variety of publications. She graduated from Ball State University with bachelor's degrees in public history and media studies and completed a master's degree at New York University's Gallatin School of Individualized Studies, with focuses on biographical and star studies. Her first book, *Lew Ayres: Hollywood Conscientious Objector*, was published in 2012. She resides in New York City, in Astoria Queens.